The Digital Reading Condition

This volume offers a critical overview of digital reading practices and scholarly efforts to analyze and understand reading in the mediatized landscape. Building on research about digital reading, born-digital literature, and digital audiobooks, *The Digital Reading Condition* explores reading as part of a broader cultural shift encompassing many forms of media and genres.

Bringing together research from media and literary studies, digital humanities, scholarship on reading and learning, as well as sensory studies and research on multimodal and multisensory media reception, the authors address and challenge print-biased conceptions of reading that are still prevalent in research, whether the reading medium is print or digital. They argue that the act of reading itself is changing, and rather than rejecting digital media as unsuitable for sustained or focused reading practices, they argue that the complex media landscape challenges us to rethink how to define reading as a mediated practice.

Presenting a truly interdisciplinary perspective on digital reading practices, this volume will appeal to scholars and graduate students in communication, media studies, new media and technology, literature, digital humanities, literacy studies, composition, and rhetoric.

Maria Engberg is Associate Professor at Malmö University, Sweden, and an Affiliate Researcher at Georgia Institute of Technology, U.S.A. She holds a Ph.D. in English from Uppsala University, Sweden.

Iben Have is Associate Professor in Media Studies in the School of Communication and Culture, Aarhus University, Denmark. She holds a Ph.D. in Musicology from Aarhus University.

Birgitte Stougaard Pedersen is Associate Professor in Aesthetics and Culture in the School of Communication and Culture, Aarhus University, Denmark. She holds a Ph.D. in Aesthetics and Culture from Aarhus University.

Routledge Research in Digital Humanities

The *Routledge Research in Digital Humanities* series is an interdisciplinary monograph series that publishes current research into the field of digital humanities. The books in the series address methodological and conceptual digital humanities issues and explain how the software or the techniques used broaden the possibilities for digital humanities and their respective field.

In the same series:

Mapping Space, Sense, and Movement in Florence
Nicholas Terpstra and Colin Rose

Visualizing Venice: Mapping and Modeling Time and Change in a City
Edited by Kristin L. Huffman, Andrea Giordano, Caroline Bruzelius

Mapping Deathscapes: Digital Geographies of Racial and Border Violence
Edited by Suvendrini Perera and Joseph Pugliese

Hidden Cities: Urban Space, Geolocated Apps and Public History in Early Modern Europe
Edited by Fabrizio Nevola, David Rosenthal and Nicholas Terpstra

Afrofuturism and Digital Humanities: Show Me and I Will Engage Differently
Bryan W. Carter

The Digital Reading Condition
Edited by Maria Engberg, Iben Have, and Birgitte Stougaard Pedersen

The Digital Reading Condition

Edited by Maria Engberg,
Iben Have, and
Birgitte Stougaard Pedersen

LONDON AND NEW YORK

First published 2023
by Routledge
4 Park Square, Milton Park, Abingdon, Oxon OX14 4RN

and by Routledge
605 Third Avenue, New York, NY 10158

Routledge is an imprint of the Taylor & Francis Group, an informa business

© 2023 selection and editorial matter, Maria Engberg, Iben Have, and Birgitte Stougaard Pedersen; individual chapters, the contributors

The right of Maria Engberg, Iben Have, and Birgitte Stougaard Pedersen to be identified as the authors of the editorial material, and of the authors for their individual chapters, has been asserted in accordance with sections 77 and 78 of the Copyright, Designs and Patents Act 1988.

All rights reserved. No part of this book may be reprinted or reproduced or utilised in any form or by any electronic, mechanical, or other means, now known or hereafter invented, including photocopying and recording, or in any information storage or retrieval system, without permission in writing from the publishers.

Trademark notice: Product or corporate names may be trademarks or registered trademarks, and are used only for identification and explanation without intent to infringe.

British Library Cataloguing-in-Publication Data
A catalogue record for this book is available from the British Library

ISBN: 978-1-032-07576-1 (hbk)
ISBN: 978-1-032-07812-0 (pbk)
ISBN: 978-1-003-21166-2 (ebk)

DOI: 10.4324/9781003211662

Typeset in Sabon
by MPS Limited, Dehradun

Contents

List of figures viii
Contributors ix

Introduction 1
MARIA ENGBERG, IBEN HAVE, AND
BIRGITTE STOUGAARD PEDERSEN

SECTION I
Historical and Sociocultural Perspectives on Reading 9

Introduction to Section I 11

1 Reading and materiality: conditions of digital reading 14
MARIA ENGBERG

2 History of media cultures from the perspective of
multisensory reading 26
IBEN HAVE

3 The condition of reading in a digital media culture 35
JAY DAVID BOLTER

4 Reading toward multiliteracies: understanding reading
comprehension and reading experience 46
BIRGITTE STOUGAARD PEDERSEN AND IBEN HAVE

SECTION II
Multisensory Reading 55

Introduction to Section II 57

5 Reading and the senses: cultural and technological perspectives 59
BIRGITTE STOUGAARD PEDERSEN AND MARIA ENGBERG

6 Reading a literary app for children 68
AYOE QUIST HENKEL

7 Trends in immersive journalism 79
IBEN HAVE AND MARIA ENGBERG

8 Multisensory reading of digital audiobooks 88
IBEN HAVE AND BIRGITTE STOUGAARD PEDERSEN

9 How to read a network, or the internet as unfinished demo 98
LORI EMERSON

SECTION III
Reading Engagement: Aspects of Digital Reading 109

Introduction to Section III 111

10 Deep, focused, and critical reading between media 113
MARIA ENGBERG AND BIRGITTE STOUGAARD PEDERSEN

11 Reading digital interfaces and audiobooks: media-specific and multisensory aspects of immersion 124
BIRGITTE STOUGAARD PEDERSEN AND AYOE QUIST HENKEL

12 Motivations for audiobook reading in modern everyday lives 135
IBEN HAVE

SECTION IV
Young Readers Between Media 145

Introduction to Section IV 147

13 Digital reading in education: a situated disciplinary literacies perspective 149
NIKOLAJ ELF

14 Different modes of reading – eighth-grade students' interaction with a digital narrative 162
AYOE QUIST HENKEL AND SIGNE HJORT NIELSEN

15 Transmedial reading 173
SUSANA TOSCA

16 Readers between media: sixth-grade students tuning in to literature in different formats 184
AYOE QUIST HENKEL

SECTION V
Aesthetics and Digital Reading 195

Introduction to Section V 197

17 Situated reading 200
MARIA ENGBERG AND BIRGITTE STOUGAARD PEDERSEN

18 Reading: atmosphere, ambience, and attunement 208
BIRGITTE STOUGAARD PEDERSEN

19 Resonance and the digital conditions of reading 219
LUTZ KOEPNICK

Conclusion: the digital reading condition 230
MARIA ENGBERG, IBEN HAVE, AND
BIRGITTE STOUGAARD PEDERSEN

Index 236

Figures

3.1	Four categories of digital textuality	43
4.1	What media types do you prefer when experiencing stories?	53
6.1	Screenshot from Burup et al. (2016). *Sofus and the Moonmachine*. The Outer Zone	70
6.2	Screenshot from Burup et al. (2016). *Sofus and the Moonmachine*. The Outer Zone	72
6.3	Screenshot from Burup et al. (2016). *Sofus and the Moonmachine*. The Outer Zone	74
9.1	TCP/IP overview	103
13.1	A design model for inquiry-oriented teaching of modes and media of Hans Christian Andersen	155
14.1	Screenshot from Hübbe et al. (2018), chapter 29	163
15.1	A transmedial experience model (Tosca 2017, based on McCarthy and Wright)	174
16.1	Screenshot from Hübbe and Meisler (2013) iPad-version	186
18.1	A screenshot from *The Cartographer's Confession* by James Attlee, illustration by Grace Attlee, app producer: Emma Whittaker	212
19.1	A scene from *MS Slavic 7* (2019) by Sofia Bohdanowicz and Deragh Campbell	222
19.2	A scene from *MS Slavic 7* (2019) by Sofia Bohdanowicz and Deragh Campbell	226
19.3	A scene from *MS Slavic 7* (2019) by Sofia Bohdanowicz and Deragh Campbell	227

Contributors

Jay David Bolter is Professor and Director of Computational Media, Wesley Chair of New Media, School of Literature, Media, and Communication, Georgia Tech, U.S.A.

Lori Emerson is Associate Professor and Program Director at Intermedia Art, Writing and Performance, University of Colorado Boulder, U.S.A.

Maria Engberg is Associate Professor at Malmö University, Sweden, and an Affiliate Researcher at Georgia Institute of Technology, U.S.A. She holds a Ph.D. in English, from Uppsala University, Sweden.

Nikolaj Frydensbjerg Elf is Professor at the Department for the Study of Culture and the Department for Education, University of Southern Denmark.

Iben Have is Associate Professor in Media Studies in the School of Communication and Culture, Aarhus University, Denmark. She holds a Ph.D. in Musicology from Aarhus University.

Ayoe Quist Henkel is Associate Professor at VIA University College, Denmark, and holds a PhD from Centre for Children's Literature and Media, Department of Communication and Culture, Aarhus University, Denmark.

Lutz Köepnick is Gertrude Conaway Vanderbilt Professor of German, Cinema and Media Arts, Vanderbilt University, Nashville, U.S.A.

Signe Hjort Nielsen is Assistant Professor at the Department of Education, UCL University College.

Birgitte Stougaard Pedersen is Associate Professor in Aesthetics and Culture, School of Communication and Culture, Aarhus University. She holds a Ph.D. in Aesthetics and Culture from Aarhus University, Denmark.

Susana Tosca is Associate Professor, Department of Communication and the Arts, Roskilde University, Denmark.

Introduction

Maria Engberg, Iben Have, and Birgitte Stougaard Pedersen

This volume proposes an interdisciplinary critical overview of digital reading practices and the scholarly efforts to analyze and understand reading in the current media landscape. What does it mean to read digitally today? How does what we call the digital reading condition encourage us to read in new ways? What are some of the key reading practices that have emerged after the first three decades of the World Wide Web, amidst an increasing number of digital devices and an incessant digitally mediated information flow? The volume brings together research from media and literary studies, digital humanities, aesthetics, scholarship on reading and learning, as well as sensory studies and research on multimodal and multisensory media reception. Our aim is to address and challenge print-biased conceptions of reading that are still prevalent in much of research, whether the reading medium is print or digital. Concepts such as deep or focused reading are often implicitly or explicitly associated with print-based formats that often only contain text. To fully understand what the current digital reading condition entails, we argue that the act of reading itself is changing, and rather than rejecting digital media as not suitable for sustained or focused reading practices, the complex media landscape that includes all kinds of media forms and remediated practices – including reading – challenges us to rethink how we should define reading as a mediated practice. Also, the digital reading condition foregrounds the importance of understanding how senses are explicitly invoked while reading digital material that often includes images, sounds, movement, and interactive elements in addition to text. Building on existing research into born-digital literature and audiobooks, our volume brings in these scholarly perspectives to understand what we see as part of a broader cultural shift now that 'the digital' is a matured and multifaceted category including many different forms of media and genres. The current media moment requires us to understand digital reading as a condition of multiple shapes and forms of experience.

The Digital Reading Condition analyzes how the ways in which we meet texts (broadly speaking) are rapidly changing in contemporary media culture, in part due to the effects of far-reaching digitization of media. As texts are published using the multimodal affordances and network capacities

DOI: 10.4324/9781003211662-1

offered by digital media, our understanding of how reading and writing function needs to change along with the changing circumstances of publication and consumption. In this book, we will analyze the current reading and writing practices, as mediated in digital forms, and their shift toward using more semiotic resources (e.g., language, voices, gestures, images) and modalities (e.g., visual, aural, haptic, tactile). We are particularly interested in texts that create aesthetic experiences (rather than texts for purely informational purposes), texts that strive for a reading experience that goes beyond the deciphering of printed text, often achieved by including images, sounds, and interactive elements.

We investigate different dimensions of what we call the 'digital reading condition', borrowing from Jerome McGann's concept of the textual condition (1991). McGann's inspirational contribution to textual and literary studies at the time was to develop a theory of *textuality* based on writing and production, recognizing that *textuality* practices and literary works are fundamentally dependent on socio-historical conditions and examining aspects of stability and instability. McGann insisted on a material understanding of how texts brought about reading:

> Reading appears always and only as text, in one or another physically determinate and socially determined form. This is not to deny either the reality or the importance of silent and individual reading. It is merely to say that textuality cannot be understood except as a phenomenal event, and that reading itself can only be understood when it has assumed specific material constitutions (1991, 20).

These material conditions, the circuit encircling book production, publishers, and writers, have been changing since the 1990s due to digitization. This book expands on McGann's analysis of the textual condition to consider the influence that digitization has had on reading practices. A 'condition' means a particular state that someone is in or the circumstances or factors affecting the way in which people live or work. With this book, we seek to shed light upon how reading habits and modes of reading fundamentally change the conditions under which we perform reading in a digitized society and community.

We argue that the key to this shift in mediation is a series of sensorial modes through which reading takes place. The book investigates and reflects upon the intensified relation between digital, expanded textual and reading practices that call upon a wider range of senses to be used when listening, seeing, touching, and interactively engaging with digital texts. Therefore, concepts such as the 'multisensory', 'embodiment', and 'literary materiality' in their digital contexts will form a conceptual basis for much of the discussion in the following chapters.

We focus on aesthetic or media-intensive experiences first and foremost with literary or narrative texts that exist in a number of digital formats:

standalone apps, websites, audiobooks, etc. Literary culture is not exempt from the societal processes of digitization that have touched nearly every other aspect of human life and changed other art forms in recent decades, including film, TV, gaming, and music. Thus, we outline a series of literacies, some that borrow heavily from print-based practices, others that are born-digital forms and seem to challenge the very concept of 'reading'. One such example is the literary app for touch screen mobile devices that build on the aesthetics and practices of, for example, computer gaming and verbal-visual literary forms; another is the digital audiobook that allows you, like any other sound media, to walk around or do something else while listening.

Research on digital reading practices is now found in many disciplines: communication studies, literary studies, digital media studies, education and pedagogical research, and psychology, to name a few. During the past two decades, many critical voices have lamented what they perceive to be a decline in or substantial challenges to reading because of digital networked media (e.g., Carr 2010, Wolf and Barzillai 2009). The dire numbers in the National Endowment for the Arts 2004 study *Reading at Risk: A Survey of Literary Reading in America* seemed to summarize the fears that many felt and still feel regarding reading in the age of digital media – in spite of the fact that a 2009 study by the NEA, *Reading on the Rise: A New Chapter in American Literacy*, showed that literary reading among American adults was in fact increasing. Despite the decade or more that has passed, and the exponential growth of digital reading (in terms of platforms, digital genres, and actual numbers of readers), these fears and misconceptions still persist. Both scholarly and more popular accounts often remain focused on particular forms of reading, for instance in the context of comprehending information or reading in the context of education. Reading activities and the learning and experience that ensue are associated with particular media forms, specific layouts and print conventions, and, finally, certain genres of literature. Often, such studies, whether in linguistic or cultural contexts, tend to ignore multimodal emergent digital reading media in favor of the still more prevalent print-mimicking electronic publishing forms (pdf, epub, etc.). Such a media-deterministic or narrow approach often concludes that there is a decline as regards to 'deep' or focused reading. The volume will challenge the preconceptions of the print book as the primary medium and role model for what constitutes reading.

Theoretical and methodological framework

This volume will provide answers to key questions and concerns regarding the fate of reading in a digital age by examining the phenomenon from a multitude of scholarly perspectives on various reading practices. Those questions include: How do digital interfaces and technologies impact the current reading situation? How are sensory aspects to be understood as part of the digital reading experience? How can concepts of reading be expanded to include contexts and situations, not just medium and genre?

The interdisciplinarity of the book is also reflected methodologically. The authors represent different scholarly disciplines, each with its own interests, methodological traditions, and theoretical framework in the study of digital reading practices, which together offer a multifaceted picture of the digital reading condition. In addition to introducing digital reading practices from a number of disciplines, we hope to establish a meaningful and fruitful exchange of approaches to reading in digital manners that can contribute to new dialog between perspectives. We present a prism of negotiations of concepts of digital reading that hopefully will create ideas for new scholarly conversations.

Several of the contributions to the book share an epistemological grounding in phenomenological theories along with a general interest in the meeting and the relation between the material world of texts, media, and technologies on the one hand and the sensing and perceiving body and mind in a situational social and cultural environment on the other. The book includes several empirical studies – qualitative as well as quantitative. Some are original and presented in this book for the first time, others have been reported on previously and the authors here refer to insights that are pertinent to discussions about digital reading. Methodologically, several chapters employ thick descriptions in order to capture different phenomenological experiences of reading, both historically and contemporaneously, followed by theoretical and analytical discussions and arguments.

Since the book is grounded in media studies, media archeology, and phenomenology it foregrounds a humanistic and sociological approach to digital reading and readers. That means that other highly relevant methodologies such as neuroscience and cognitive psychology will not play a major role in the book. In recent years, these positions have gained ground as extensions of the cognitive theoretical approach to reading (e.g., Mangen 2013). Mangen has for instance developed the concept of 'embodied cognition', which links a bodily and a neuroscientific approach in effects studies, comparing reading on paper with reading of the same text as a scanned pdf version followed by surveys and informant interviews. These results are generally critical toward the outcome of digital reading, enhancing the lack of haptic and bodily feedback in digital formats (ibid.).

This volume investigates the sensory aspects of interacting with born-digital phenomena, and by adding and foregrounding the phenomenological and sensory perspective to reading interfaces in the digital reading condition, we seek to establish a dialogue with these positions and believe that valid answers can be found in combining the paradigms. Several chapters in this book include and discuss cognitive and neuroscientific studies, but the overall aim is to present alternatives to the experimental evidence-seeking approaches.

This book seeks to bring together a wealth of methodological and theoretical perspectives to expose the normative perspectives on mediation that often underlie research into digital reading practices. We remind the reader of well-established print-based assumptions of reading that are at times underscored by digital interfaces which seek to draw on the readers' experience of reading printed works. At other times, however, this print bias precludes a richer understanding of the varied situations that occur in the current media landscape. Each chapter accounts for its own theoretical and methodological grounds while addressing the overarching concern of the book: the digital reading condition that permeates many, if not most, contemporary text encounters.

Framing reading

In this book, we will not adhere to one single definition of reading. In fact, we firmly believe that there cannot be one shared definition to such a complex practice. In this, we are in line with many other scholars who have recently noted that reading has in fact never had an agreed-upon definition across disciplines. Rather, it remains a fluid concept at the heart of several academic disciplines and fields, continuously debated and discussed during the development of modern academic disciplines. As Price and Rubery (2020) note, reading is debated as a method, as a practice, as a generative term engaged in contradictory statements. And they correctly point out that the advent of digital technologies has sped up the process with which reading is analyzed, probed, questioned, combined with qualifiers such as distant, deep, serious, hyper, and so on. Yet, also, it remains a practice in which we are all invested, and which is a cornerstone of education.

Any statement beginning with 'reading is' in this book will be followed by arguments that may be contradicted in another chapter. In some chapters, you will find that the authors refer to audiobook reading, which others might first and foremost consider as a listening activity only. The book aims to foreground different conceptions of the term and to describe different facets of reading practices and to underscore that understanding reading means recognizing that it is and has always been more than a cerebral activity. When practices change, concepts regarding these practices also need to be revisited. And most people can recognize that reading texts happens on different devices today: screens, books, audio files on smartphones, as well as different sensory input: eye reading, listening, touching, and so on.

The materiality of the reading situation – of the work, of the situation, the embodiment of the reader, and so forth – is part of how we address what we are calling the digital reading condition. Barthes's distinction between *readerly* and *writerly* types of literary text (in French *lisible* and *scriptible*) can serve as a symbolic reminder of some of the distinctions that we wish to address. Barthes used the terms to distinguish between texts that are straightforward and demand no special effort to understand (*readerly*) and those whose meaning is not immediately evident and demand some effort on the part of the reader (*writerly*). Digital technologies seem to have made many textual encounters *writerly*; they change the practices of reading and writing, as millions of people engage in digital reading and writing through various digital platforms and services that in turn are shaped by hardware and software technologies.

Reading is and has always been defined in relation to the material that is being read and the context and situation in which the practice occurs, even though this perspective has not always been foregrounded in scholarship. It is these material elements that the chapters in this book seek to analyze, describe, understand. Therefore, we argue that discussions of reading as a practice, as a method, as a phenomenon, need to include those elements. The hope is that cumulatively the chapters will present different facets of understanding reading today and form a more complete picture. While the emphasis in many of the examples that the book puts forth is on those moments of reading that may seem foreign, awkwardly shaped by unusual new media objects, or misunderstood as something other than reading, rather than the everyday, habitual reading practices to which we have become more accustomed, the goal is not to suggest that other kinds of definitions of reading are not valid. Quite the contrary. We wish to contribute to an opening up of the concept, rather than supplant reading with some other term since reading is and continues to be so central to human culture.

The book is divided into five sections. The first section focuses on how mediation, materiality, and reading have been analyzed and understood, primarily in literary and media studies. The chapters foreground the importance of understanding that the history of reading is intimately bound with the history of various media forms. The second section's chapters bring us closer to how technologies and sensory perception are connected, and how reading practices foreground and rely on different sensory engagements. The chapters also delve more deeply into specific digital reading practices and ways of understanding the digital reading condition as linked to digital networked media. The third section analyzes how reading practices have been connected to specific modes of engagement: deep reading, distracted reading, audio reading, and immersion across media are some examples. The chapters in the fourth section foreground empirical studies of reading practices, with an emphasis on transmedial reading and reading by young readers. This includes studies of children and youth and their encounters with digital reading material across media.

The fifth section moves beyond the intersection between reader and the reading material to look at the situation, site, and context of reading. The section both studies this as concrete everyday reading practices and involves more philosophically invested reflections that consider relationships between materiality, background, and reading.

In the concluding chapter of the book, we reframe the aspects of multisensory and situated reading, pointing toward sociologically framed studies on personal and social reading as well as discussing the result of the book in terms of digital plenitude, post-critical reading, and new institutional infrastructures changing the landscape of reading practices.

References

Carr, Nicholas. 2010. *The Shallows: How the Internet is Changing the Way we Think, Read and Remember*. New York: WW Norton & Co.

Mangen, Anne. 2013. "Putting the body back into reading." In *Pædagogisk neurovidenskab*, edited byTheresa Schilhab, 11–32. Aarhus, Denmark: Danish School of Education, Aarhus University.

Mangen, Anne. 2016. "The digitization of literary reading." *Orbis Litterarum* 71, no. 3: 240–262. 10.1111/oli.12095

McGann, Jerome. 1991. *The Textual Condition*. Princeton, New Jersey: Princeton University Press.

National Endowment for the Arts. 2004. *Reading at Risk: A Survey of Literary Reading in America*. NEA, June 2004.

National Endowment for the Arts. 2007. *To Read or Not to Read: A Question of National Consequence*. NEA, November 2007.

National Endowment for the Arts. 2009. *Reading on the Rise: A New Chapter in American Literacy*. NEA, January 2009.

Rubery, Matthew, and Price, Leah, eds. 2020. *Further Reading*. Oxford: Oxford University Press.

Wolf, Maryanne, and Barzillai, Mirit. 2009. "The importance of deep reading." *Educational Leadership* 66, no. 6: 32–37.

Section I
Historical and Sociocultural Perspectives on Reading

Introduction to Section I

This introductory section provides a background for the following sections and for the book's overall argument that reading as an intellectual, emotional, and embodied practice must be recast in a different light that considers, and does not reject, the importance of the "digital." To analyze and understand the current sociocultural, material, economic, and analytic condition of reading practices in a computational age, it is imperative that we also include a wider lens on the contemporary digital media condition. The four chapters of the section lay out the framework for our understanding of the current reading condition, impacted by the last few decades of digitalization. The ways in which we perceive the world through and with media are forged through the materiality and context of those instances of perception. Reading a digitally produced and distributed work requires material understanding as much as conventionally printed books do, even though the latter may feel more natural and familiar than the former. The materiality of the digital shares some qualities with the materiality of print, but also has distinct qualities.

During the past several hundred years, literature and literary scholarship have been connected to printed books. In the chapters the authors revisit the history of media technologies, thoroughly analyzed in media and communication studies, textual studies, book history, and publishing studies, in order to illustrate how sensory-based concepts of perception have been linked to the very definitions of those media forms. Building on the aspects of the mass production of text from a media matrix characterized by orality to one dominated by printed words and visual reading (McLuhan 1964; Ong 1982), the chapters point toward an expanding of the concept of reading in the digital condition. The argument of the whole book is that such an expansion is key to avoiding binary assumptions about what kinds of experience print-based reading on the one hand and digitally produced and distributed reading on the other produce. Although our emphasis is not on learning and literacy, these fields of practice and research become important touch points as we seek to explain our culture's ocularcentric understanding of reading, even though demonstrated Chartier, McGann, and

DOI: 10.4324/9781003211662-3

other textual scholars have demonstrated that other senses are always involved in reading.

This first section's chapters, therefore, have a two-pronged agenda. First, these chapters overview the material changes brought about by the mediatization of literature – changes analogous to those of other artforms, such as music, film, and TV, in recent decades. These changes are documented by the work of literary scholars such as Hayles and Pressman (2002, 2008, 2010; Hayles & Pressman 2013), John Cayley (2018) and Scott Rettberg (2019) in their studies of electronic literature as a born digital phenomenon with strong ties to print culture. Second, the chapters will introduce some of the sensory and multisensory registers that digital media increasingly make possible as material for literature (and other texts, using that term broadly). Today there exists a plethora of formats and different modes of engaging with literary and other kinds of texts, and they keep multiplying. The impact and increasing popularity of audiobooks and ebooks, albeit perhaps unevenly distributed, constitute one such development that puts pressure on the traditional concept of reading. Do we read, rather than listen to, audiobooks? If so, how can we understand that reading? With an interactive ebook, readers can highlight, annotate and copy text, but they can also link to reading communities online in order to read and discuss the comments and analyses of others and share their reviews and comments in wider social networks. These born-digital activities offer an expanded reading experience that, although it resembles print-based practice in some ways, nevertheless takes on a distinctly digital flavor.

In the first chapter, "Reading and materiality: conditions of digital reading," Maria Engberg introduces the thesis of the book: that there is a materiality of reading and it takes different shapes depending on the medium in which texts are presented. She discusses how digital environments now constitute the material conditions for our consumption of all texts: born-digital, digitized, and print literature. In the second chapter, "History of media cultures from the perspective of multisensory reading," Iben Have introduces the so-called Toronto school's theory regarding the relationship of culture and media technologies and shows how the digital can fit into the oral-written-print-electronic schema of media and communication technologies, and consequently the conditions for reading. This chapter thus presents the progression of materialities through various media eras. In the third chapter, "The condition of reading in a digital media culture," Jay David Bolter describes how computers and digital media have shaped production, distribution, and consumption of texts in the past forty years and he argues that the processes of extension, intensification, and innovation in the digital reading condition can be classified under four rubrics: hypertextual, multimodal, collective, and locative. Finally, in the section's fourth chapter, "Reading toward multiliteracies: understanding reading comprehension and reading experience," Birgitte Stougaard Pedersen and Iben Have lay the foundation for understanding the link between reading comprehension and reading experience. They discuss in detail different concepts of literacy and show how literacies are giving way to multiliteracies, or in what Bolter elsewhere has called the digital plenitude (2019). Their chapter also points to the foundational understanding of reading as a means to develop democratic and cultural values through reading, primarily as children are raised and educated.

References

Cayley, John. 2018. *Grammalepsy: Essays on Digital Language Art*. 1st ed. New York: Bloomsbury Academic. 10.5040/9781501335792.
Hayles, N Katherine. 2008. *Electronic Literature: New Horizons for the Literary*. Notre Dame, IN: University of Notre Dame Press.
Hayles, N Katherine. 2010. "How we read: Close, hyper, machine." *ADE Bulletin* 150, no. 18: 62–79.
Hayles, N. Katherine. 2002. *Writing Machines*. Cambridge, MA: MIT Press.
Hayles, N. Katherine, and Pressman, Jessica, eds. 2013. *Comparative Textual Media: Transforming the Humanities in the Postprint Era*. Minneapolis: University of Minnesota Press.
McLuhan, Marshall. 1964. *Understanding Media: The Extensions of Man*.New York: New American Library Inc.
Ong, Walter J. 1982. *Orality and Literacy: The Technologizing of the Word*. London; New York: Methuen.
Rettberg, Scott. 2019. *Electronic Literature*. Cambridge, Massachusetts, USA: Polity.

1 Reading and materiality: conditions of digital reading

Maria Engberg

All reading activities are grounded in the material body of that which is read. Reading activities are shaped by the material conditions of the circumstances of the reading and how, when, and by whom it is conducted. Today, for anyone who has lived through the past 30 years during which digital technologies have permeated almost all areas of human activity, the impact of digital technologies on media channels and on the modes of production of texts and audiovisual media in all forms should be evident. This chapter builds upon the previous chapter in which the role of reading in mass media cultures was discussed. The aim here is to draw some of the broader strokes of influential ideas on the material nature of reading and specifically digital *materialities*. Of course, in some sense, the entire volume is devoted to the analysis of the conditions of digital reading and the necessary scholarly and philosophical work that is undertaken to account for those conditions. Our overall emphasis is on foregrounding the multisensory dimensions of digital media technologies today. However, while the sensory registers involved in perception figure in the discussion here as well, I am casting a wider net to catch some key thoughts on the material conditions of reading and their impact on the understanding of current digital transformations of reading.

Since the increased use of personal computers and the advent of the world wide web in the 1980s and 1990s, the *materiality* and particular conditions of reading on digital platforms have been continuously studied in various scholarly fields: within more experimental forms of literary writing, such as born-digital literature (Hayles 2002, 2012, Rettberg 2019), as well as in the more widespread forms of digital children's literature (Quist Henkel 2018) and digital audiobooks (Have and Stougaard Pedersen 2017, Rubery 2016). As Simone Murray has pointed out, literary culture and practices are now equally formed by digital environments and shaped by literary discourse (2018, 3). Murray argues that there is a "literary-digital mutual interpenetration that demands detailed analysis" (ibid., 3). Indeed, this "literary-digital" loop has had a profound impact on the humanities in the last two-three decades, not least evident in digital humanities scholarship, but we still find that there is a need for analyzing and considering the social, economic, or technological conditions of the production

DOI: 10.4324/9781003211662-4

of literary texts and the material instantiations in which those texts reach their audiences. Such analyses should reformulate the definitions and inherent material assumptions that girdle foundational concepts, including text, reading, and, for that matter, writing.

Reading in a digital age has for some "defamiliarize[d] the act of reading" (Hammond 2016, 4), while others have grown up in a hybrid reading environment that encompasses print and digital formats and may not see reading digitally as defamiliarizing (read more about literacy in Chapters 4 and 14). The conditions and practices of reading depend on so many factors: socioeconomic and geographical circumstances, the cultural specificities of your country or community, the ways in which digital formats are embraced, or not, in the educational system, and individual readers' engagement with digital media, to name a few. While this chapter paints a picture in broad strokes, the ensuing chapters will address aspects of the digital reading condition in detail, homing in on specific facets and circumstances. It is impossible to map all the dimensions of what we call the conditions of digital reading in one chapter. However, the chapter will begin to outline some of the relevant questions regarding the material, technological, and aesthetic conventions and assumptions implicated in the concept of a digital reading condition.

To understand the conditions of digital reading today, it is useful to revisit some of the developments – technological and scholarly – that occurred in a crucial time for the development and establishment of the personal computer, just before the birth of the world wide web, in addition to more recent developments of mobile and tactile media platforms (primarily smartphones and tablets). In the late 1980s and early 1990s, digital technologies became known as "textual machines" that were very useful for word processing and digital publishing. Step by step, as computers and later networked computers overtook other technologies, scholars of book history and reading as well as scholars interested in the impact of digital technologies on writing and reading began to query the material conditions of reading. In his highly influential work, Roger Chartier laid out the case for scholarship that attends to the *materiality* of reading and writing. In the 1992 essay "Laborers and Voyagers: From the Text to the Reader," Chartier presents the task of the scholar who needs "to reconstruct the variations that differentiate the "readable space" (the texts in their material and discursive forms) and those which govern the circumstances of their "actualization" (the readings seen as concrete practices and interpretive procedures)" (1992, 50). He maintained that readers always confront texts in their material forms, as objects to apprehend and comprehend. Arguing against purely semantic definitions of text, Chartier foregrounded the physical form as the locus of interpretation of text:

> We must also realize that reading is always a practice embodied in gestures, spaces, and habits. Far from the phenomenology of reading,

which erases the concrete modality of the act of reading and characterizes it by its effects, postulated as universals, a history of modes of reading must identify the specific dispositions that distinguish communities of readers and traditions of reading. (ibid., 51)

But Chartier's ideas were not the reigning viewpoint in literary studies at the time, occupied then with poststructuralist and postmodernist notions of texts that radically de-emphasized the material conditions of production and of reading. At the same time, computers were increasingly used for writing, and their growing and future potential importance for books, book publishing, and reading was being noticed. Writing at the same time as Chartier, Jay David Bolter's influential scholarship into what he at the time termed "the coming of the electronic book" appeared in *Writing Space: The Computer, Hypertext and the History of Writing* (1991). Bolter was one of several scholars who began to analyze and to a certain degree argue for the benefits of electronic text. Choice, changeability, and ease of access were important aspects of electronic texts for Bolter, who argued that "if we combine the dynamic writing of the word processor with the dynamic reading of the bulletin board or textual database and add the interactivity of computer-assisted instruction, then we do have a textual medium of a new order" (ibid., 6). The aged references aside, the understanding of digital texts as malleable and changeable, dependent on the reader's choices, and thus not confined to a physical artifact is still useful today. Although the available literary hypertexts were perhaps few, and digital texts still cumbersome to read on the computers of the early 1990s, in scholarship into the material conditions of digital texts, reading was seemingly open to *readerly* choice. The reader could choose when and where to find information and read texts in a "textual network"; electronic reading, it was suggested, meant an alteration to the "nature of an audience's shared experience of reading" (ibid., 8). While Bolter, Lanham (1993), Landow (1992), Douglas (2000), and many other scholars argued at this time for the benefits of digital *textuality*, fears started to grow about how digital technologies profoundly impacted the entire media landscape, creating digital entertainment that would vie for potential readers' attention and time.

In 2007, when the National Endowment for the Arts (NEA) in the U.S. released the report *To Read or Not to Read: A Question of National Consequence*, which followed the even more alarming sounding *Reading at Risk* report from 2004, scholars of electronic or digital *textuality* critiqued both the methods by which the NEA reports reached their conclusions and the reports' view of reading altogether. In the NEA's reports, and others like them, reading is often conceived of primarily as a textual skill – literacy – that needs to be acquired and mastered. As the then president of the NEA, Dana Gioia, clearly intimated, reading is equated with reading literary texts published in (printed) books, and he provocatively stated:

Reading a book requires a degree of active attention and engagement. Indeed, reading itself is a progressive skill that depends on years of education and practice. By contrast, most electronic media such as television, recordings, and radio make fewer demands on their audiences, and indeed often require no more than passive participation. Even interactive electronic media, such as video games and the Internet, foster shorter attention spans and accelerated gratification.

(Gioia 2004, preface)

Nancy Kaplan (2008) and Matthew Kirschenbaum (2007) were among those who voiced their concerns about the two reports and "the NEA's narrow conception of (literary) reading" (Kaplan 2008, 201). Indeed, media scholars such as Kirschenbaum, N. Katherine Hayles, and Lori Emerson have produced influential scholarly work that has shown how digital *materiality* influences *textuality*. So, why retread the ground of discussions held 30, 20, or even 10 years ago, given the exponential growth of digital platforms for reading that has occurred? Surely, the projected fears or benefits of literary reading in the face of the digitization of the 1990s have been resolved by now. As various platforms for digital *textuality* – not to mention audiovisual materials – have emerged (and disappeared again to give way to new ones) and some platforms such as social media and publishing formats for fiction and non-fiction in the form of e-books and audiobooks have become well-established in our contemporary media culture, the question of the conditions of digital reading should no longer be viewed as a simple comparison to printed texts. And yet, questions of what kind of reading and what kinds of material conditions are most suitable, preferable, or amenable to reading and learning continue to be hotly debated. The basic tenet, that reading is an intellectual activity primarily suited to the printed medium, still undergirds most of the discussions and the framework of research into digital forms of reading practice. This is a debate that this book wants to be a part of, though starting from the premise that *plenitude* (Bolter 2019) characterizes the multifaceted engagements with texts that are offered by the contemporary media landscape.

To understand the material conditions of digital reading one must first acknowledge the extent to which print and digital practices are still intricately bound together. Many digital texts are still made to emulate print conventions. Contrary to some predictions of the 1980s and 1990s that digital formats would take over, the present-day media culture is one of plenitude and co-existence of printed and digital formats. Printed texts are still very much at the heart of many societies' economic and legal structures, and fiction as well as non-fiction material is routinely printed and sold through both digital and brick-and-mortar marketplaces. Digital text formats, word-processing software, layout and page design software (for instance Adobe InDesign, QuarkXPress, and Microsoft Publisher) rely on remediating print conventions of how a text should look, what functions and layout options should exist, and how these should be named. For some readers, these remediated digital pages make the material easier to relate to and to learn how to read in this newish format. Other aspects of interacting with a digital device involve a learning curve – different for each reader – from the earliest digital texts to one of the most commonplace document formats today, the Adobe PDF, and to more interactive or changing digital formats. Digital texts often mimic the layout and look of the printed page and augment it with the benefits that digital technologies offer. The one glaring – and massively popular – exception to this type of remediated digital reading is social media. Although they certainly are amalgamations of remediated practices – news pages, photo albums, letters, television and video, radio, and so forth – social media are probably the most common digital reading space in the world. And, all put together, they do not have an immediate connection or family resemblance to printed texts.

A day in a life

What does the current moment in our history look like from a media consumption and reading standpoint? Borrowing from Sarah Pink's sensory ethnographic approach of attending to the "sensory embodied and affective routines of everyday life" (Pink and Leder Mackley 2013, 678), I want to capture some images of how, where, and with which media and materials reading can happen in one person's everyday life. This is just one image; there will be countless other versions, culturally, geographically, socio-economically, and materially different from this one.

> *Imagine the following scene: You are an academic teacher and researcher. You wake up and you reach for your smartphone to check the newspaper and social media notifications that have popped up during the night. There are a few text messages too. During the morning you have a quick glance at national and local newspapers, and you run through your social media feeds on your iPad while eating breakfast. Apps and digital subscriptions make it easy (but perhaps increasingly expensive) to keep track of all kinds of news outlets: newspapers, magazine, as well as TV channels and purely digital news aggregators. You are not a social media fan, but you have a few accounts anyway: Twitter, Facebook, Instagram. The last is your favorite channel at the moment: You like reading through accounts that focus on cooking and gastronomy. In fact, your smartphone and iPad are constant companions and reading platforms throughout your day. This is where you can check your text messages, emails, and other direct digital communication, but also read books, whether via an e-book app or by listening to audiobooks. Lately, you have found yourself reading mostly through audiobooks, and Amazon products*

(the Kindle app for e-books and Audible for audio) dominate, for now, on your smartphone and tablet. At work, you are grading some papers which have been handed in digitally in PDF format, and you use the comment and review functions to provide comments and feedback. You also need to grade some tests, written down on paper with pencil, since the test was taken in a classroom. Next semester the university will upgrade to digital exams only, and the students overwhelmingly supported that decision since they prefer writing on a keyboard, and many do not like to write in longhand. You understand that feedback: Some students' handwriting is really difficult to decipher.

As your day progresses, you read material in digital and print formats interchangeably. You write digitally and by hand. You have not owned or even seen a typewriter for quite a while, although they have not disappeared by any means. On brightly colored sticky notes, you write down to-do tasks and a note on what to buy for dinner. Throughout the day, reading is a constant task that changes quality depending on what kind of reading is required: casual and quick reading of notes and messages, more prolonged and engaged reading as you grade and comment on tests and papers. As you read an academic article for your research, you take notes, carefully annotating portions of the article on your iPad with the digital pencil. Throughout the day, you need to engage with each individual material and its properties, interfaces, and potentialities, not that this necessarily requires much afterthought. You have developed functional habits of reading and writing digitally, except perhaps when software products change. Recently, you had to learn some of the new features of Adobe PDF, and you are still not fully capable using all that Microsoft Word has to offer, although you use it every day and have done for decades. As you are walking home from work, you listen to a novel for a bit and then switch to a podcast that reads out long articles in audio form. At home, you switch to watching Apple TV+ on your iPad – you are into one of their series about an alternative future of NASA astronauts at the moment. While you are cooking dinner, the iPad is perched atop a bowl. After dinner, you work for a while, writing emails. Before you fall asleep, you listen briefly to an audio mediation to calm your thoughts, the phone lying next to your pillow.

I invite you, too, to sketch the reading (and writing) activities of your day. While the details will surely be different, I am willing to venture that, for most of us, reading occurs in print/paper and digital formats, depending on the context and what needs to be done. For N. Katherine Hayles and Jessica Pressman, the current state of digital *textuality* in a multitude of forms has led them to propose a field of comparative textual media studies: an approach to texts that "pursues [textual] media as objects of study and as methods of study, focusing on the specificities of the technologies as well as the cultural ecologies they support, enable, and illuminate" (2013, x). We can see the echoes of the insistence on *materiality* and social context from Chartier, McKenzie, McGann, and Bolter 20 years earlier.

Of course, scholars have paid attention not only to reading as if it was a uniform activity but also to various practices of reading. And with the expansion of digital media, the list of suggested modes of reading continues to grow: casual or distracted reading (Phillips 2015), hyper reading (Hayles), deep reading (Wolf and Barzillai 2009), and distant reading (Moretti 2013). Anne Mangen asks "[i]s it important for us (and, perhaps in particular, for young people), in the digital age, to read literature?" (Mangen 2016, 241). Mangen answers her own question by calling for a truly interdisciplinary scholarship, arguing that the question must move beyond literary studies, something which we subscribe to in this volume. However, Mangen's understanding of literary reading remains surreptitiously invested in cultural hierarchies of low-brow or high-brow literary genres and in long-form books, whether in digital or printed form (2016). Lutz Koepnick (2016) reminds us that any concept of reading is historically contingent, and that "the true challenge is in understanding digital reading as an expansion of previous models of reading" rather than "seeing expanded practices of reading in the digital age as the downfall of concentrated reading" (ibid., para. "Rethinking Reading"). Rita Felski has proposed that reading involves four affective and cognitive parameters or categories: recognition, enchantment, social knowledge, and shock (2008, 14). This goes for scholarly reading and interpretation, reading for pleasure, and everything in between. Hers is a phenomenological or, in her own terminology, neo-phenomenological stance, turning primarily to an academic audience who has, Felski charges, favored an overly critical engagement with literary texts over one that does justice to readers. Felski's invocation of "thick descriptions of experiential states" (ibid., 19) aligns with the methodological approach behind many of the contributions of this volume.

The digital reading condition importantly includes community-forming activities supported by social media platforms. Simone Murray points toward virtual reading communities as an important phenomenon to bring into academic scholarship if we are to understand digital reading activities, and as late as in 2018, she asks why the intellectual work of understanding reading online still has not been done (ibid., 147). Murray thus brings in yet another dimension of the conditions of digital reading: that it is often social, connected through online communities, and that it in various ways takes advantage of what the web offers. E-book formats regularly offer opportunities to share and access comments on the text. In Kindle, you can access popular highlights made by others while you are reading "your" digital copy of a book. Readers share their thoughts, reviews, and interpretations on community platforms such as Goodreads (currently owned by Amazon). Such communities of readers can be seen as merely digitally supported interpretative communities (Fish 1980), but because of digital affordances, contemporary readers have much more agency in these social contexts: they can publish their own interpretations and discuss texts with other readers and sometimes also with authors who are active on specific reading platforms or via social media.

So, is a discussion of the conditions of digital reading doomed to be caught between diverging opinions in a minefield of diverging interdisciplinary theoretical and methodological approaches? Sidestepping the answer to an admittedly skewed question, what we are suggesting is that asking questions about the *materiality* of reading and how to best address them must be part of what has alternatively been called "the late age of print" (Bolter 1991, 2001, Striphas 2009) and "an era of veritable digital incunabula" (Murray 2018), even if it could be argued that we are now beyond incunabula. The material conditions of digital reading cannot be settled by fixed definitions of reading or of digital materials. Through "thick descriptions of experiential states" (Felski 2008) and "media-specific analysis" (Hayles 2004) which consider texts as "embodied entities" and *materiality* an "emergent property" (ibid.), the *materiality* of literature is to be determined in the particular, the individual, the specific, and not in the general or in larger but ultimately not very elucidating categories of "print" or "digital."

Jerome McGann's influential book *The Textual Condition* (1991), which informs our suggestion of a digital reading condition, may be a peculiar choice for a book that foregrounds reading. McGann developed a theory of *textuality* based in writing and production, in the sociohistorical conditions that brought the texts into being, and then how they are regenerated over time through reprints and by authors, editors, typographers, marketers, and the like. Just as McGann was concerned with textual stability and instability in print, and the impact on reading and interpretation, we are concerned with elucidating the textual stabilities and instabilities in digital forms, and how they shape reading practices. McGann's long-term collaborator, Johanna Drucker, has shown, in her work on artists' books in particular, how various forms of books that question textual stabilities and foreground materially prominent reading practices that challenge minimal physical engagement have always existed. Instead, such books bring forth physical, textual, and visual forms as integral parts of perception and meaning-making (Drucker 2013).

Digital interfaces

Let us return to the specific *materialities* that digital technologies offer literature. The act of reading is enmeshed with digital culture in many instances of our everyday lives, even if individual readers may not always realize the extent to which digital technologies are involved even in the production of printed books. Perhaps more conspicuously "digital," computationally based book formats (via apps, the web, or in specific software formats on bespoke devices) necessitate a grounded material stance on each occasion to address the digital interfaces that are created. The dichotomy between print and digital that still resonates in some popular and scholarly discourse obscures the true multifaceted nature of both *materialities*. Lori Emerson (2014), John Cayley (2005, 2017), Scott Rettberg (2019), and N. Katherine Hayles (2010) are among the many scholars who have addressed digital media as (a) reading (of) interfaces. In different ways, they analyze how literary text intersects with the interfaces of digital technologies. In Lori Emerson's words, "that interface is a technology – whether it is a fascicle, a typewriter, a command line, or a GUI – that mediates between reader and the surface-level, human-authored writing, as well as, in the case of digital devices, the machine-based writing taking place below the gloss of the surface" (2014, x). Emerson suggests that each occasion of engaging with interfaces becomes a *readingwriting*, "the practice of writing through the network, which as it tracks, indexes, and algorithmizes every click and every bit of text we enter into the network, is itself constantly reading our writing and writing our reading" (ibid., xiv). John Cayley goes further in acknowledging that reading in newer digital formats such as e-books is what he would call "electronic" reading: "As a form or practice of reading, it is not experienced as fundamentally distinct when compared with reading from print. And yet, it is formally different, both in itself, subtly, and also with regard to real, novel affordances offered by both textual digitization and connection to the network (Cayley 2017, 76). For Cayley, an important aspect of the digital reading condition today is that of "social reading and annotation" (ibid., 77), which, he argues, changes reading. In N. Katherine Hayles's work, we find similar articulations of what kind of reading digital interfaces invite: "In digital environments, hyperreading has become a necessity. It enables a reader quickly to construct landscapes of associated research fields and subfields; it shows ranges of possibilities; it identifies texts and passages most relevant to a given query; and it easily juxtaposes many different texts and passages" (2010, 66, see more in Chapter 1.1). Rather than replacing close reading or focused and sustained reading as a literary scholarly method over time (whether those texts are literary or not), hyper reading is now well established as a mode of engaging quickly with hyperlinked texts. While we may not still use the terminology of hypertext and hyperlinks, the architecture of the web is full of networked and connected texts (and images, videos, audio, and so on). As Hayles notes, and this discussion is already more than a decade old, several empirical studies showed that hyperlinked reading tended to degrade comprehension (2010, and these studies have been repeated with both supporting and diverging results in the interim years (Fitzsimmons et al. 2019) While such studies may show that hyper reading does not suit the reading of certain texts (long, complex, information-rich), it does not follow that hyper reading is not useful at all, nor that digital technologies cannot support rich, long, and complex reading material. Lisa Gitelman's assertion that it is more useful to focus on specific practices and structures at defined sites, rather than lose ground into more general media theories (Gitelman 2013), is well heeded, and as Hayles and Pressman suggest in the same volume, "concept, object, and practice coevolve and codetermine one another" (2013, xxviii).

The concept of reading in a digital cultural context will certainly "coevolve" with the discussions of digital literary objects and practices throughout this volume, and the chapter that you have just read hopes to have opened up some of the discussions and stakes that are at play. More specifically, the perceived dichotomy between so-called digitally born and digitized materials does not delineate a border between "digital" and "print" reading, even though many of the assumptions about the latter still permeate perceptions of what is more valuable to read. Even in work that lists the pros and cons of various reading media, print holds prime. The virtues of print seem more assumed than actual, for every kind of reader and every kind of reading situation: "[Print is] well suited for thinking through abstract concepts or reading long texts" (Baron 2021, 2). Nor is the dismissal of e-books' print likeness, which can be seen in some academic work devoted to electronic literature, a useful path to go for understanding the multitude of aesthetic options, models of distribution, and tools for consumption that exist today.

The kinds of analyses that Chartier, McGann, Bolter, and later Hayles and Emerson among others have brought to the understanding of literary materiality in print and digital forms are, this chapter has suggested, what is needed if we are to understand reading today. Although I am suggesting that the current media moment brings about a "digital reading condition," I do not mean to imply that it does not include print, audiobooks, printed books in all forms, as well as a multitude of digital forms. Rather, we live in a complex, interlocking media economy that includes all those forms. Rather than suggesting that the digital means cyberspatial or cybernetic existence, divorced from material concerns and import on our practices of production and consumption, this chapter has sought to bring material matters to the fore, which will run through the rest of the book as a foundational prerequisite for how to understand the changes that reading practices are undergoing.

References

Baron, Naomi. S. 2021. *How We Read Now: Strategic Choices for Print, Screen, and Audio*. Oxford University Press USA.

Bolter, Jay David. 1991. *Writing Space: The Computer, Hypertext, and the History of Writing*. Hillsdale, New Jersey: Lawrence Erlbaum Associates.

Bolter, Jay David. 2001. *Writing Space: Computers, Hypertext, and the Remediation of Print*, 2nd ed. Mahwah, New Jersey: Lawrence Erlbaum Associates.

Bolter, Jay David. 2019. *The Digital Plenitude: The Decline of Elite Culture and the Rise of New Media*. Cambridge, MA: The MIT Press.

Bradshaw, Tom, and Nichols, Bonnie. 2004. *Reading at Risk: A Survey of Literary Reading in America. National Endowment for the Arts*. Washington DC: National Endowment for the Arts. Report.

Cayley, John. 2005. "Writing on complex surfaces." *Dichtung Digital*, no. 2. https://www.dichtung-digital.org/2005/2/Cayley/index.htm.

Cayley, John. 2017. "The advent of aurature and the end of (electronic) literature." In *The Bloomsbury Handbook of Electrornic Literature*, edited by Joseph Tabbi, 73–91. Bloomsbury.

Chartier, Roger, and Gonzalez, J. A. 1992. "Laborers and voyagers: From the text to the reader." *Diacritics* 22, no. 2: 49. 10.2307/465279.

Douglas, Yellowlees J. 2000. *The End of Books – or Books Without End?* Ann Arbor, Michigan: University of Michigan Press.

Drucker, Johanna. 2013. "Reading interface." *PMLA/Publications of the Modern Language Association of America* 128, no. 1: 213–220. 10.1632/pmla.2013.128.1.213.

Emerson, Lori. 2014. *Reading Writing Interfaces: From the Digital to the Bookbound*. Minneapolis, Minnesota: University of Minnesota Press.

Felski, Rita. 2008. *Uses of Literature*. Malden, Massachusetts and Oxford, United Kingdom: Blackwell.

Fish, Stanley. 1980. *Is There a Text in This Class? The Authority of Interpretive Communities*. Cambridge, Massachusetts: Harvard University Press.

Fitzsimmons, Gemma, Weal, Mark J., and Drieghe, Denis. 2019. "The impact of hyperlinks on reading text." *PLOS ONE*, no. 14: 2. 10.1371/journal.pone.0210900.

Gitelman, Lisa. 2013. "Print culture (other than codex): Job printing and its importance." In *Comparative Textual Media: Transforming the Humanities in the Postprint Era*, 183–197. Minneapolis, Minnesota: University of Minnesota Press.

Hammond, Adam. 2016. *Literature in the Digital Age: A Critical Introduction*. Cambridge University Press.

Have, Iben, and Stougaard Pedersen, Birgitte. 2017. *Digital Audiobooks: New Media, Users, and Experiences*. New York and London: Routledge.

Hayles, N. Katherine. 2002. *Writing Machines*. Cambridge, Massachusetts: MIT Press.

Hayles, N. Katherine. 2004. "Print is flat, code is deep: The importance of media-specific analysis." *Poetics Today* 25, no. 1: 67–90. 10.1215/03335372-25-1-67.

Hayles, N Katherine. 2010. "How we read: Close, hyper, machine." *ADE Bulletin* 150, no. 18: 62–79.

Hayles, N Katherine. 2012. *How We Think: Digital Media and Contemporary Technogenesis*. Chicago, Illinois: University of Chicago Press.

Hayles, N. Katherine, and Pressman, Jessica (eds.). 2013. *Comparative Textual Media: Transforming the Humanities in the Postprint Era*. Minneapolis, Minnesota: University of Minnesota Press.

Kaplan, Nancy. 2008. "To Read, Responsibly." *Public Library Quarterly* 27, no. 3: 193–201. 10.1080/01616840802229297.

Kirschenbaum, Matthew. 2007. "How reading is being reimagined." *The Chronicle of Higher Education*. https://www.chronicle.com/article/how-reading-is-being-reimagined/.

Koepnick, Lutz. 2016. "Reading in the digital era." In *Oxford Research Encyclopedia of Literature*. Oxford University Press. 10.1093/acrefore/9780190201098.013.2.

Landow, George P. 1992. *Hypertext: The Convergence of Contemporary Critical Theory and Technology*. Johns Hopkins University Press.

Lanham, Richard A. 1993. *The Electronic Word: Democracy, Technology, and the Arts*. Chicago, Illinois: University of Chicago Press.

Mangen, Anne. 2016. "The digitization of literary reading." *Orbis Litterarum* 71, no. 3: 240–262. 10.1111/oli.12095.

McGann, Jerome. 1991. *The Textual Condition*. Princeton, New Jersey: Princeton University Press.

McKenzie, Donald Francis. 1999. *Bibliography and the Sociology of Texts*. Cambridge: Cambridge University Press.

Moretti, Franco. 2013. *Distant Reading*. London and New York: Verso.

Murray, Simone. 2018. *The Digital Literary Sphere: Reading, Writing, and Selling Books in the Internet Era*. Johns Hopkins University Press.

National Endowment for the Arts. 2004. *Reading at Risk: A Survey of Literary Reading in America*. NEA, June 2004.

National Endowment for the Arts. 2007. *To Read or Not to Read: A Question of National Consequence*. NEA, November 2007.

National Endowment for the Arts. 2009. *Reading on the Rise: A New Chapter in American Literacy*. NEA, January 2009.

Phillips, Natalie M. 2015. "Literary neuroscience and the history of attention: An fMRI study of reading Jane Austen." In *The Oxford Handbook for Cognitive Approaches to Literature*, edited by Lisa Zunshine, 55–84. Oxford University Press.

Pink, Sarah, and Leder Mackley, Kerstin. 2013. "Saturated and situated: Expanding the meaning of media in the routines of everyday life." *Media, Culture & Society* 35, no. 6: 677–691. 10.1177/0163443713491298.

Pold, Søren Bro, and Andersen, Christian Ulrik. 2021. "Interface." In *Uncertain Archives: Critical Keywords for Big Data*, edited by Nanna Bonde Thylstrup, Daniela Agostinho, Annie Ring, Catherine D'Ignazio, and Kristin Veel, 299–304. Cambridge, Massachusetts: MIT Press.

Quist Henkel, Ayoe. 2018. "Exploring the materiality of literary apps for children." *Children's Literature in Education* 49, no. 3: 338–355. 10.1007/s10583-016-9301-7.

Rettberg, Scott. 2019. *Electronic Literature*. Cambridge, United Kingdom: Polity Press.

Rubery, Matthew. 2016. *The Untold Story of the Talking Book*. Cambridge, Massachusetts: Harvard University Press.

Striphas, Ted. 2009. *The Late Age of Print: Everyday Book Culture from Consumerism to Control*. New York, NY: Columbia University Press.

Wolf, Maryanne, and Barzillai, Mirit. 2009. "The importance of deep reading." *Educational Leadership* 66, no. 6: 32–37.

2 History of media cultures from the perspective of multisensory reading

Iben Have

Historically, the changing conditions of reading are closely related to the development of media technologies. How we read is influenced by the dominating media technologies available at a certain historical time, cultural environment, and geographical place.

The big history of media and communication technologies and how they influence culture and society can be told along many lines and from different perspectives. But in media and communication studies, one narrative has dominated them all for decades. That is the "oral-literate-electronic" schema, to borrow a term from Jonathan Sterne (2011, 208), which divides the history of media and communication into three major media matrices, sometimes four, depending on whether print culture is included as separate from the literate. The theoretical tradition behind this schema is referred to as the Toronto School, Medium Theory, or media ecology and includes thinkers like Harold Adam Innis (1894–1952), Herbert Marshall McLuhan (1911–1980), Walther Jackson Ong (1912–2003), and Joshua Meyrowitz (1949–); but also the works of Elisabeth Eisenstein (1923–2016), Eric Alfred Havelock (1903–88), and John Durham Peters (1958–) can be included. Regardless of their different approaches and interests, what unites these scholars is an interest in describing and discussing how developments of media technology afford social, cultural, and psychological changes in societies and human beings historically as well as in present times.

What characterizes the Toronto School is also the idea that every historical period in the schema has its own sensory bias, depending on the dominating communication technologies of the time. Both McLuhan and Ong base their arguments about the relation between culture and media technology on the assumption that new media, transforming one media matrix toward the next, reconfigure the balances of the senses either toward the visual or the acoustic.

The "oral-literate-electronic" schema can be useful to discuss in a book like this about the digital reading condition – for two reasons. First, we can use it as a framework for discussing how reading cultures have changed historically into the digital reading condition of today, and second, the idea of the pendulum swinging between visual and acoustic biases can be challenged by the notion of multisensory reading.

In the rest of this chapter, I will first briefly outline different understandings of "reading" to be able to discuss these in the following audit of the "oral-literate-electronic" schema and to add a fourth digital link to the sequence. This leads us to a discussion of a more multifaceted and multisensory conceptualization of reading following from the digital reading condition of modern times. In other words, it is the aim of this chapter to present a media-historical perspective on reading and a reading perspective on the history of media and to challenge the notion of sensory biases and normative conceptions of visual, auditory, and multisensory reading.

Conceptions of reading

Before assessing the different media matrices, we need to focus on understanding reading as something more than just decoding black letters on white paper or screens – an approach resonating with the general interests of this book (see also Section II). The aim is not to provide a definitive broad definition of reading, but to pave the way for more inclusive conceptions of reading than we usually meet – conceptions rooted in the historically changing *materialities* of reading. The following four points can be identified along a scale toward greater inclusion.

In the *Oxford Learner's Dictionaries*, reading is defined as "to look at and understand the meaning of written or printed words or symbols" (Oxford Learners Dictionary n.d.). Based on that definition, reading always includes a specific medium such as a rock, clay, paper, or a screen, and according to the Toronto School, it is inextricably linked to sight ("to look") and written or printed symbols.

If we acknowledge that you can read audiobooks or braille, then we need to rephrase the definition above to something like *to perceive and understand the meaning of linguistic symbols*. That would include audio reading and tactile reading, but be limited to linguistic symbols and exclude pictures and moving images.

By replacing the linguistic perspective with perception in general, reading may also be understood as *human perception of symbolically coded signs of all kinds made by humans to be decoded by humans*. Based on that definition, human communication and storytelling through all times and media is included as an act of reading: we have read smoke signal, cave paintings, and grunts long before we began talking, writing, and printing languages. This position includes reading with all the senses.

The most extreme definition of reading would be an act not excluded to either symbols or humans, but including *all species' experience of their surroundings*, cultural as well as natural (landscapes, facial expressions, movements, social interaction, sounds etc.). By using the term "experience," however, this definition becomes so holistic and all-including that it seems to dilute reading as a phenomenon in itself.

Each step along this scale challenges existing normative conceptions historically associated with reading. Among academics as well as the broader public, you still find the stance that proper reading is something you do alone, with your eyes, and with a printed book in your hands. In this volume – despite its form as a printed paper book itself – we move toward a more inclusive conceptualization of reading (though not the most radical all-including definition above), and from the perspective of a digital multisensory reading condition, we challenge existing cultural hierarchies associated with "proper" reading. It is our aim to disrupt the predominant understanding of reading and disturb existing cultural media and reading hierarchies and the associated hierarchies of senses and perception.

It is in this context of questioning dominant ideas of reading, storytelling, and the origins of linguistic communication that the present chapter should be read. In his book *The Descent of Man* (1871), Darwin was inspired by bird song when he suggested that the human language may have roots in singing and be related to the expression of complex emotions. In the article "The integration hypothesis of human language evolution and the nature of contemporary languages," a group of researchers from the Massachusetts Institute of Technology picks up on Darwin's hypothesis and adds that the human language is a unique evolutionary combination of two existing proto-linguistic mechanisms: bird song and the grunting and screaming of primates (Miyagawa et al. 2014). It is important to keep this point in mind – that language was originally oral and only much later became literate – when I next present an outline of the shifting hierarchies in the cultural and media-historical development.

The canonized "oral-literate-electronic-digital" schema

The "oral-literate-electronic" schema has influenced Western media and communication theory for decades with its macro perspective on the shifting cultures following from the dominating media technologies at the time. In this section, I briefly present the schema one link at a time and relate it to conceptualizations of multisensory reading.

According to the Toronto School, oral cultures are based on speech and are among the oldest known form of human communication. And since oral cultures leave no traces of oral practice, their historical origin is unknown. In oral cultures, communication and narration are synchronized in time and space, and stories are stored in people's minds and passed on through word of mouth to the next generation. However, this mono-sensory approach is too simplistic because in addition to the voice, the media of these cultures also included body language and body movements (dance), facial expressions, singing, cave paintings, etc., and therefore call for a multisensory approach to communication.

Literate cultures – also called "manuscript cultures" (Ong 2012, 117) or "scribal culture" (McLuhan 2004, 71) – emerged in Mesopotamia, Egypt, and China in the years 4,000 to 3,000 BC and later in Mesoamerica. If we follow the narrow definition of reading as "to look at and understand the meaning of written or printed words or symbols" (*Oxford Learner's Dictionaries* n.d.), then the practice of reading as we typically understand it origins from this introduction of writing (Sampson 2015). From a Eurocentric perspective, print cultures emerged around the German smith and engraver Johannes Gutenberg's invention of the printing press in 1450. But we find block printing in China around 600, and moveable types were widespread in China before 980.

In literate cultures, stories were written down, and people who were able to read could read them aloud in churches, theatres, and other public or private places. Even though most early manuscripts were meant for reading aloud, the spreading of specific stories was no longer limited to the memory of human beings, but could relatively easily be transported around the world and even translated into other languages and passed on through generations. It was in the period of literate cultures that reading in the narrowest sense of the word – a visual decoding of letters on a flat, light material – was consolidated, and the distribution of print copies accelerated in time and space. From this period emerged the codex book as we know it, which has dominated our understanding of reading ever since, reflected in the entry on reading in the *Oxford Learner's Dictionaries*. But even when reading became a solitary and silent practice among the European bourgeoisie during the 17th century, oral storytelling and reading aloud continued to be widespread among all social classes alongside singing, dancing, painting, talking, and other communicative practices. The communicative practices of oral cultures did not disappear, but continued side by side and merged with literate cultures, which makes it hard to argue for the sensory dominance of vision.

Electronic cultures emerged with the electric telegraph in the United States in 1843 and in Europe in 1847, followed by an increasing number of media based on the use of electricity and energy processes for symbolic purposes. Most significant is Alexander Graham Bell's invention of the telephone (1876) and the Thomas Edison phonograph (1877), but important are also radar, the tape recorder, radio, television, video, the electric typewriter, cinema, etc. In relation to these media, reading must be understood as "human perception of symbolically coded signs of all kinds," and in modern media semiotics, it is still common to use the extended notion of "text" and, following from that, "reading" as including all kinds of media content, including audio and audiovisual material.

We need to update the original "oral-literate-electronic" schema by adding the digital as a fifth element. One of the first people to do that, still following the logic of the schema, was the Danish Internet researcher Niels Ole Finnemann in his book *Internettet i mediehistorisk perspektiv* (*The

Internet in a Media-Historical Perspective) from 2005. Digital culture has its roots in Alan Turing's definition of the principle of the universal computer from 1936 and in the building of the first computers 10 years later; though the Internet first appeared as a publicly accessible open network in the 1990s. Finnemann describes the binary digital alphabet and the computer reading the letters 0 and 1 as a renaissance of written cultures. In digital media culture, the term "reading" has taken on yet another layer of meaning, which is not present in the four definitions above, namely when the technology itself, and not just living biological creatures, is reading and reading *us* through algorithmic data analysis of our digital footprints. The Internet has facilitated an increase in written communication in general, but since Finnemann wrote his book at the beginning of the millennium, the audiovisual, audio, and interactive content – what he calls the "multi-semiotic potential" (Finnemann 2005, 142) of the Internet – has increased as well, which brings us to the idea of a multisensory digital reading culture.

The "oral-literate-electronic-digital" schema has been widely criticized for being media-deterministic and based on white male, religious ideologies (see for instance anthropologists like Scribner and Cole (1981) and Feld (1986) or Finnemann (2005) and Sterne (2011)). Despite this important critique, this media-specific schema has had an enormous influence on studies on media history and discussions of how media and technology have always influenced culture and society and hence also reading.

Coarse as it is, it may, at first sight, seem obvious to transfer the logic and the historical idea of the "oral-literate-electronic-digital" schema developed by the Toronto School to a corresponding history of an "oral-literate-electronic-digital" reading condition. As the following section will show, the literature behind the "oral-literate-electronic-digital" schema suggests that each culture is dominated by either the acoustic or the visual. But as indicated above, we can in fact identify practices of multisensory communication and reading in every culture, and the emergence of digital media culture has made it increasingly important to study reading as a multisensory activity.

Ideas of sensory biases

What characterizes media ecologists like McLuhan, Ong, and Meyrowitz is the idea that each media matrix has a bias toward either the visual or the acoustic. In *Understanding Media: The Extensions of Man*, McLuhan describes the development from oral to print culture as a cultural transformation from an acoustic to a visual space of perception. According to McLuhan, writing and especially the invention of the printing press in the 15th century led to the domination of vision over the other senses. McLuhan is particularly interested in the transition between written/printed culture and electronic media and argues that with the introduction of electronic media the pendulum returns to the acoustic space, where – like hearing – information comes from all around you in a 360-degree circle instead of from a delimited visible space where you focus on one thing at a time.

One must be aware that when McLuhan differentiates between the visual and the acoustic, he is not claiming that we use our ears more than our eyes in the electronic age. He uses the sensory metaphors to argue that the character of the electronic media culture – the amount of information sources and the way in which communication takes place – calls for a form of multisensory perception based on audio characteristics.

> Acoustic space is a dwelling place for anyone who has not been conquered by the one-at-a-time, uniform ethos of the alphabet [...] There are no boundaries to sound. We hear from all directions at once. But the balance between inner and outer experience can be precise [...] Sound comes to us from above, below and the sides.
> (McLuhan 2004, 68)

Obviously, it is easy to argue against McLuhan's stereotypical dichotomy between visual and acoustic perception, since we also use sight in a non-rational way, for instance, to orientate ourselves in the world, and we are also able to perceive sounds logically and sequentially, for instance when listening analytically to audiobooks (Have and Stougaard Pedersen 2016, see also Sterne 2011). But in the context of this volume, we can use the framework behind his metaphors to extend the concept of reading, understanding it to be something that can be practiced through several senses (simultaneously) and which includes analog as well as digital book formats. Multisensory reading includes sensory impressions from all directions and all senses and balances the inner cognitive and emotional experience with the outer materiality of the book and the surroundings.

Ong and oralities

McLuhan's observations are interesting regarding the different normative views on the experience of eye and ear reading, respectively; historically the latter has been considered a form of second-rate reading (see Have and Stougaard Pedersen 2016). In the book *Orality and Literacy: The Technologizing of the Word* (1982), Ong focuses on the transition between oral cultures of communication and written and printed ones, and he argues that silent reading, the dominant form for centuries, followed from that shift.

Inspired by McLuhan, Ong talks about closure as the heritage of print (Ong 2012, 135). He complains that "words are grounded in oral speech, [and] writing tyrannically locks them into a visual field forever" (ibid. 12). Following that reasoning, audiobooks must be a liberating medium, releasing the word and letting it return to the free oral world of storytelling.

However, audiobooks are still strongly dependent on the structure and form of the written book. Hence, the conditions of the audiobook today are not the same as the conditions found in oral cultures, simply because a written text structures the oral narration (Have and Stougaard Pedersen 2016), and digital audiobooks are today endlessly distributed across time and space.

Ong conceptualizes the shift from "primary orality" in oral cultures to "secondary orality" in the electronic age:

> I style the orality of a culture totally untouched by any knowledge of writing or print, 'primary orality'. It is 'primary' by contrast with 'secondary orality' of present-day high-technology culture.
> (Ong 2012 (1982), 11)

Stories and narratives in oral cultures are stored in memory. When stories are written down, they become silent. So, you may say that the audiobook restructures writing, returning it to secondary orality, freeing the words from what Ong has called the "tyranny of writing." But you may also argue that the controlling voice of the audiobook creates closure of the printed source in relation to pace and free interpretation, and that the recorded sound is just as fixed in time and space as the printed text (Have and Stougaard Pedersen 2016).

All electronic texts are, according to Ong, "secondary," in the sense that they are technologically powered, unlike "primary" orality, which uses absolutely no tools or technologies. Some researchers have suggested an updating of Ong's oralities to a "tertiary orality" of digital media (Finnemann 2005, Logan 2010, Have and Stougaard Pedersen 2016). Finnemann adds the term to the fifth media matrix above, including different kinds of digitized speech, synthetic speech, voice response systems, speech recognition systems, etc., and Robert K. Logan suggests a tertiary orality or "digital orality" based on the conversational nature of text-based Internet communication. According to Logan, this would include the orality of emails, blog posts, list services, text messaging, etc. – written text transmitted through the Internet (Logan 2010, 103).

Dissolving the sensory hierarchy of reading

The way we read in our daily life and in our interaction with our surroundings has changed historically in line with the shifting media matrices and their dominating media technologies. In other words, the reading condition of a specific period is defined as the interplay between available reading technologies and the way people use those technologies. As media and culture scholar John Hartley puts it in the foreword to the 30th-anniversary edition of *Orality and Literacy*, "Ong popularized the idea that knowledge is a product of language, and that the medium in which language is communicated – by voice, writing, print – makes us think along certain path-dependent lines" (Hartley in Ong 2012, xiv).

Media, communication, and reading have always been multisensory because we as human beings cannot limit our perception of the world to one sense only. The sensing body is always present in all kinds of reading. It is not the media or media-historical periods that are biased toward visual or acoustic perception. It is the hierarchies around dominant concepts of reading, knowledge, etc. that feed these normative ideas and discourses. The reading condition of modern digital times makes it easier to challenge these ideas and argue for a dissolution of the sensory hierarchy with shifting sensory attention and intentionality.

It has been the aim of this chapter to nuance and critically discuss notions on the changing cultural media matrices and the associated hierarchies of senses and perception in favor of an account of a more multifaceted reading environment in the digital media matrix of the present. The digital reading condition naturally affords an equalization of both sense and reading hierarchies.

References

Darwin, Charles. 1871. *The Descent of Man, and Selection in Relation to Sex*. London: John Murray. 10.1037/12293-000. https://www.gutenberg.org/ebooks/2300.
Feld, Steven. 1986. "Orality and consciousness." In *The Oral and the Literate in Music*, edited by Tokumaru Yosihiko, and Yamaguti Osamu, 18–28. Tokyo: Academia Music.
Finnemann, Niels Ole. 2005. *Internettet I Mediehistorisk Perspektiv*. Copenhagen: Samfundslitteratur.
Have, Iben, and Stougaard Pedersen, Birgitte. 2016. *Digital Audiobooks: New Media, Users, and Experiences*. New York: Routledge.
Innis, Harold. 1991 (1951). *The Bias of Communication*. Toronto: University of Toronto Press.
Logan, Robert K. 2010. *Understanding New Media: Extending Marshall McLuhan*. Peter Lang.
McLuhan, Marshall. 2004. In *Audio culture: Readings in modern music*, edited by Christoph Cox, and Daniel Warner. New York: Continuum
Meyrowitz, Joshua. 1986. *No Sense of Place: The Impact of Electronic Media on Social Behavior*. Oxford University Press.
Miyagawa, Shigeru, Ojima, Shiro, Berwick, Robert C., and Okanoya, Kazuo. 2014. "The integration hypothesis of human language evolution and the nature of contemporary languages." *Frontiers in Psychology*, 9 June 2014. 10.3389/fpsyg.2014.00564.
Ong, Walter J. 2012 (1982). *Orality and Literacy: The Technologizing of the Word*. New York: Routledge.
Oxford Learners Dictionary. Entry for definition of the verb "read." https://www.oxfordlearnersdictionaries.com/definition/english/read_1?q=read.

Peters, John Durham. 1999. *Speaking Into the Air: A History of the Idea of Communication*. Chicago: University of Chicago Press.
Sampson, Geoffrey. 2015. *Writing Systems*, 2nd edition. Sheffield, United Kingdom: Equinox.
Scribner, Sylvia, and Cole, Michael. 1981. *The Psychology of Literacy*. Cambridge: Harvard University Press.
Sterne, Jonathan. 2011. "The Theology of Sound: A Critique of Orality." *Canadian Journal of Communication* 36, no. 2, The Senses of Technology.
Sterne, Jonathan. 2003. *The Audible Past: Cultural Origins of Sound Reproduction*. Durham, North Carolina: Duke University Press.

3 The condition of reading in a digital media culture

Jay David Bolter

Chapter 2 laid out a broad historical schema, "oral-written-print-electronic-digital." In this chapter, we focus on the historical and material development of the fifth element of that schema. The first electronic, stored-program computers, the Manchester Mark I and the EDVAC, date from 1949, and the first personal computers for word processing and spreadsheets appeared in the 1970s and 1980s. This length of time compares to the span between the decade of Gutenberg's first printed books, which were made to resemble medieval manuscripts, and the early 16th century, when many of the characteristics of the modern printed book were being established. That historical parallel suggests that we may now be able to say something definitive about the impact of digital technology on our practices of reading and writing.

In the past half century, there have been significant changes in our assumptions about reading as a cultural practice. The range of texts that we read and encourage or expect young people to read as part of their education has become significantly more diverse. The definition of what counts as reading and writing has become less stable; for many it now includes audio (books) and hypertexts, if not video. We cannot ascribe any of these developments solely to the advent of digital media. For one thing, the changes began before the computer had matured as a medium. The computers of the 1960s were large and very expensive, available only to a technical elite and used almost exclusively for science and engineering, the military, and business. There were no word processors as we understand them now, and a few pioneers such as Ivan E. Sutherland were only beginning to conceive of the machine as a medium for visual display (Sutherland 1965). The first widely used desktop computers appeared in the 1980s, and it was only in the 1990s that computer-graphics capable machines and the World Wide Web emerged as important elements in the existing media economy of television, film, radio, and print. Efforts to enlarge the canon of literature and the definition of reading – gradual and intermittent as they were – gained ground through this period and were the result of a range of cultural and economic influences independent of the development of these digital media platforms and technologies (Bolter 2019).

DOI: 10.4324/9781003211662-6

When digital media did mature, however, they provided an ideal platform for the ongoing redefinition of reading and writing on a vast scale. Desktop and laptop computers redefined production (writing) more quickly and easily than consumption. In the 1980s and early 1990s, word processing became the preferred way to produce texts – at least texts for publication and for academic and research purposes. But these texts were usually still printed out and read on paper. The quality of computer screens made it uncomfortable to read for longer periods, and laptops were simply not as convenient to hold and carry as printed books. One of the factors that doomed the early movement for literary hypertext was that these "born-digital"texts had to be read at the computer. The novelist E. Annie Proulx expressed the judgment of most in the literary community when she wrote in 1994: "Nobody is going to sit down and read a novel on a twitchy little screen. Ever" (Proulx 1994). In 2007, when Amazon released the Kindle, whose screen was indeed small but not at all twitchy, sales of e-books rose immediately and dramatically. This early exponential growth led some, inevitably, to predict that e-books would replace print. But market shares for e-books reached a plateau in the early 2010s, and since then e-book sales have gone up and down in relation to print, most recently up during the pandemic. E-books have now become part of a heterogeneous economy with printed books and audiobooks. It seems no more likely that e-books will disappear than printed books will, although the relative popularity of these media forms may vary.

Heterogeneity is in general a defining characteristic of our contemporary media culture. Digital technologies play an indispensable role, but often that role is to serve as platforms for delivering other, older forms of recorded audio and video, photography and text. Meanwhile, other *materialities* and platforms continue to survive and even thrive. Printed books, magazines, brochures, pamphlets are still popular in various communities for various purposes. Theaters for live drama, art galleries, museums, and concert halls still attract large audiences. People still go to movies in theaters too, as the return to relative normalcy in the waning days of the pandemic shows. These obvious facts need to be mentioned simply because digital media enthusiasts have often predicted that all media will be rendered obsolete by some single digital platform (e.g., virtual reality) or media form (e.g., interactive video games). Throughout 40 and more years of digital development, what we have seen is not convergence toward a single platform or form of entertainment, but continued diversification of devices and forms, while "traditional" non-digital forms survive. Yet this is not to deny that digital media have had a tremendous impact: the digital is currently the dominant form that inflects our understanding of media culture as a whole.

This situation suggests one way to understand the digital reading condition. Digital media increasingly define modes of production and reception of texts of all sorts. In so doing, digital media now play a role in defining our assumptions about all forms of reading (and writing). There is a sense in which the digital condition influences us even when we are reading printed or written materials on paper. The influence may be most obvious in the case of experimental fiction that plays with the breaking down of traditional features of print, such as Mark Danielewski's *House of Leaves*, which N. Katherine Hayles characterized as a "writing machine" (Hayles 2002). But the influence is more often expressed in subtler ways. As digitally literate readers, we know while reading a printed book that we can always turn to our computer and google for references, and many of us do. That is, we can realize our own links for printed texts and make our reading experience a hybrid of analog and digital media. Prior to the advent of digital media, those literate in the previously dominant technology of print no doubt also appreciated the interconnectedness that print provided by vastly increasing the numbers and availability of texts. The great national and academic libraries and archives of the 19th and 20th centuries were physical expressions of that interconnectedness. But digital networking is of a different order. The ease of digital search and retrieval and the availability of online libraries and bookstores now encourage readers to view each text in dialog with a universe of other texts. Here as elsewhere, the digital reading condition extends or intensifies qualities that we can identify as beginning in the age of print or earlier eras (see Chapter 2). Poststructuralists in the 20th century, who had little or no interest in digital media, developed the concept of intertextuality to explain how texts functioned in the late age of print. What was esoteric literary theory then has become a standard practice of digital reading today.

The processes of extension, intensification, and innovation in the digital reading condition can be classified under four rubrics: hypertextual, multimodal, collective, and locative. Each of these can be identified as a creative response to technological innovations, which became widely available in roughly this chronological order during the period from the 1980s to the present. The responses were both practical and theoretical. Writers and readers began producing and consuming texts with these characteristics, and researchers and critics began to promote or debate the value of these new reading and writing practices. In each case, the material conditions and sense ratios of reading changed as a result.

Hypertextual

When Ted Nelson coined the term in the 1960s, his vision of a universal library of hypertexts could not come close to realization with existing technologies. But by 1989, Tim Berners-Lee and colleagues were able to create the protocols and software necessary for the World Wide Web, which led to an ever-expanding network of texts. They were in the first instance scientific texts and data, then commercial texts and advertising, but soon information from all sorts of governmental and private groups and individuals, and eventually traditional literary and scholarly texts as well. As this platform came to be available for millions of users, it promoted the reading practice that N. Katherine Hayles has labeled as "hyper reading" (see Chapter 1). Hyper reading has been contrasted, somewhat controversially, to "close" or "deep reading," often associated with reading a printed book (see Chapter 4). As important as following links for this new practice was the use of search engines (e.g., Altavista in 1995 and Google in 1998), which allowed users effectively to create their own hyperlinks in real time.

Early enthusiasts claimed that hypertext would lead to a new kind of writing, in which links defined multiple, equally valid paths for the reader to follow – hence, a new kind of dynamic or interactive fiction and new forms of argument (Coover 1992, Joyce 1995, Landow 1992). Such experimental hypertexts, however, have never attracted more than a modest reading audience, and the form was resoundingly rejected by the literary community, as exemplified by *The New York Times* article from Annie Proulx mentioned above. Hypertext links have indeed become a standard feature of online discursive writing today (but not for fiction). In many "serious" online publications (e.g., the *Atlantic*, *Slate*, *Salon*, op-ed section in *The New York Times*, and so on), hyperlinks take the reader to articles on related topics and thereby buttress the author's argument. The argument itself, however, is still made in linear fashion from beginning to end. In many cases, the same article is published online and in print. Perhaps one of the most popular online publications to make extensive use of hyperlinks is Wikipedia. Every major Wikipedia entry is shot through with links to related entries. Readers often read part of one entry before branching to another, which can fairly be called hyper reading, and the pace of such online hyper reading would be impossible to achieve in reading a printed encyclopedia. Nevertheless, the Wikipedia articles themselves are written to make sense as a linear reading experience. If the reader chooses to branch to another article, that new article is equally linear and does not adjust to accommodate where the reader has come from. Hyperlinks in these articles are the remediation of the footnotes in printed books. They are simply much faster and easier to follow. This persistence of traditional, linear structure within a hypertextual platform is an example of what Simone Murray has called the "literary-digital interpenetration" (Murray 2018, 3).

Taken together, the new and remediated practices of digital *textuality* have contributed to a changing understanding of the textual universe in which we function. The web as a network of pages and links is both a metaphor and a mechanism (see Chapter 9). As a mechanism, it is hierarchically organized, with a backbone and routers and central servers as main nodes spreading out to smaller servers and end nodes at individual computers. But from the user's perspective, technological hierarchy is invisible, and the network appears flat. The user's perception is that any page or site can in principle be reached from any other. There is no center to the Internet and no periphery. Already in the 1990s, digital media enthusiasts were touting the web as a medium that democratizes communication. In principle, anyone with the resources to acquire a computer, Internet connection, and service provider could publish their own website, which (again in principle) was just as accessible to millions of users as were the sites for CNN or *The New York Times*. In practice, the ratio of producers to consumers of websites remained relatively low, until the rise of social media. Nevertheless, Internet publication did make a wider range of texts (and eventually images and video) available to readers throughout the developed world, and this increased access accorded with and probably promoted a sense that the older hierarchies no longer applied. Information hierarchies were breaking down as readers could begin to search online rather than in library stacks. The move to include more women and minority authors in school and university curricula owed nothing in particular to the rise of the web. But the web did provide an operational metaphor for a culture that lacks a universally agreed center and single canon of authors and texts.

The hypertextual condition also facilitated passage back and forth between reading and writing, especially since the rise of blogs and social media. When users read a Twitter feed, they are invited to add likes or write comments, which are then available for other readers to respond to. To cut and paste text or links from a website into tweets or a Facebook page is to pass from reader to writer, now the normal practice in social media. This is another obvious, but important change from earlier eras of literacy, where readers have always outnumbered writers to a significant degree. We may actually be approaching the ironic condition where there are more "published" authors than readers. That is, many write comments that no one may ever read.

Our digitally networked media environment also facilitates the interrelating of media forms. Audiobooks are increasingly regarded as a legitimate form of reading, becoming even more popular during the pandemic. When a customer searches for a book on Amazon, they are often given the choice of paperback, e-book, or audiobook, suggesting that they are all equivalent formats for the same product. With Amazon's Whispersync feature, the customer who chooses both audiobook and e-book can move seamlessly back and forth between the two. Storytel is a European service with a similar feature (see also Chapter 4).

Multimedial

From about the same time as the advent of hypertext, the contemporary space of reading and writing began to include visual media, at least in the form of static images, and audio media such as audiobooks. The development of computer graphics and the graphical user interface in the 1970s also led to the emergence of multimedia computers in the following decades, with the Apple Macintosh leading the way to greater availability. Multimedia machines came into widespread use as the World Wide Web was growing in the 1990s. In the second half of the 20th century, the academic disciplines of literary theory, semiotics, and visual cultural studies had all come to regard visual artifacts such as films, television shows, and pictorial advertising as texts. By the end of the century, that perspective came to be shared in practice by web users who had never heard of these academic disciplines. The practices of professional and amateur remix (e.g., hip hop) show that multimedia texts can be produced and distributed almost as easily as they can be read (Navas et al. 2015, Lessig 2008).

The computer was not by any means the first popular medium for visual and aural representation: we can point to the entire history of what Benjamin called technologies of mechanical reproduction. Benjamin concentrated on photography and film in his "The Work of Art in the Age of Mechanical Reproduction" (1968), but audio recording, radio, and television belong to this list as well. The reception of each of these media depended on the cultural standards and hierarchies of their day, and none of them were regarded as repositories of our culture's most important texts; print retained that status throughout this entire period. Neither film nor television, for example, succeeded in replacing or even seriously challenging the textbook as the main instrument of education. All through the 1950s and 1960s, in fact, television viewing was seen as a major obstacle to the educational goal of getting students to read and attend to important printed texts. In contrast, after a relatively short period of contestation in the 1990s, the computer was regarded as appropriate and then important for education. In the United States, the special status of the computer become apparent in the rhetoric of the Clinton Administration – the Internet was an "information superhighway" – and has been true since (although adoption of computers has been different in different parts of the world). Computers became accepted educational tools with a place in both the classroom and students' home. As multimedia websites were now ubiquitous and as computers now featured tools for manipulating images, remixing audio and video, and building websites, it was natural to think that digital literacy required the ability to read and manipulate images and video and audio as well as text. Today it is no longer at all unusual for students to be making their own websites as part of school projects in a variety of classes as well as extracurricular activities. In the university community, we can discern a gradual, sometimes ambivalent, acceptance of digital research and publication.

Reading multimedia texts engages the sense of sight more fully or at least in a different way from reading alphabetic print alone, and audio texts obviously add another sense altogether. Multimedia *textuality* also suggests a new role for embodiment and polyaesthetic reception in the reading condition (see Chapter 1). Readers engage multimedia texts in what media communication researchers characterize as a "multimodal" fashion; their concept of multimodality is particularly useful for understanding the emerging digital condition of reading (see Chapter 4).

Collective

The ways in which the digital reading condition has become collective or communal also suggest similarities and continuities to earlier eras. Reading aloud to an audience has been practiced for centuries, indeed millennia, starting as early as the writing phase of the "oral-written-print-electronic-digital" schema, which Chapter 2 addressed. Reading aloud to one's children has been a standard element in parenting since the 19th century, and multi-authored forms of writing also have a long history. Nevertheless, the paradigm of silent, individual reading remained certainly dominant in the 20th century, as was the paradigm of the single-authored article or monograph. Both reading and writing as individual practices remain extremely common on digital platforms. But precisely because blogs and social media have broken down the boundary between consuming and producing texts, they have also facilitated collective reading and writing on a scale that dwarfs any earlier form of literacy. Practically any text (verbal or multimedia) on the Internet is available for comment and revision by others. Adding highlights, comments, and even emojis is now the digital equivalent of reading a printed text with a pencil in hand. The difference is that when the text is a shared social media document, your "reading" of the text becomes a paratext that others can also read and add to. Twitter feeds are designed to facilitate this practice, as are Facebook pages. YouTube videos are evolving collective texts, as are more lasting products such as Wikipedia articles. All such applications suggest a writing space, in which the status of the author becomes negotiable. (At least this insight of poststructuralists such as Barthes and Foucault has survived into the digital era). With the technology of print, the writing space, the printed page, is (apparently) fixed and belongs to the author or authors: writing is public, and reading is generally viewed as not only private but also derivative. The reader can make notes on the page, but those notes can never enter into the text itself. On the computer, the writing space does not seem to belong to any single author in the same way.

Just as the printed book and newspaper were said to define a metaphorical republic of letters and a public square, digital writing spaces redefine the notions of public and private. In the case of social media, the redefinition of public and private is becoming a source of urgent social and political contestation and is the subject of a massive amount of research in the social sciences and humanities. Definitions of appropriate political discourse in the public square mediated by print and even 20th-century mass media no longer seem adequate in this new space, where the distinction of public and private is radically altered, if not obliterated, as discussed below.

Locative

The fourth characteristic is the least well researched because its technologies are still emerging and large-scale use is relatively recent. Mobile devices with their location-based applications are now very common in the developed economies of Europe, North America, and East Asia (O'Dea 2022). Most often, these applications gather and display location-relevant texts, images, or videos on the user's screen. For example, a grocery store app tells the user on what aisle a product is located, and mapping apps indicate restaurants or businesses in the area. Such techniques, using GPS, WIFI, or cellular tracking, have become so common that a user's phone may at any time be running a dozen or more apps in the background – all tracking their position, which raises serious privacy concerns. A specific class of location-based and image-based applications use augmented reality (AR) techniques to display information registered on the screen over the live video of the user's current environment. One of the most commonly used geo-location apps, Google Maps, now offers a Live View feature, which helps the user navigate by locating directions or labels over the landmarks around them.

Such applications suggest a new kind of *materiality*, a blending of textual space and physical space. Admittedly, such locative texts are usually practical or commercial rather than literary in nature. But geo-location is also a feature of many cultural heritage applications: an app designed as an audio tour of a heritage site. An AR application in a museum might use image recognition or even QR codes to determine which artifact that visitor is standing in front of and deliver appropriate text, audio, or visuals. More and more museums and exhibition site are experimenting with AR and VR to enhance the visitor's experience (Bekele et al. 2018).

This kind of reading in and of place is both radically contemporary and quite traditional. Inscribing on wood, bronze, or stone monuments is a practice that dates back millennia and of course continues today, and stone inscriptions probably constitute the most lasting form of writing. The obvious and important difference is precisely that monumental inscriptions are designed to communicate exactly the same message indefinitely to all potential readers. Locative applications on mobile devices are contextual, sometimes tailored to the individual user, and relatively easily updated with new information.

We can already see how this locative dimension of the digital *textuality* is joining with the collaborative nature of social media to realign the categories of public and private. In the hybrid space of AR, the digital world merges into the physical even more palpably and completely than with previous mobile applications. AR thus takes our media culture further, both in making private space public and in appropriating public space for private use (see Bolter et al. 2021, chapter 9). Bringing public or commercial data into our homes has clear utility – for example, to display furniture that we are thinking of purchasing in our living room. By contrast, when we are in a public space and ask our mobile device to display all the data of interest to us (our favorite restaurants or friends' tweets), we are personalizing that space, at least in the moment. Again, the techniques of 3D mapping and

The condition of reading in a digital media culture 43

scene recognition used by AR devices have serious implications for individual privacy and security (Hosfelt 2019).

Layered *materialities* and the digital reading condition

These four categories (hypertextual, multimedial, collective, and locative) can be illustrated on a timeline as follows (Figure 3.1).

As noted above, hypertextual and multimedial qualities emerged first. The graphical user interface was pioneered in the 1970s at Xerox Parc and then perfected and made available to consumers in the Apple Macintosh in the 1980s, although it was not until the 1990s that multimedia computers came into their own. The commercialization of the Internet and the development of the World Wide Web in the 1990s made collective writing and reading feasible, but it was the rise of social media in the 2000s that inaugurated the practice on its current scale (literally billions of writers and readers sharing texts). Finally, smart mobile devices such as the iPhone introduced locative reading and writing on a similar scale in the 2010s. AR headsets and glasses have yet to achieve a broad user base, if they ever will, although industry giants such as Apple and Google are apparently committed to bringing them to market. As the timeline indicates, these qualities are cumulative rather than successive. The digital reading condition is still hypertextual and multimedial today, and the dominance of social media platforms guarantees that it will continue. It remains to be seen how important a facet of our media culture locative reading and writing will prove to be.

The implications of these four qualities together are significant for all sorts of cultural and societal practices, not least for the functioning of

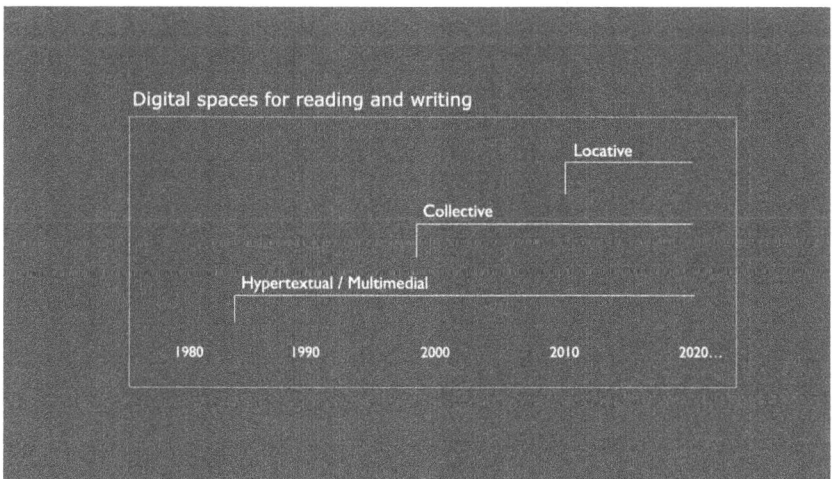

Figure 3.1 Four categories of digital textuality.

democracy in technologically advanced societies, as has become apparent since 2015. These implications form the subject of many later chapters in this volume. As this brief chapter indicates and later chapters will reiterate, the digital reading condition is characterized by a tension between forces of change and inertia. Reading and writing of print and other technologies remain important, even definitive, today, even if they are now often remediated by and presented in digital platforms. At the same time, digital media accelerate the flattening of cultural hierarchies we identified at the outset, and they do so through their *materialities*, as discussed in Chapter 2. That is, the hypertextual networking of our textual universe, including older printed texts now available online. Multimedia applications enhance the status of video and audio as texts in that universe. Social media applications do the same for practices of collective reading and writing. Finally, locative applications suggest that texts need not be in a separate, implicitly high realm of the mind, but can also exist in intimate relation to our embodied existence in the world. How all these multiple literacies coexist in today's media culture is the subject of the next chapter.

References

Bekele, Mafkereseb Kassahun, Pierdicca, Roberto, Frontoni, Emanuele, Malinverni, Eva Savina, and Gain, James. 2018. "A survey of augmented, virtual, and Mixed reality for cultural heritage." *Journal on Computing and Cultural Heritage* 11, no. 2: 1–36. 10.1145/3145534.

Benjamin, Walter. 1968. "The work of art in the age of mechanical reproduction." In *Illuminations*, 217–251. New York: Schocken Books.

Bolter, Jay David. 2019. *The Digital Plenitude: The Decline of Elite Culture and the Rise of New Media*. Cambridge, Massachusetts: MIT Press. https://mitpress.mit.edu/books/digital-plenitude.

Bolter, Jay David, Engberg, Maria, and MacIntyre, Blair. 2021. *Reality Media: Augmented and Virtual Reality*. Cambridge, Massachusetts: MIT Press.

Boyd, Danah. 2014. *It's Complicated: The Social Life of Networked Teens*. New Haven, Connecticut: Yale University Press.

Coover, Robert. 1992. "The end of books." *New York Times Book Review*.

Hosfelt, Diane. 2019. *Making Ethical Decisions for the Immersive Web*. ArXiv paper 1905.06995. May 14, 2019. http://arxiv.org/abs/1905.06995.

Have, Iben, and Stougaard Pedersen, Birgitte. 2015. *Digital Audiobooks: New Media, Users, and Experiences*. New York and London: Routledge.

Hayles, N. Katherine. 2002. *Writing Machines*. Cambridge, Massachusetts: MIT Press.

Joyce, Michael. 1995. *Of Two Minds*. Ann Arbor, Michigan: University of Michigan Press.

Landow, George. P. 1992. *Hypertext: The Convergence of Contemporary Critical theory and Technology*. Johns Hopkins University Press.

Lessig, Lawrence. 2008. *Remix: Making Art and Commerce Thrive in the Hybrid Economy*. Bloomsbury.

Murray, Simon. 2018. *The Digital Reading Sphere: Reading, Writing, and Selling Books in the Internet Era*. Illustrated edition. John Hopkins University Press.

Navas, Eduardo, Gallagher, Owen, and Burrough, Xtine. 2015. *The Routledge Companion to Remix Studies*. Routledge, Taylor & Francis Group.

O'Dea, S. (2022, March 14). Global smartphone sales to end users 2007–2021. *Statista*. https://www.statista.com/statistics/263437/global-smartphone-sales-to-end-users-since-2007/.

Proulx, E. Annie. 1994. "Books on top." *New York Times*, May 26, 1994.

Sutherland, Ivan E. 1965. "The ultimate display." *Proceedings of the IFIP Congress*, 506–508.

4 Reading toward multiliteracies: understanding reading comprehension and reading experience

Birgitte Stougaard Pedersen and Iben Have

Reading competencies as well as the exploration of these competencies often enhance cognitive aspects of decoding and understanding texts. The concept of reading which is explored in this volume deals with an understanding of digital literacy that moves an interest in reading toward a focus on the reading *experience* and, by extension, a more sensory-based approach to the concept of literacy. This is especially evident and important when it comes to reading in the digital age, where we read an increasing number of texts via computer screens, tablets, and smartphones – texts often combined with images, film, and sound. Furthermore, the portability of the smartphone makes it easy to move around in shifting environments when experiencing podcasts or audiobooks. Hereby we are drawing a parallel to notions of media literacies, since the development of digital technologies is not just textual, but includes all kinds of multimedia, multisensory dimensions, complicating the issue of reading and literacies.

In this chapter, we discuss concepts of literacies from different perspectives: digital literature, didactics and pedagogical research, multimodality (social semiotics), and multiliteracies. These fields of research form the scholarly basis of this chapter. Building on Chapter 2, we combine insights from the academic communities that study digital reading and digital forms of literature with national areas of study concerning reading related to language and education. We do this in order to grapple with the concept of literacy as well as multiliteracies, which is one of the research backgrounds for this volume's proposed notion of multisensory digital reading (see Section II). We will end this chapter by discussing cultural and democratic values, long attached to the issue of literacy, in the context of multimodal media texts and a survey from 2020 exploring experiences of narratives, reading habits, and crossmodal everyday media use among 12- to 14-year-old children in Denmark.

Text practices and the digital reading condition

Digital technologies challenge the debates around media and literacy competencies. This is evident in various scholarly fields, especially in

DOI: 10.4324/9781003211662-7

didactic contexts in which technologies have pointed to the need of developing new skills for reading in a digital landscape.

By raising aspects of literacy, we add to and nuance current debates on reading by offering a slightly new perspective – we are generally focusing on types of texts that have not received ample scholarly attention: audiobooks and born-digital narratives that produce both new types of works and new sensorial ways of reading.

Considering the reflections on multisensory reading that run through this volume, we point to the value discussions within the sociocultural landscape in which the debates of reading are situated. Reading as politically guided national contexts of language and education deals with the development of technology as well as with concepts such as multimodality and multiliteracies. Even though for instance the Danish national goals for primary and secondary schools mention and reflect multimodal text practices, reading competencies still to a wide extent are connected to ideas of literary reading as something that takes place in a book (see Chapter 13). By introducing a fuller understanding of human sensory perception in relation to multimodal communication and multiliteracies, we can broaden the understanding of what a reading experience in our digital age comprises.

Digital reading

Digital reading is widely debated in many academic fields. In a subfield of literary studies often called digital or electronic literary studies, we find scholars who are interested in understanding how the digital condition is changing conceptions of literature and reading (in their digital technological contexts). Some scholars – N. Katherine Hayles, Jessica Pressmann, David Ciccoricco, Scott Rettberg, Chris Funkhouser, Alice Bell, Astrid Ensslin, Hans Kristian Rustad, and Dene Grigar, to name but a few – have engaged in an international community invested in understanding how specifically born-digital literature intersects with earlier literary technologies. Poets and writers such as John Cayley, Maria Mencia, Talan Memmott, and Kate Pullinger who also work as scholars in the field have also produced important theoretical contributions. Starting with studies of early hypertext literature, the field today analyzes various types of born-digital literature, many of them with a clear avant-garde modernist aesthetic, others influenced by other art and media forms (such as comics or children's literature), and some exploring the very nature of digital, that is, algorithmically generated text.

The reason why it is relevant to introduce discussions on digital literature reading when discussing multiliteracies is to draw attention to the specific conditions of the digital text: that born-digital text formats add new ways of reading – for instance, hypertexts that challenge the linearity of the text as well as digital texts that include visuals and audio. These formats make us read in new ways, just as they create new ideas of what is considered deep, close, or distracted reading (Hayles 2010, see also Chapter 10). In that sense, digital texts force us to reconsider what it means to read – and they shed light on the close relationship between *materiality* and the reading activity. Printed books afford the material and sensory reading situation in one specific way, digital text in a different way, and audiobooks in a third.

Reading in educational contexts

The educational field concerning reading in national political contexts includes a broad variety of approaches and perspectives, such as cognitive science, social semiotics, and various learning and educational approaches to reading competencies. The chapters in Section IV discuss the didactic perspectives in detail, while in this chapter we present them primarily to outline the path toward the notion of literacies.

In a Danish context, the ideas of decoding and language comprehension are central to the didactic approaches to reading (Bråten 2008, Elbro 2001). Decoding leads to identification of written words – meaning, sound, and grammatical properties – and is reserved for text formats. Language comprehension relates to how we as readers imagine meaning from the decoded words and how the words activate prior knowledge of the described world. Language comprehension is not reserved for text format, but relates to language and communication in general. We do for instance read an audiobook when it comes to comprehension but not when it comes to decoding in the sense of apprehending written signs.

Decoding and language comprehension cover the entire cognitive apparatus that is activated while reading. However, a number of other aspects are also central to the understanding of reading competencies, particularly in our everyday lives, including interpreting signs and symbols and reading maps. Different national contexts of reading research and didactic and pedagogical education across the world of course cover a variety of approaches such as reading processes, reading contexts (classroom studies), as well as research focusing on aesthetic aspects of reading, but generally cognitive aspects are seen as decisive for understanding of and researching reading in a school context.

Multimodality and reading

The discussions on multimodality are founded in social semiotics (see Kress 2010, Jewitt 2014) and focus on the significance of contextual aspects of reading practices – in a school context often implemented in an increasing focus on audiovisual culture and products. If we use the defined goals of the Danish Ministry of Children and Education as an example, multimodal texts are implemented in the goals for the L1 teaching (native language) in primary schools. Digitization creates new concrete and differentiated contexts that we need to understand in order to be able to respond in a creative and qualified manner. According to van Leeuwen, very young children are able to communicate with the means at hand, and they find it easy to explore the limits for how different media can be used for communication (Van Leeuwen 2017). This ability is however continuously and increasingly being *culturalized* through primary school into a value-based situation, in which text and language are presented and recognized as more valuable and compelling than for instance sound and images (ibid.).

Multimodality studies thus investigate the learning potentials of semiotic resources and how the role of multimodal aesthetics has changed its position, gaining more impact on the means of communication. According to van Leeuwen, multimodal literacy has added an aesthetic dimension to everyday forms of communication that were formerly regarded as more functional and monomodal. This fosters forms of communication that combine functionality (a focus on the job that a given piece of communication is intended to perform) with the use of aesthetic design ideas meant to communicate corporate or personal identities and values (Van Leeuwen 2017, 10).

The multimodal agenda is part of a movement within reception aesthetics that has developed since the 1970s and which represents a more and more extended notion of what a text is (Iser 1976). Multimodality was raised by social semiotics during the 1990s and stems from changes in the social and technological contexts in which we meet texts. At the same time, related notions of literacy have developed, partly due to the increasing digitization. Readers need to develop new types of literacies to thrive in a digitized society, and the digital condition is thus pushing reading acts and reading strategies in new directions.

This has resulted in an increasing use of the term literacy, partly replacing the notion of reading – changes in the *materiality* of texts lead to changes in the concept of reading as well as to new demands regarding pedagogy and technical terms related to educational contexts.

Literacy and multiliteracies

A broader concept of text as well as an increased awareness of reading as a way of taking part in society are some of the underlying agendas of the term literacy. According to the broad UNESCO definition,

> Literacy is the ability to identify, understand, interpret, create, communicate and compute, using printed and written materials associated with varying contexts. Literacy involves a continuum of learning in enabling individuals to achieve their goals, to develop their knowledge and potential, and to participate fully in their community and wider society (UNESCO Institute for Statistics 2005).

In the UNESCO definition, values like learning, independency, setting own goals, and self-development stand out; only in the last paragraph does the definition refer to how these individual goals are important for taking part in society, for participating in communities. We can also note that literacy in this edition is continuously defined as focused entirely on *written* texts.

According to the founders of the so-called New London Group, the notion of multiliteracies has since the 1990s been addressing this ver2 problem by broadening the focus on written texts belonging to the concept of literacy. According to Cope and Kalantzis (2009), there is a need for multiliteracy skills to develop the single citizen's capability to take part in a digitized democratic society. According to the authors, this is done by developing multimodal skills in relation to technology, also taking into account that children have differentiated skills regarding modal expressions and practices and that all children ought to be recognized in contributing to knowledge production in a didactic context (Cope and Kalantzis 2009). Multiliteracies thus enhance the multimodal dimension of literacy. According to Cope and Kalantzis, several modalities of meaning are needed to cover and mobilize several literacies that are part of understanding multiliteracies, including writing, speak, visual representation, auditory representation, tactile representation, gestures, spatial representation, and self-representation (ibid., 15–6).

Research into multiliteracy thus pays attention to multimodality as a way of supporting transports between senses, also called synaesthesia, an ability that children possess, but which is unlearned in school (Van Leeuwen 2017). One of the reasons for this is that our cultural schemas regarding knowledge are divided into separate conceptional paradigms that do not necessarily support cross-modal learning. Synaesthesia as related to meaning-producing processes can, according to Cope and Kalantzis, be performed as a didactic strategy in a school context since children have natural competencies for this transport between the senses – competencies that need to be maintained and developed instead of pushed out, as is often the case in more strictly text-based learning environments.

The notion of multiliteracies is thus part of an increasing articulation of, and need for, rethinking reading competencies in this expanded field of multimodal text practices. Digital literacy as well as multiliteracies have a strong focus on the semiotic resources that are available and needed in a digital community. Multimodality in the theoretical framework of Kress and van Leeuwen comprises context-based social semiotic notions of reading practices and means of communication from a broad perspective. The idea of digital literacy that we point toward in this volume, as a corrective or nuancing of the multimodal apparatus of both the research positions of multimodality studies and the New London Group, is developing *sensory* reading competencies. In that sense, we do not primarily draw on literacy as the understanding or handling of either written text or technology. Rather, we work on qualifying and developing skills that consider the fact that digital texts also change the sensory aspects of reading competencies by changing the ratio or pace at which various senses are employed. When reading digital texts, readers interact with the digital interface, for instance by following links, searching online, etc. We enhance the situational aspects of reading, but from a more aesthetic, situated understanding of each reading situation as affording new sensory-specific and unique reading experiences. We do this by drawing on an open-minded attitude toward actual current digital reading practices.

Critical and curious approaches toward digital reading

According to research in multiliteracies, all kinds of communication – visual, spatial, auditory – are *culturalized* expressions that need to unfold as a critical, reflexive practice. These critical aspects are thus foregrounded in multiliteracy theory (1996, 2009) building on a *critical* notion of being a citizen in society and taking this aspect of citizenship seriously. The theory of multiliteracies passes on these ideas from critical theory, that to become this competent citizen, you need to develop a clear critical consciousness toward politics. In that sense, paradoxically, the theory of multiliteracies reproduces a rather normative and intellectual conception of the citizen who needs *Bildung* to gain the correct critical consciousness. Cope and Kalantzis, and the rest of the New London Group appear open to alternative approaches to knowledge and learning. However, such approaches still seem to take place within a rather institutionalized idea about what is considered valuable to learning.

When you are reading on your smartphone via a streaming service such as Storytel or Mofibo today, you can seamlessly switch between an e-book and an audio format for reading. This everyday use of literary texts represents an expanded concept of texts which makes us curious about rethinking the concept of reading as well as of literacies from a sensory perspective. What are the challenges hereof, how we can name and understand these everyday experiences, and how are they discursively outlined in relation to aspects of cultural values?

We will now discuss these aspects in connection with a Danish investigation of young people's reading and media habits. As we will address in further detail in Chapters 10 and 11, there exists a strong critique of screen reading as more distracted, hyper and less engaged and immersed than paper book reading. Underneath this critique runs a dystopian narrative of the way human beings bit by bit lose the ability to deep reading – intensified by the digital reading condition (Baron and Mangen 2021). We acknowledge this concern, however adding our notion of the importance of including the sensory aspect of reading to a higher degree to frame a position that embraces the pre-cognitive, embodied aspects of reading experiences. This relates to the need for more multifaceted modal representations, as stated by Cope and Kalantzis, supporting their critical perspective of how every single citizen will need to become a competent (partaker) participant in society. In our perspective, this also needs to include and recognize aesthetic elements of embodied experiences, including listening, touching, moving bodies, as important partakers in meaning processing. As we have shown in Section I, digital reading practices cover numerous multifaceted reading practices. Therefore, the theoretical approach to these practices also needs to develop a curiosity toward different forms of multisensory and multimodal attention. The theoretical ideas above are implemented in a survey we did in 2020 exploring experiences of narratives, reading habits, and cross-modal everyday media use among 12- to 14-year-old children in Denmark. Empirical studies of reading have been conducted in various academic fields such as didactics, information studies, literature studies, cultural studies, and media studies. From a Danish context, it is our impression that studies of existing reading habits and media use take different approaches to *Bildung*-related normative discussions of good and bad text practices or good and bad reading cultures. Compared to studies anchored in literary studies fields, we find it significant that surveys investigating media use from a media studies perspective often address the qualities of all aspects of culture, including popular culture, and we believe that the Danish context represents trends found throughout the world. This is a perspective we wanted to include in a Danish study.

The study is a part of the research project *Reading Between Media*, to which both authors of this chapter have contributed. It is a survey including 565 respondents in a Danish secondary school in the municipality of Silkeborg. The overall aim of the study is to investigate Danish children's multisensory digital reading practices and experiences. We wanted to investigate how being a young reader in the digital age implies that reading happens via screens and through headphones with the ability to shift easily between interfaces while reading a specific story or being in a specific story world. Starting from the premise that multiple literacies and media competencies co-exist among the children, we deliberately formulated the questions in the survey to include a broad range of narrative media. We wanted to create a wider space for the experience of narratives based on the belief that experience and engagement are interrelated. The study shows that children's media habits change radically from the 6th to 8th grade (age 12–13 and 14–15 years). This influences the students' reading habits – reading of traditional printed books decreases and the consumption of film, TV series, podcasts, music, and social media increases.

The Silkeborg study demonstrates how the children's reading culture and media culture converge and provides insight into the practice of multitasking. About 87% say that they use different media simultaneously (p. 30 in the report), for instance, videos, social media, gaming, audio, traditional reading, and drawing (p. 113) and combine them in different ways.

When we look at a broader context of reading, we see that the participants are guided not so much by the media technology itself, but by the transmedia content. The popularity of transmedia storytelling and transmedia story worlds such as *Harry Potter*, *World of Warcraft*, and *The Lord*

Reading toward multiliteracies 53

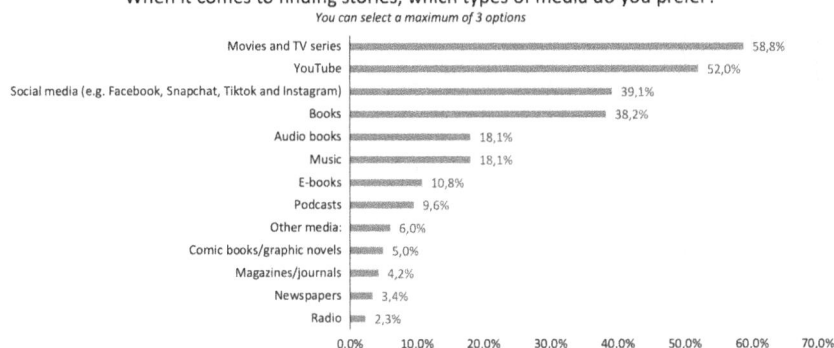

Figure 4.1 What media types do you prefer when experiencing stories?

of the Rings confirms the need for a broader and alternative media perspective when studying children's multisensory reading experiences.

We wanted to meet the students with a curious and less hierarchical understanding of their media use and asked them in which medium they had last met an engaging story. We can see that most students prefer to experience narratives in film and TV series, followed by YouTube, books, and social media (Figure 4.1).

The survey shows how the readers experience and actively engage in narratives in multiple ways, afforded by digital media. Different media require different kinds of literacies and different sensory and technological competencies, and the children navigate sophisticated media and reading strategies and show us that paths to knowledge and narratives are complex and manifold.

Both the multiliteracies perspective and the growing interest in technology comprehension, which in Denmark is about to become a mandatory subject in primary school, reveal an interest in educating children to better handle technology and navigate a digitized society. The perspective that we have foregrounded in this chapter is the *investigation and development of the aesthetic and embodied potentials of reading*. This is done by bringing forward a need for building competencies regarding a broader sensory approach to meaning creation to support the development of sensory-based digital literacy. By doing so, we seek to develop an understanding of reading with the senses, not just as something that delivers an add-on to the text-based approach to knowledge and experiences, but as something that democratizes meaning-making processes – or in other words, reading with the senses that acknowledge the multitude of technologies that support an understanding of reading as matters of the body, the senses, and our surroundings.

References

Baron, Naomi S. 2021. *How We Read Now: Strategic Choices for Print, Screen, and Audio*. Oxford University Press.
Baron, Naomi S., and Mangen, Anne. 2021. "Doing the reading: The decline of long long-form reading in higher education." *Poetics Today* 42, no. 2: 253–279.
Bråten, I. 2008. "Læseforståelse: Komponenter, vanskeligheder og tiltag." In *Læseforståelse. Læsning i videnssamfundet: Teori og praksis*, edited by I. Bråten, 47–83. Klim.
Cope, Bill, and Kalantzis, Mary. 2009. "Multiliteracies: New literacies, new learning." Pedagogies (Mahwah, N.J.) 4, no. 3: 164–195. Taylor & Francis.
Ehri, Linnea C. 1995. "The emergence of word reading in beginning reading." In *Children Learning to Read: International Concerns. Volume 1. Emergent and Developing Reading: Messages for Teachers*, edited by Pamela Owen and Peter Pumfrey, 9–31. The Falmer Press.
Elbro, Carsten. 2001. *Læsning og Læseundervisning*. Copenhagen: Gyldendal.
Hayles, N. Katherine. 2010. "How we read: Close, hyper, machine." *ADE Bulletin* 150.
Iser, Wolfgang. 1976. *Die Akt des Lesens*. Munich: W. Fink.
Jewitt, Carey. 2014. *The Routledge Handbook of Multimodal Analysis*. London: Routledge.
Jewitt, Carey, and Kress, Gunther. 2003. *Multimodal Literacy*. New York: Peter Lang.
Kress, Gunther. 2010. *Multimodality – A Social Semiotic Approach to Contemporary Communication*. New York: Routledge.
Kress, Gunther, and van Leeuwen, Theo. 2001. *Multimodal Discourse. The Modes and Media of Contemporary Communication*. Bloomsbury.
New London Group. 1996. "A pedagogy of multiliteracies: Designing social futures." *Harvard Educational Review* 66: 60–92.
Underwood, Ted. 2017. "A genealogy of distant reading." *Digital Humanities Quarterly* 11, no. 2.
UNESCO Institute for Statistics. 2005. http://uis.unesco.org/en/glossary-term/literac
Van Leeuwen, Theo. 2017. "Multimodal literacy." Videnomlaesning.dk. https://www.videnomlaesning.dk/media/2127/21_theo-van-leeuwen.pdf.

Section II
Multisensory Reading

Introduction to Section II

The chapters in this section analyze how different sensory inputs and combinations of sensory engagement written into the text itself shape the reading. Reading, in particular silent reading, is most often understood primarily as an activity of the eyes: You decode signs with your vision as you read. (For blind readers, of course, this decoding occurs via touch). However, reading has always occupied more of the human senses, not just vision. When reading a printed book, the activity involves approaching the text with our eyes (appreciating both visual design elements as well as the signs needed to be decoded), turning the pages with our fingers. Perhaps we become aware of our whole body's position, and while we read, we cannot help but register our auditory surroundings. When we learn to read (spell, write, decipher signs), we also use different senses when we listen to the words (auditory faculties) and learn to pronounce them (kinetic faculties). However, these multisensory dimensions of reading often have to give way to a predominantly ocular emphasis. During the last two to three decades, digitization has changed contemporary reading practices, and there is an increasing prevalence of works that purposefully invoke multisensory reading patterns and reawaken our appreciation of how reading can involve multiple senses.

Current acts of reading are fundamentally conditioned by the changing materialities of our digital age. Media scholars and sensory studies scholars, among others, have theorized how engagement with digital media can be studied and understood. The authors in this section contribute to and transform those insights into detailed studies of reading as a practice and as a concept. The chapters analyze digital literature, experimental audiovisual texts, audiobooks, and even the structure of the Internet itself in its networked form as examples of how material experimentation foregrounds multisensory mediations. At the heart of the issues lies how we can understand the embodied reading of media forms that activate most, if not the whole, of the human sensorium.

The reading experiences that are addressed in the chapters include narrative and informational texts that use haptic interfaces, immersive technologies such as Virtual Reality, sounds, and audio – multisensory narrative

DOI: 10.4324/9781003211662-9

media experiences that take advantage of most of what newer mobile devices such as smartphones and tablets offer.

The first chapter, "Reading and the senses: cultural and technological perspectives" by Birgitte Stougaard Pedersen and Maria Engberg, charts the ways in which the senses have been understood in philosophy and, more recently, sensory studies. The chapter argues that any discussion of reading needs to take full account of the sensory aspects of experience in order to understand the full sensory impact of a reading situation. The second chapter, "Reading a literary app for children," compliments the first chapter's more theoretical discussions by including empirical studies of how children read digital literary apps. In this chapter, Ayoe Quist Henkel explores the materiality and specific *textuality* of literary app formats for children. In the section's third chapter, "Trends in immersive journalism", Iben Have and Maria Engberg go outside of literary texts to explore how immersive and audio formats have been used in innovative ways to produce journalistic pieces that call upon the reader to engage more senses and other modes of engagement than they might otherwise have become accustomed to in web-based newspapers and news reporting. Sound plays a big part in immersive journalism, and the fourth chapter of the section, "Multisensory reading of digital audiobooks" by Iben Have and Birgitte Stougaard Pedersen, analyzes in depth how listening can in fact be seen as a multisensory activity and how the materiality of engaging with digital audiobooks creates multifaceted reading experiences. The section's fifth and last chapter, "How to read a network, or the internet as unfinished demo" by Lori Emerson, points our attention to how the very foundation of digital networked media, which supports the various media formats and literary digital works discussed in the book, relies on networked structures created in specific historic contexts. Emerson proposes ways to "read" complex, connected technologies such as Transmission Control Protocol/Internet Protocol (TCP/IP), the structure that drives the Internet.

5 Reading and the senses: cultural and technological perspectives

Birgitte Stougaard Pedersen and Maria Engberg

How do humans sensorially perceive their surroundings? This question is wide-ranging and has been researched and debated within different academic fields with various aims, methods, and intentions. For the purposes of this book, studying multisensory aspects of reading digital interfaces, academic disciplines, and fields of study that are of particular interest to us include everyday aesthetics, sensory studies, anthropology, (digital) media studies, and studies of digital reading. As David Howes (2003), Caroline A. Jones (2006), and Mark Paterson (2007) have discussed, the confluence of reading practices, digital technologies that increasingly support reading devices, and human perception may also be a sign of a kind of "sensory turn" as a metaphor, beyond debates in philosophy.

In this chapter, we argue that any discussion of reading needs to take full account of the sensory aspects of experience because these aspects are part of both aesthetics and knowledge production. The chapter begins with a discussion of traditional views and hierarchical paradigms of general sense perception and goes on to address how these paradigms seem to be re-negotiated when reading through digital technologies and interfaces.

Philosophy has debated the senses throughout history, and sensory aspects of our perception have been acknowledged to be both historically and culturally variable. According to David Howes, sense perception has only been acknowledged on specific and historically variable terms. He argues: "In Modern Western Culture, there is a strong tendency to *separate* senses for scientific and aesthetic purposes [...] I have [...] suggested that any theory of aesthetics, if it is cross-cultural and not merely pertain to the West, will necessarily be multimodal, and the same goes for any scientific theory of perception" (2011, 177–8).

Howes is here building on Husserl, claiming that we do not perceive the world through five separate senses, but with our senses as such (Ree 1999). Similarly, inspired by Michel Serres, Steven Connor describes our senses as "ways" of perceiving, interconnected as a knot. Connor stresses that the way the senses operate is often experienced as a course of events rather than as simultaneous (Howes 2005). In that sense, he regards sensory perception as both temporally and spatially organized.

DOI: 10.4324/9781003211662-10

In the course of the 20th century, we have witnessed a significant development among phenomenologists in explaining consciousness itself: while they originally favored a primarily cognitive approach, they later came to prefer a more bodily understanding of phenomenology and aesthetic responses, which is the understanding we find in the writings of Maurice Merleau-Ponty (1994, 1999) and Mikel Dufrenne (1973), respectively.

Conceptions of sensory engagements with the surroundings serve as the point of departure for the phenomenology of mind and body. Although sensory engagement is a universal precondition for any phenomenology, sensory studies must also take into account the influence of cultural contexts on the interplay of the senses and on sense hierarchies.

Senses, knowledge, and cultural hierarchies

In general, cultural periods have tended to organize the senses (particularly seeing and hearing) into hierarchies of modality. This has led to totalizing conceptions of *visuality* and *sound*.

Steven Connor states that, historically, visuality has been considered better suited to creating distinctions, while sound has been regarded as something that drags us in and spreads us out at the same time (2008) – building on a spatial understanding of the relation between sound and listener.

Along with Jonathan Sterne and others, Connor is responding somewhat critically to the conception of sound, as opposed to visuality, which occupies a privileged position in discussions of our sensory relation to interfaces and surroundings. Connor writes:

> [I]t puts us in some sense in the world in a richer and more three-dimensional way than seeing, which seems by contrast to make of the world a flat screen, or the other senses, that seem to give us only small slugs or slices of the sensible totality of the world. For we can hear textures and qualities, or at least judge of them by their sounds, and we can thus hear the insides of things, while we can only ever see their outsides – which is why we speak of sounding things and may refer to something as "sound." (2008, 2)

Connor stresses the three-dimensional sensory aspects of the auditory experience. However, he also adds to and builds on the general critique that Western culture has emphasized the dominance of language in relation to other sensory modes of meaning. He argues that the visual approach to the world has been put forward at the expense of, for instance, sound.

In critiquing the primacy of visually mediated language, sound studies researchers tend to privilege the experience of sound over sensory experiences.

Instead of enhancing the importance of multisensory modes of perception, listening is highlighted as a special case of bodily experience. This tendency of foregrounding sound is already identifiable in Don Ihde's book *Listening and Voice* (1976), where Ihde, building on Heidegger's philosophy, underlines how Western thought privileges visuality and the visual as the primary sensory source of knowledge. The dominant position of visuality manifests itself in for instance the way language subscribes meaning. For instance, this is the case when metaphors are related to the visual domain: you have an "overview," you can gain "insight."

Ihde's contention, an argument we also find in Howes (2005) and Emerson (2014), is that the sensory experience in itself is culturally coded and colored by a hierarchy of the senses, where visuality historically has been dominant. In that sense, Ihde establishes a dichotomy between listening and seeing, also stated by several other scholars, including Jonathan Sterne, which does not necessarily seem nuanced or fruitful (Ihde 2007). Ihde's perspective has been important for the development of a vocabulary for discussing sonic experience within sound studies as well as for the development of sound studies as a discipline.

Jonathan Sterne, who researches the interplay between sound and technology, opposes this tendency. Already in *The Audible Past* (2003) and in many of his later writings on the subject, for instance "The Theology of Sound" (2011), Sterne presents what he calls an "audiovisual litany," performed by a number of sound studies scholars. He describes it as a conceptual gesture that gives preference to the mode of sound and sonic phenomena and hereby converts the dominance of *ocularcentrism*. He states that "the audiovisual litany [...] idealizes hearing (and, by extension, speech) as manifesting a kind of pure interiority. It alternately denigrates and elevates vision: as a fallen sense, vision takes us out of the world. But it also bathes us in the clear light of reason" (Sterne 2003, 15).

Sterne also criticizes Walter J. Ong for extrapolating this litany and opposes the idea that there should exist a fundamental and ahistorical hierarchy of the senses. In that sense, Sterne holds a critical position toward the privileged status of sound that was already predominant in the writings of Marshall McLuhan, who we will return to (see also Chapter 2). Sterne states that some sound studies researchers continue to maintain and even extend this dichotomy. Sterne is primarily addressing the relation between the conceptions of the audible and the visual. Howes is critical of the predominant view that oral language and writing are the primary sources of gaining cultural knowledge. Sterne has observed the same biases: "Literate culture is visual culture, structured by the dominance of visual epistemologies such as the split between subject and object and the ability to externalize memory and institutional form through the power of writing and eventually print" (Sterne 2011).

We need a more nuanced approach to the cultural and historical understanding of the senses, acknowledging that researchers have always contested the degree and nature of the interconnections between the senses. In what follows, we point out the importance of exploring how the senses are related to concepts of writing and text and attendant notions of knowledge production. We then consider how we can include haptics as well as multisensory experience modes in current conceptions of digital reading practices.

The hierarchy of the senses is without a doubt historically as well as culturally embedded and changeable, and this notion, that the figures presented in relation to listening and seeing are not universal, does make it interesting to work on developing a cultural-historical rethinking of the print-centric aspects of our culture in relation to understanding sensorial aspects of cultural and social systems. This is also the claim of Howes. He advocates for a more "full-bodied understanding of culture and experience" and stresses that sensory experiences are embedded in social values: "[T]astes, sound, touch are imbued with meaning and carefully hierarchized and regulated so as to express and inforce the social and cosmic order" (Howes 2011, 3).

We can now consider what a sense-based investigation of the digital reading condition may look like. Scientific paradigms are influenced and developed in dialog with perceptual paradigms, as Howes puts it, and here the impact of the visual domain is predominant, as also argued by Ihde and Connor. The idea of deliberately connecting the sensory aspects of experience to the concept of reading, which is the ambition of this volume, is to challenge the classical opposition between sense and intellect and replace it with a less binary and more dynamic way of thinking.

When it comes to digital and audio reading, value-related debates regarding sense hierarchies are still evoked and may seem relevant with regard to, for instance, audio reading (foregrounding hearing/listening) and the visually dominant technologies of Virtual Reality (VR). It may be the case that sound studies has *essentialized* sound as especially connected with a more primary, first-hand sensory experience; however, when it comes to reading experiences this does not seem to be the case at all. On the contrary, audio reading has historically been and still is regarded as a more passive, lazy kind of reading than reading with the eyes. A kind of shortcut or cheating (Kozloff 1995, Birkerts 1994), leading to shallower reading experiences. In what follows, we will continue to discuss how digitization compels us to rethink the conceptions of the sensory, hereby also renegotiating the sensory aspects of reading on updated terms. This chapter builds on the earlier discussions of historical and hierarchical interplays regarding general perception paradigms as it moves toward an investigation of how the sensorial aspects are interconnected with mediated, digital technologies and interfaces.

Technology, digital media, and the senses

Reading takes place through technologies, and any text that discusses media and the senses will have to deal with Marshall McLuhan's influential, bewildering, thought-provoking, and inconsistent writing on the matter.

McLuhan's thoughts on the relationship between perception, the human sensorium, and mediated experiences, objects, and situations are still influential, despite his technological determinism which over time has affected the reception of his ideas. As Janine Marchessault has pointed out, McLuhan places the human senses in the center of human cognition (2004, 14). In *The Gutenberg Galaxy* (1962), we find the central McLuhanesque idea that, as Marchessault puts it, "specific technologies work on sensorial experiences, and [...] these technologies privilege certain senses over others" (Marchessault 2005, 76). And electronic media technologies are at the heart of McLuhan's interests. Whatever important insights and provocations McLuhan imparts, what is foundational in his work is the insistence that there is an important relationship between technologies and whatever is communicated and conveyed. At the time of his scholarship, the media landscape was at the beginning of the proliferation of media technologies: the electric age that for McLuhan meant that we needed to understand the ways in which our technologies – or extended senses – engaged in interplay. As Marchessault notes, McLuhan's ideas draw from the medieval theory of sensory perception, which maintains that all senses play a part in experience (Marchessault 2005, 125), a thought that this book sympathizes with. To the observer of the contemporary digital cultural moment, it should be clear that McLuhan's largely metaphoric or philosophical musings on the role of the senses in perceiving media technologies have now been realized, as technologies, devices, and media channels directly call upon multisensory perception in their very interfaces and machinations.

Here we foreground contemporary thinking of sensory perception in relation to mediations – rather than the real world. Computational devices with a widening set of user input systems are moving to include other modes of engagement and perception than, say, inputting alphanumerical characters via a keyboard, as we are doing now, and calling upon the reader to decipher them along learned and conventional patterns of apprehension of text, as you are doing now. Digital technologies have taken over and remediated most other media forms into convergent digital multimodal platforms and media forms. The devices with which we engage with those digitized or born-digital objects now often include touch and movement-tracking capabilities such as the smartphone, tablet, and the like, or even more complex: head-mounted displays and hand controllers. Understanding the relationship between technologies and the senses, then, requires a situated approach, as different technologies may foreground different aspects of sensory engagement or combinations of senses in the meaning-making process. A tablet can foreground *tactility* and proprioception because the technology affords those capabilities.

In her 2005 discussion of writing machines, N. Katherine Hayles foregrounds what she calls "technotexts": "[A] literary work interrogates the inscription technology that produces it, it mobilizes reflexive loops between its imaginative world and the material apparatus embodying that creation as a physical presence" (2005, 25). These "active" works – whether realized in print or digital forms – "envision subjects who are formed through and with the inscription technologies these works employ. The writing machines that physically create fictional subjects through inscriptions also connect us as readers to the interfaces, print and electronic, that transform us by reconfiguring our interactions with their materialities" (ibid. 131). The result, Hayles argues, is that reading of technotexts, perhaps especially borndigital ones, "redefine what it means to write, to read, and to be human" (ibid. 131). Hayles argues that attention must be paid to those interfaces, print or electronic, so that we may understand how this type of materially "aware" *textuality* functions – a digital *textuality* in which the aesthetics and reading structures bring to the forefront issues of perception, deciphering of text and images, and comprehension of multisensory registers made up of sounds, movement, and touch.

For scholars such as Parisi et al. (2017), or Pold and Andersen (2018), learning how to read digitally means understanding the haptic interfaces of digital media technologies. Parisi et al. (2017) argue that there is a need to move beyond the "metaphorization of touch," referring to McLuhan in particular, to a more detailed study of the "practices of touching or being touched by mediation technologies" (2017, 1517). Within media scholarship, there are studies that foreground metaphorical or *ekphrastic* notions of the sensory. Laura Marks's invocation of a haptic *visuality* (2008) combines sight with touch and *kinaesthetics*, as she seeks to understand spectatorship of, for instance, video art.

On the other hand, as Parisi, Paterson, and Archer point out, such wide approaches to the haptic and sensory turns in mediation risk deemphasizing how digital media make possible actual sensory reading modes that directly engage for instance our sense of proprioception or understanding of spatial sounds. Recently, as VR technologies are coming into wider use as consumer technologies, moving from research labs and experimental or fringe technologies into the general media landscape, sensory dominant discussions about how we understand digitally mediated experience have begun to return with renewed urgency. Using a head-mounted display with hand controllers to play digital games or engage with a textual or visual-spatial experience entails a very different embodied experience than, say, playing a board game or even the same game on a flat 2D screen with keyboard and mouse as input. As interfaces such as VR headsets become more complex, digitally mediated reading follows suit. From more experimental work such as Australian author Mez Breeze's VR literature made up of 3D sculptures and text in interactive VR spaces, to tactile digital works such as *Pry* by Tender Claws, it becomes clear that engaging with these born-digital literary works is a multisensory activity. Mez's work forces the reader to make navigational choices, often a feature of digital narrative structures, but here they are laid out spatially, creating what Mez calls "microstory spaces" (Breeze 2021).

From the senses to the multi*sensory*

The so-called immersive technologies such as VR exemplify interfaces that require more senses than vision and trivial or minor physical engagement (such as scrolling or clicking to advance digital pages or turning the pages of a printed book). Rather than attempting to isolate or understand the sensory input one sense at a time, we align ourselves with more recent studies (Velasco and Obrist 2020) that suggest that senses intermingle and rely on each other in a multisensory manner (Howes 2005). In understanding how mediated experiences relate to and call upon the senses, we have in prior research used the term *polyaesthetics* (Engberg 2014). For instance, if a reader is experiencing a 360-degree immersive journalistic piece that combines written text, images, video, and 3D models, she will have to move her body around with the device (or the headset) to engage with the material. The combined sensations of proprioceptive engagement with the work, along with reading and taking in other media elements, become an experience characterized by multiplicity. The aesthetic is here understood as perception of the lived world, and in particular the perception of mediation, and the prefix "-poly" naturally indicates a multitude and, further, an intermingling of the senses. Related to the notion of the multisensory, then, the *polyaesthetic* also seeks to foreground how artistic and aesthetic mediations proliferate and multiply.

Thus far, we drawn lines from the role of the auditory and the visual to historical notions of sense hierarchies and pointed to how scientific domains and not least cultural artifacts and technologies currently renegotiate the status and cultural values of the senses. This can be further understood when we look at the increasing use and distribution of such audio formats as podcasts and audiobooks. When asked in surveys, adult audiobook users often mention the flexibility of the audiobook experience as a key advantage (see also Chapter 12). You can read an audiobook in a number of multisensory situations – walking, running, knitting, cleaning. These reading activities are characterized by crossing sensory as well as cognitive and bodily borders. One of the main aspects that we have wished to highlight here is that digital reading experiences such as audiobook reading or reading of born-digital interfaces, for instance VR, actually distribute the bodily sensorium on new conditions, involving, which is also the argument of Howes, the entire body in the production of meaning.

If sound studies point to how sound potentially spreads us out and inclines us to experience the world with our bodies as a whole, then sound studies is in fact advocating for a synesthetic approach to perception that is bodily and phenomenologically based. On the one hand, this could be said to privilege the role of sound, as Sterne critically engages with the audiovisual litany. On the other hand, the audiobook reading experience in a mobile setting emerges from the feeling that, when listening in a specific situation, you actually spread out your bodily attention and experience spaces, experiencing interplays between sound, body, sight, surfaces, and surroundings. Bodily movements such as cleaning, running, walking, and knitting become part of the reading experience; the movements become rhythms with which we read.

From the perspective of sound studies, sound is always experienced and conceptualized through specific contexts, meaning that sound is colored by the spaces within which it is experienced and the concrete cultural habitus of the ears listening. What is true of sound now applies to the interplay of senses in digital reading practices such as born digital and audiobook interfaces: this interplay is colored by particular spatial and cultural contexts. Current practices of audiobook reading as well as the haptics of the VR experience suggest a distribution of our senses on terms that are fundamentally multisensory. The evidence of digital reading refutes the idea that sound is especially privileged and instead highlights listening as an important part of a broad-spectrum experience in which all the senses are mobilized and interact in new ways.

References

Birkerts, Sven. 1994. *The Gutenberg Elegies: The Fate of Reading in an Electronic Age*. Boston: Faber and Faber.

Breeze, Mez. 2021. "V[R]ignettes." Mez Breeze Designs. https://www.mezbreezedesign.com/vr-literature/vrignettes/.

Connor, Steven. 2008. "Ear room." Audio Forensics Symposium. IMT Gallery, London, 30 November. http://stevenconnor.com/earroom.html.

Dufrenne, Mikel. 1973 (1953). *The Phenomenology of Aesthetic Experience*. North Western University Press.

Emerson, Lori. 2014. *Reading Writing Interfaces: From the Digital to the Bookbound*. Electronic Mediations. Minneapolis, Minnesota: University of Minnesota Press.

Engberg, Maria. 2014. "Polyaesthetic sights and sounds: Media aesthetics in The Fantastic Flying Books of Mr. Morris Lessmore, Upgrade Soul and The Vampyre of Time and Memory." *SoundEffects – An Interdisciplinary Journal of Sound and Sound Experience* 4, no. 1. 10.7146/se.v4i1.20370.

Howes, David. 2003. *Sensual Relations: Engaging the Senses in Culture and Social Theory*. Ann Arbor, MI: University of Michigan Press.

Howes, David. 2005. *Empire of the Senses: The Sensual Culture Reader*. New York and Oxford: Berg.

Howes, David. 2019. "Multisensory anthropology." *Annual Review of Anthropology* 48, no. 1: 17–28. 10.1146/annurev-anthro-102218-011324.

Howes, David. 2011. "Hearing scents, tasting sights: Toward a cross-cultural multimodal theory of aesthetics." In *Art and the Senses*, edited by Francesca Bacci and David Melcher, 161–181. Oxford: Oxford University Press.

Howes, David, and Classen, Constance. 2014. *Ways of Sensing: Understanding the Senses in Society*. New York: Routledge.
Husserl, Edmund. 1989. "Fænomenologi." *Tid Skrift* 11.
Ihde, Don. 2007. *Listening and Voice – Phenomenologies of Sound*. New York: State University of New York Press.
Ingold, Tim. 2000. *The Perception of the Environment*. London: Routledge.
Jones, Caroline A., ed. 2006. "The mediated sensorium". In *Sensorium: Embodied Experience, Technology, and Contemporary Art*. Cambridge, Massachusetts: MIT Press.
Kozloff, Sarah. 1995. "Audiobooks in a visual culture." *Journal of American Culture* 18, no. 4: 83–95.
Marchessault, Janine. 2005. *Marshall McLuhan: Cosmic Media*. London: Sage Publications.
Marks, Laura U. 2008. "Thinking multisensory culture." *Paragraph* 31, no. 2: 123–137.
McLuhan, Marshall. 1962. *The Gutenberg Galaxy: The Making of Typographic Man*. Toronto, Canada: University of Toronto Press.
Merleau-Ponty, Maurice. 1994 (1945). *Kroppens Fænomenologi*. Frederiksberg: Det Lille Forlag.
Merleau-Ponty, Maurice. 1999 (1945, 1960, 1964, 1969). *Om Sprogets Fænomenologi*. Gyldendal.
Parisi, David, Mark Paterson, and Jason Edward Archer. "Haptic media studies." *New Media & Society* 19, no. 10 (October 2017): 1513–1522. 10.1177/1461444 817717518.
Paterson, Mark, 2007. *The Senses of Touch: Haptics, Affects, and Technologies*. Oxford; New York: Berg.
Pold, Søren Bro, and Christian Ulrik Andersen. 2018. *The Metainterface: The Art of Platforms, Cities, and Clouds*. Cambridge, Massachusetts: The MIT Press.
Ree, Jonathan. 1999. *I see a Voice*. Great Britain: Harper Collins.
Sterne, Jonathan. 2003. *The Audible Past: Cultural Origins of Sound Reproduction*. Durham, North Carolina: Duke University Press.
Sterne, Jonathan. 2011. "The theology of sound: A critique of orality." *Canadian Journal of Communication* 36, no. 2: *The Senses of Technology*.
Velasco, Carlos, and Obrist, Marianna. 2020. *Multisensory Experiences: Where the Senses Meet Technology*. Oxford: Oxford University Press.

6 Reading a literary app for children[1]

Ayoe Quist Henkel

Introduction

Owing to digital developments, the literary text for children is undergoing significant changes. The media through which a text is realized are not neutral, but on the contrary, play an important part in the meaning-making process, just as the basis of reading culture changes as literature moves onto digital devices. Viewing children's literature from this perspective of materiality may help to identify levels and aspects involved when it is realized as apps, and, furthermore, it may capture some of the paradoxical conditions of the app, which arise in the relationship between materiality and immateriality and in the ambiguous movement between various formats, genres, and media.

A typical example of the concretization of some of the foregoing changes is the app *Sofus and the Moonmachine* targeted at 6- to 8-year-olds by Burup et al. (2016), which constitutes the analytical example in this chapter. It navigates between computer games and children's literature in book format, and it presents itself as a book as well as an app, for example by having "chapters" and a "turn-over-the-page function," as in a book, and a "menu" with its origin in the logic of the app format and interface. The interface is here to be understood as the boundary and contact surface between the electronic device and the reader. *Sofus and the Moonmachine* positions itself in a liminal space between, on the one hand, the strong tradition of nonsense lyrics in children's literature and, on the other hand, animated movies; between children's stories about a traveling protagonist and the quest structure of the computer game; and between transparency and the meta-consciousness of the media. As the materiality perspective reveals, the app exemplifies both the open and subtle relationship between text, reader, technical device, and the context in which the reading of children's literature takes place.

Research on materiality is rooted in many different academic traditions, and the concept of materiality is far from indisputable. In this chapter, I attempt to crystallize three aspects that may shed light on both literary apps for children and cross-media reading from a general cultural perspective. I draw on approaches within literary and digital studies of materiality, and on general reflections on the cultural impact of materiality. As digital

DOI: 10.4324/9781003211662-11

artifacts, literary apps for children have their own ways of being texts, and thus create their own specific materiality, by virtue of integrating written words, pictures, sound, animation, and interaction, and being realized in an interface. In her theoretical work, N. Katherine Hayles emphasizes the materiality of literature – both paper-based and digital – and develops a material inquiry into the interface (Hayles 2002, 2004, 2008, 2013); Hayles is a consistent theoretical reference in this chapter, combined with cultural theory on materiality and children's literature theory. First, the app is introduced, and central aspects of research on materiality in the context of children's literature are explored. Second, three material aspects of *Sofus and the Moonmachine* are analyzed under the headlines: (1) "Intrinsic material qualities – the embodiment of the literary app for children," (2) "The physicality of the app," and (3) "The mode of existence of the app – the cultural scope of materiality."

Ambiguous app – *Sofus and the Moonmachine*

When readers touch the app icon for *Sofus and the Moonmachine* on their tablet computer or cell phone, they first see a short animation with a "spacey" soundtrack and then the logo for the company, The Outer Zone, which published the app. This introduction to the app imitates the introduction to a game app, where one often sees a short sequence with the manufacturer's name and logo before the game starts. The next slide or entry the reader sees provides a stark contrast to this in terms of sound and visuals (Figure 6.1): the visuals have many dynamic forms and harmonic shades of green and brown. The soundtrack is a pleasant little tune, repeated until the reader touches the text.

In Figure 6.1, which, from the perspective of the book, would be the cover, stands a doodled figure that first waves at the reader (a metafictional touch) and then looks toward the title of the app, *Sofus and the Moonmachine*, guiding the attention of the reader. Under the title, the words "Start the journey" vibrate, enticing the reader to touch the screen. This, however, is no ordinary cover. First, there is no author mentioned on the "cover," nor any illustrator or composer, since the text is an interplay between words, pictures, and sound. Second, the bottom third of the cover consists of a "menu" of touch buttons with "settings" and various choices based on the logic of the interface and app format and divided into chapters following the logic of the book format. Third, the screen shown in Figure 6.1 is not a conventional and physical cover either, being embedded in the oblong format and digital interface of the tablet computer or cell phone with its limitations and possibilities.

Examples of research on materiality

Sofus and the Moonmachine is but one example of literary apps for children being realized as texts. The origin of the word *text* is the Latin *textus*, which

Figure 6.1 Screenshot from Burup et al. (2016). *Sofus and the Moonmachine*. The Outer Zone.

means weaving, closely connected to the weaving of textiles, and this meaning takes on new significance in the case of the weaving and construction of digital texts. The literary app for children has its own distinctive *textuality*, that is, its own quality as a text, and its own materiality. Thus, analyzing a literary app means seeing its manifestation as text, its embedment in a medium, and its manner of being and interacting with the world. This focus on physical manifestation and being-in-the world is in accordance with the orientation to materiality that has recently become prevalent, especially in archaeological, cultural, and anthropological research (e.g., Miller 2006, Damsholt et al. 2009, Bille and Sørensen 2012).

This development has been called "the materiality turn" (Knapp and Pence 2003, Damsholt et al. 2009, 14, Bille and Sørensen 2012, 16 and 31, Munster 2014), and it is seen as a response to the so-called "linguistic turn" – although caution is required when terms such as "paradigm shift" or "turn" are applied. The materiality turn concerns the significance of materiality in the attribution of meaning and the relationship between things, the body, and technology. It thus contributes perspectives on the relationships between digital devices, reading, and creation of meaning, in this case where the realization of children's literature as an app is concerned. To a certain degree, the materiality turn has been the object of research in literature, where materiality has been stressed by book historians (Malm et al. 2009), and in studies of the book as object (McGann 1991, Brügger 2003). Hayles argues that literature primarily has been seen as "immaterial verbal constructions" (2002, 19), that the book as a physical object has been neglected in literary criticism, and that the growth of electronic literature makes it even more natural and pressing to centrally situate the materiality of the literary artifact in literary studies. By defining the book as object as a "material metaphor," Hayles focuses on "the traffic between words and physical artifacts" (ibid., 22). She points out that paper literature in book form is embedded in physical and historical conventions established by 500 years of printing art, which structure the definition of a page, the reading direction, and so on. As a result, we have a naturalized relationship to the conventions for reading literature. A literary app such as *Sofus and the Moonmachine* absorbs such book-based conventions while breaking free of the conventions for the cover and title page and employing interactive and game-aesthetic elements. A result of "the traffic" between the word and the physical artifact – which in the case of the literary app for children is between words and other representational forms, on the one hand, and the interface of the tablet computer or cell phone, on the other – is that the literary app for children materializes in the world in its own manner, and this has a decisive influence on meaning making. Within research on children's literature, studies of the aesthetics of picture books have for many years included analyses of the materiality of picture books by way of analyses of the format, cover, endpaper, and so on, and the picture book has been perceived as a medium (Rhedin 1992, Christensen 2003, 2014, Druker 2008). Thus, there has been an orientation toward the materiality of the picture book, its physicality and way of being in the world, without explicitly applying the term and concept of materiality. In the following, the earlier mentioned three material aspects of a literary app will be analyzed:

Intrinsic material qualities – the embodiment of the literary app for children

Sofus and the Moonmachine is about the "forest gnorf," Sofus, who lives on the planet of Goya. He collects scrap and is building a privy when something happens: The Moonmachine stops and the sun cannot shine: "When the Moonmachine's still, there's no sun to shine,/and all planets will die: every oak every pine." This is serious: it is a question of survival and of existence, of light versus darkness, of life versus death. Scrap is falling from the Moonmachine, and with the help of the reader (i.e., the reader catches pieces of scrap with their fingertips), Sofus manages to collect the scrap. It turns out that the parts may be assembled into a space rocket, which Sofus builds with help from the reader. He flies to the Moon, and, in the best fairytale style, he undergoes a series of trials. The characteristic of the intrinsic materiality of the app is that various representational forms cooperate in telling the story of Sofus and his journey to the Moon. Written text, pictures, animation, sound, music, and various forms of interaction are integrated into the storytelling. An example of this is the sequence rendered with a screenshot in Figure 6.2, where the sound universe consists of a voice reading, an instrumental piece of music, an unsettling space sound, and a cicada song. This sound universe continues until the reader has completed the task of collecting scrap and touched the "page-turning button" in the bottom right corner. At the same time, the screen displays constant movement, provided by shimmering, animated, flying dots in the bottom left corner and by Sofus, who winks at the reader. The sound, the green circles, and the two small animations generate indeterminate alternation between dynamic and static elements, superimposed on a static picture page. The picture depicts a futuristic, dark, and almost barren universe, now that the universe no longer has a sun, and the winding path and the hills in the background establish perspective.

In several entries, the reader must help Sofus to collect things, shake down a rocket part, switch on a light, get through a maze, and so on, and often Sofus addresses the reader directly and asks for help: "Well, hello!" Sofus said, "Have I met you before? / Would you be so kind as to open that door?" At one point, a little game sequence occurs, where the reader must

Figure 6.2 Screenshot from Burup et al. (2016). *Sofus and the Moonmachine*. The Outer Zone.

lose a game in order to help Sofus progress (!). This is an ironic comment on the game format, and it teases the reader/player, who initially decodes this as a game where he has four lives, when the game element is momentarily suspended, and he cannot move on until he has lost. Thus, the app thematizes and explores the format at the intrinsic material level, that is, the level of the narrative. As these examples from *Sofus and the Moonmachine* illustrate, the intrinsic material text qualities of this app are characterized by a complex sound universe, a screen picture charged with meaning, and an advanced relationship between static, dynamic, and interactive elements.

The physicality of the app

It may seem paradoxical to speak of the materiality of a digital text, since from an extrinsic perspective it may be characterized as being immaterial: it is embedded in an electronic device, a tablet computer or a cell phone, and does not have the same unique materiality as a physical book, for example, whose central qualities are concrete physical aspects, such as format, thickness, paper quality, and illustrations. The materiality of the literary app for children is subtler, as it is stored as a computer software program and realized on a touch screen, that is, a specific interface. Hayles writes about the way the interface addresses the reader materially: "Even when the interface is rendered as transparent as possible, this very immediacy is itself an act of meaning-making that positions the reader in a specific material relationship with the imaginative world evoked by the text" (2002, 107). The distinctive physicality of the tablet computer or cell phone implies specific material conditions for an app such as *Sofus and the Moonmachine*. It invites touching, and its smooth, seamless surface invokes transparency and immediacy; according to Hayles, this is central to the meaning making, as experienced when the act of reading is transferred to the fingertips roaming across the pages, for example in Figure 6.3, where handles and switches invite touch. However, when touching, the reader realizes that the handles and switches are not materially manifest, but visual and virtual representations. An interface appears to be especially suitable for setting up transparency and materiality by presenting the physical presence of objects, which is then immediately retracted. It pretends to be what it is not. In such sequences, the reader's interaction with the text is intuitive, whereas in other cases it is thematized visually, through action-prompting elements such as the previously mentioned green hotspot circles, or quite concretely, through iconic renderings of the digital device placed on the surface of the screen.

The characteristic of the app as a format is its position in the schism between materiality and immateriality, so its essential qualities are both its physicality, owing to its embedment in a technical device, *and* its relational character. The relational aspect manifests itself in various ways: technologically, by virtue of the relation between the interface and the

Figure 6.3 Screenshot from Burup et al. (2016). *Sofus and the Moonmachine*. The Outer Zone.

underlying programming of layered codes; relationally, in the relationship between the various layers of background, animations, and foreground; and in the interaction between the app, the reader, and the context, in what Paul D. Miller refers to as "a dynamic tension between code and culture" (2014, 7). In other words, the app format is positioned in a range of tensioned and relational conditions, conferring on the app a "metaphorical character" (ibid. 11) as well as an assemblage character (Matviyenko 2014, 18). For the literary app for children, this is the case both technically and substantially, by way of its absorption of a series of media, formats, and genres. As previously mentioned, various expressive forms are involved in *Sofus and the Moonmachine*, such as pictures, music, literature, computer games, and animation, and characteristically they figure in a non-hierarchical assemblage relationship. The app consists of digressions by way of the many layers of pictures and the playfulness of the computer game, combined with the narrative, the sequential nature of the animations, and the narrative drive of the verse tale of Sofus. The sound and music alternate between creating pleasant intermissions and contributing narrative sequences.

The mode of existence of the app – the cultural scope of materiality

At a third and general level, the materiality perspective exposes the position of the literary app for children in a general (reading) cultural perspective. By focusing on the relationship between man and object, between reader and artifact, and how these dimensions and relationships are embedded in a cultural framework, we may examine how the app carries and creates meaning. According to materiality research, it is difficult to overestimate the scope and meaning of materiality, as pinpointed by Jerome J. McGann: "[T]he intercourse that is being human is materially executed: as spoken texts or scripted forms" (1991, 3). In a more low-key manner, and with reference to digital texts, Anna Munster writes: "Materiality should not be now mistaken for a simple quality or property of digital technologies. Instead, it can be discerned as an expanded approach to analyzing neglected questions and areas in computation and culture" (2014, 328). In any case, from this perspective, reader and material artifact are in continual interaction and mutually constitutive, so that, in principle, it is not possible to isolate the reader, the app, or the context, because here the point at issue is the way social and material phenomena belong together and define each other. A literary app for children positions its reader in a different reading situation: tablet computers and cell phones are not necessarily expected to be used for reading literature; the reader must employ his visual, auditory, tactile, and sometimes even kinaesthetic senses, and the reading may be a cooperative, not an individual, activity. Thus, the literary app for children may thematize and render visible the reading of literature, with which we (adults) have a naturalized relationship.

The hybrid *textuality* and broad cultural reference horizon of *Sofus and the Moonmachine* is also conveyed through its positioning of itself among other texts. It has clear, intertextual references to both Shaun Tan's literary universe for children and to a computer game such as *Machinarium*, and it invites the reader to partake in a special interaction with the text, explicitly pointing this out. In other words, the contract between the reader and fiction becomes very concrete and is constantly a subject for thematization. This happens in both direct and metafictional addresses to the reader, similar to those in, for example, Hans Christian Andersen's fairytales, and in direct invitations to participate in the story and help Sofus to build the rocket, shake down rocket parts from a tree, turn on a light, or light fires or candles because Sofus cannot do it himself and needs help. The contract with the reader becomes articulated, concrete, and very insistent – verbally as well as in the interface, when the triangular page button says when to turn a page. Applying a concept from Barbara Bader's "the drama of the turning page," Ulla Rhedin points out that the act of reading picture books involves a physical and tension-creating activity (1992, 18). This "drama" is concretized and often articulated in this app, for example when a verse ends with a "page turner" such as: "The next thing that happened was especially bad."

The text addresses the reader verbally by using different personal pronouns, such as "you," "I," and the inclusive "we." Often, the reader is addressed as "you out there," whereby the app creates an illusion of "in" and "out" of the story, which underscores its material basis: it is situated in something specifically material and so creates something specifically relational. The app also addresses the reader visually, as Sofus waves, looks, and winks at the reader. Furthermore, it addresses the reader by inviting them to interact concretely. Thus, the digital materiality and the multisensory address of the interface become significant for the app as an active phenomenon, which, by means of its embedded (and, here, quite concrete) media reflexivity, meets the reader with specific expectations of physical cooperation in the reading process. These metafictional elements create the impression that the story comes into being through the interaction between the narrator, the literary characters, and the reader, and these elements thematize the literary reading process and the status of fiction as fiction.

The literary app for children generates a peculiar reading act and possesses a peculiar cultural significance, owing to its materiality. The tablet computer or cell phone is not just a dead object, and an app is not just a piece of software, but a proactive thing that creates its context and its reader; that is, it constructs a reality. A piece of software in an electronic device incorporates expectations of touch, game, and interaction, facilitating a specific social act. So, on the one hand, people create materializations, and, on the other hand, these materializations create their readers.

Conclusion

As the literary app format is new and still under development, it is difficult to isolate and pinpoint. An app such as *Sofus and the Moonmachine* is but one example, illustrating how children's literature is read on a new material basis due to the digital reading condition. As emphasized above, materiality researchers, and especially Hayles, point out the dialectics between intrinsic and extrinsic text qualities in literature – and, one might add, other art forms – and argue that literature cannot be separated from its context. A literary app for children has specific textual qualities, being embedded in a tablet computer or cell phone and its interface, and this is crucial to the way it creates a dialog between text and reader and is embedded in a social world.

The reader's expectations of children's literature and of the app format are challenged and thematized by reading *Sofus and the Moonmachine*. On the one hand, this text follows a linear narrative and structure, keeping the "bookish" (Pressman 2020) conventions of chapters and pages with a "turning effect," and, on the other hand, it absorbs game aesthetics and interactive elements, bestowing crucial significance equal to that of the written word on expressive forms such as pictures, animations, and music.

This creates a fluctuation between narrative elements, sensory digressions brought about by the *spatiality* of the pictures and the music, and the playfulness of the game. Altogether, the literary app for children destabilizes the written and unwritten conventions of literature – should the reader approach the text with such expectations – at the same time destabilizing the conventions of games and interaction – should the reader approach the text with those expectations.

Sofus and the Moonmachine exemplifies how the literary app for children experiments with narrative genres and aesthetic effects, just as it derives inspiration from general popular culture as well as from classical and experimental movements in children's literature, animation, visual arts, and music. The literary app for children has turned into a meeting place for writers, illustrators, animators, and interaction designers, which results in a synchronism of various art forms and expressions. The tablet computer, and particularly its interface, with its immanent ambiguity between transparency and hyper-consciousness, constitutes a new basis for reading literature that causes a denaturalization of the reading process, as the material conditions of the text are reflected on and thematized. The tablet computer's mediation of its interface is not neutral, just as the socialization of the reader changes in nature owing to the changed relationship between artifact and reader. By virtue of its intrinsic text qualities, its physicality, its being a software program embedded in a tablet computer or cell phone, and its mode of existence in the world, the materiality of a literary app for children has a crucial influence on the realization and reading of children's literature. Altogether, the app format is a cultural and media phenomenon with far-reaching importance, of which we have only just glimpsed the outlines.

Parts of this chapter have been published in the article "Exploring the Materiality of Literary Apps for Children" in *Children's Literature in Education* 49 (2016): 338–55, Springer Nature.

Note

1 This chapter is an adaptation with permission of the article: "Exploring the Materiality of Literary Apps for Children," https://link.springer.com/article/10.1007/s10583-016-9301-7

References

Bille, Mikkel, and Sørensen, Tim Flohr. 2012. *Materialitet – En Indføring I Kultur, Identitet Og Teknologi*. Frederiksberg, Denmark: Samfundslitteratur.
Bolter, Jay David, and Grusin, Richard. 2000. *Remediation. Understanding New Media*. Cambridge and London: MIT Press.
Brügger, Niels. 2003."Bogen som medie – nedslag i bogobjektets historiske transformationer." *Passage* 48: 77–95.
Burup, Malte, Jensen, Kasper Sebastian Brandt, Skovmand, Pelle, and Vedel, Mikkel. 2016. *Sofus and the Moonmaschine*. The Outer Zone.

Christensen, Nina. 2003. *Den Danske Billedbog 1950-1999. Teori, Analyse, Historie*. Frederiksberg, Denmark: Roskilde University Press.

Christensen, Nina. 2014."I bevægelse. Billedbøger og billedbogsforskning under forvandling." *Tidskrift för Litteraturvetenskap* 2: 5–18.

Damsholt, Tine, Simonsen, Dorte Gert, and Mordhorst, Camilla. 2009. *Materialiseringer. Nye perspektiver på materialitet og kulturanalyse*. Aarhus, Denmark: Aarhus University Press.

Druker, Elina. 2008. *Modernismens Bilder. Den Moderna Bilderboken i Norden*. Stockholm: Makadam.

Hayles, N. Katherine. 2002. *Writing Machines*. Cambridge: MIT Press.

Hayles, N. Katherine. 2004. "Print is flat, code is deep: The importance of media-specific analysis." *Poetics Today* 25, no. 1: 67–90.

Hayles, N. Katherine. 2008. *Electronic Literature: New Horizons for the Literary*. Notre Dame: University of Notre Dame Press.

Hayles, N. K. (2013). Combining close and distant reading: Jonathan Safran Foer's Tree of codes and the aesthetic of bookishness. *PMLA*, 128(1), 226–231. 10.1632/pmla.2013.128.1.226.

Knapp, A. James, and Pence, Jeffrey. 2003. "Between thing and theory." *Poetics Today* 24, no. 4: 641–671.

Matviyenko, Svitlana. 2014. "Introduction." In *The Imaginary App*, edited by Paul D. Miller and Svitlana Matviyenko, xxvii–xxxvi. Cambridge, Massachusetts, and London: MIT Press.

Malm, Mats, Sjönell, Barbro Ståhle, and Söderlund, Petra. 2009. *Bokens Materialitet. Bokhistoria Och Bibliografi*. Stockholm: Svenska Vitterhetssamfundet.

McGann, Jerome J. 1991. *The Textual Condition*. Princeton: Princeton University Press.

Miller, Daniel. 2006. "Materiality. An introduction." In *Materiality*, edited by Daniel Miller, 1–50. Durham, North Carolina, and London: Duke University Press.

Miller, Paul D. 2014. "Preface." In *The Imaginary App*, edited by Paul D. Miller and Svitlana Matviyenko, v–xiii. Cambridge, Massachusetts, and London: MIT Press.

Munster, Anna. 2014. "Materiality." In *The Johns Hopkins Guide to Digital Media*, edited by Marie-Laure Ryan, Lori Emerson, and Benjamin J. Robertson, 327–331. Baltimore, Maryland: Johns Hopkins University Press.

Pressmann, Jessica. 2020. *Bookishness: Loving Books in a Digital Age*. Columbia University Press.

Rhedin, Ulla. 1992. *Bilderboken. På väg Mot en Teori*. Stockholm: Alfabeta.

7 Trends in immersive journalism

Iben Have and Maria Engberg

Introduction

The digital reading condition does not only influence the practices of institutional fields like the literary and the educational, which are central to this book. In this chapter, we will briefly turn our attention to the field of journalism where the use of multisensory digital texts in news communication has become part of mainstream journalism in recent years. While the bulk of the examples in this book are literary, concomitant trends in digital journalism have provided interesting challenges to digital reading by way of long-form journalistic pieces experimenting with 3D, 360° video, audio productions, or tactile interfaces. Global as well as local news organizations around the world are experimenting with new digital opportunities for presence and engagement of users, and this chapter gives some examples. While it is not possible to do justice to the whole field of digital journalism in a short chapter like this, we will use the few examples to add a journalistic perspective on the multisensory and digital reading experience that is developed in this book – a perspective with other implications and dimensions than educational or literary reading.

Journalism describes and assesses contemporary events and conditions, and because of the claim of objectivity in journalistic news, it is particularly important to discuss how different constellations of media and senses influence the digital reading condition and, ultimately, how we as readers understand, reflect on, and relate to the world around us. Whether a person reads, in a printed paper, that extreme weather caused by climate changes has resulted in flooding in Central Europe, or hears human voices accompanied by on location soundscapes giving the same information in a podcast, or is absorbed in a virtual reality (VR) representation of how it feels to escape from a flood, trying to save people around you, the specific material instantiation of the news story may result in different impressions and (re)actions. By appealing differently to the senses, the body, and the brain, news can be communicated as a sense of actually "being there," on the one hand, or as a distant reflection, on the other. Where the journalistic product places itself on that scale matters for how knowledge is constructed but also provokes critical discussions of emotional and entertaining news communication.

Historically, journalism has been communicated through different kinds of media – written (newspapers), electronic (radio and television), digitized and born-digital versions of these, and digital platforms like Danish *Zetland*, which we will return to below. In the spirit of this book, we will in this chapter give attention to journalistic texts inviting multisensory, highly digital experiences that go beyond reading printed texts. Such journalistic formats are usually compiled under the umbrella term "immersive journalism." Immersive journalistic formats experiment with digital technologies and formats to create a reading experience that is closer to a sensory experience of "being there." Immersive journalism is associated with the emergence of so-called immersive technologies – the use of 3D graphics, VR and augmented reality (AR) applications, interactive techniques such as parallax scrolling, and sophisticated use of audiovisuals. In this chapter, we will widen the umbrella to also include another trend in current digital journalism, namely the development of different formats of audio journalism. Audio and especially voices also afford immersive experiences of being present in a particular place with someone, as we have already argued in other chapters of this book (e.g., Chapters 8 and 12). Audio journalism has a history of almost a hundred years in flow radio, but the development of digital technologies has caused a branching of popular journalistic audio formats ranging from 1:1 oral readings of written published articles, over sound-designed long reads, to more composite podcast documentaries and news shows with interviews and chatty hosts in, for example, talk radio.

Journalistic considerations and choices as to how the reader should be addressed in a sensory manner as well as textually and technologically have become even more pertinent and complex with the digitization and the Internet than during the electronic media age of radio and television. Also, traditional print journalism is forced to think beyond the written text today. The Internet has provided us with additional multimodal possibilities, including reader interactivity and hyperlinked information together with videos and sound, to an extent that has not been possible before. The current media landscape offers expanded digital possibilities for multisensory engagement, which in turn raises similar discussions in journalism as the ones we find in the fields of book publishing and literary studies, namely discussions of reading, literacy, and knowledge (see Chapters 1, 2, and 4).

After a short framing of the term "immersive journalism" follow two sections that present examples of what we call VR journalism and digital audio journalism – two subareas within the broad field of immersive journalistic practices. We will focus on a discussion of how these two forms, rather distinct in other ways, share possibilities for sensory engagement and immersion.

Basic understandings of immersive journalism

New digital journalism products are often described as "immersive journalism," "interactive journalism" (or "features"), "web documentaries," "multimedia features," VR, or what is sometimes called extended reality (XR), which includes 3D, AR, and VR formats as part of digital multimodal journalistic pieces. 3D models, AR and VR, and 360° photography and videography are also used in various news outlets today to give readers a different, possibly more immediate experience. Borrowing from *The New York Times*" description of its efforts into immersive journalism, in this case particularly AR, "[it is] a new pathway that can lead away from the abstract depiction of objects and toward a more visceral sense of real-life scale and physicality" (Roberts 2018).

Immersive journalism is still in its infancy. One of the most decorated and early examples is "Snow Fall," published by *The New York Times* in 2012, which has gained international recognition and received the Pulitzer Prize for feature writing in 2013 as well as a Peabody Award. Immersive journalism experienced a greater breakthrough in 2018, when VR presentations were included in the series that was awarded the Pulitzer Prize for explanatory journalism (Uskali et al. 2021).

"Immersive" or "immersion" is often understood as "a process or condition whereby the viewer becomes totally enveloped within and transformed by the "virtual environment"" (Dyson 2009, 1). In the introduction to the book *Immersive Journalism as Storytelling* (Uskali et al. 2021), immersive journalism is defined more specifically as:

> [T]he use of immersive technologies, like 360-degree video, virtual reality, augmented reality, cinematic reality, and mixed reality in journalistic storytelling. Immersive journalism is an experiential approach that allows users to experience, and subsequently become immersed in, stories created not in the real world but in a virtual, augmented, or mixed reality.
>
> (Uskali et al. 2021, 2)

Uskali et al.'s definition represents a common understanding of immersive journalism. But if we turn to Nonny de la Peña et al. to whom the term "immersive journalism" is originally ascribed, we find a more open definition: "the production of news in a form in which people can gain first-person experiences of the events or situation described in news stories" (2010, 291). As opposed to Uskali et al.'s definition, this definition also makes room for the experience of being immersed in written texts or spoken word technologies.

Immersive journalism is per definition associated with digital technology and based on the premise of ubiquitous digital screens, but there exists a spectrum of technologies with affordances that prioritize the senses differently, which the following sections will bring examples of.

Just like being there – VR, AR, and 360° immersive journalistic narratives

Like *The New York Times*, the British news giant *The Guardian* has also created a series of VR and 3D experiences as part of its way of bringing stories to its readers. The paper's ventures into immersive journalism started in earnest with the launch of *theguardianVR app* in 2016, partly catering to its broad digital audience; *The Guardian* is the most widely read digital newspaper in the United Kingdom (Ofcom 2021). And, of course, given that this chapter was written in late 2021, the emergence of the COVID-19 pandemic and the resulting self-quarantine and many institutions shuttering their operations, digital options just seem more and more viable. In fact, 3D visualizations of the spread of the coronavirus presented in VR or AR modes have been popular inclusions in newspapers' digital reporting on the pandemic. Even before the pandemic, *The Guardian* and other newspapers used immersive technologies for explanatory or experiential purposes, adding value to their regular written stories. The first VR piece released by *The Guardian* was "6x9: A Virtual Experience of Solitary Confinement" (N.n. 2016), which focused on creating an isolated experience by placing the reader inside a U.S. solitary confinement prison cell. The VR piece focused on the sensory-charged experience of being confined to a 6x9-feet space surrounded by dreary brick walls and the resulting pressure of tediousness and claustrophobia.

In fact, many journalistic pieces that use VR take advantage of the sensory affordances offered by the media technology. In *The New York Times* story about the 2018 rescue mission in the NAME cave in Thailand, AR 3D modeling was used to show in real size how small the various openings and tunnels of the cave were (Beech 2018). In a multimodal recreation using actual audio and photos of the Apollo 11 moon landing, AR has also been used to piece together individual photographs and static as well as moving 3D models of the Apollo Lunar Module and the astronauts in a 3D computer graphics space. One of the aims of forging the story in this format is to convey a sense of the experience on site and further ground a sense of "being there" through a mix of historic material and immersive technologies. Immersive technologies in news narratives are proliferating, and while many of them rely heavily on visual modes (3D and 360° images), audio experiences are increasing as well, which leads us to the next section of the chapter, which will discuss another version of immersive journalism.

Audio news and sound as the immersive medium par excellence

The digital reading condition has imparted a growing interest in news as audio, formerly known as radio, and today, most media and news institutions offer some kind of audio output. This can be recorded versions of already written and printed articles, either in 1:1 long or abridged form, or it can be conversational podcasts summing up the news of the day or the week, sometimes including interviews. Audio journalism or audio news is not a new thing; it has existed in the radio ever since that medium was born in the 1920s. What is new in digital media culture is that audio news is no longer isolated to flow radio, but has become widespread in new formats such as the audio newspaper, audio articles, and podcasts from all kinds of media institutions.

The present expansion of audio formats in news publishing is confirmed by Nic Newman's scientific report *Journalism, Media, and Technology Trends and Predictions 2022*, which is based on interviews with 246 news leaders from 52 countries/territories:

> Growing consumption of digital audio has been a trend for a few years, driven by a combination of smartphones, better headphones, and investment in podcasts from platforms like Spotify, Google, and Amazon. But in the last year we"ve seen the rapid development of a much wider range of digital formats such as audio articles, flash briefings, and audio messages, along with live formats such as social audio.
>
> (Newman 2022, 16)

An illustrative case of the popularity of audio news is the young Danish news medium *Zetland*, which as a born-digital and digital-only medium has continuously adapted to the digital reading condition (https://www.zetland.dk). *Zetland* has been a pioneer with regard to expanding our understanding of journalistic texts. In 2012, it became the first publisher in Europe of what *Zetland* calls e-singles – long reads that are longer than articles, but shorter than books. *Zetland*'s e-singles were published outside Denmark in France, Germany, and the U.S. *Zetland* has also explored journalism live on stage through its live magazine, *Zetland Live*, which performs journalism live on different European stages, including the Royal Theatre in Copenhagen. *Zetland* is a subscription-based online streaming service, and the many initiatives are centered around the digital platform Zetland.dk and the app version integrating and activating members in virtual meeting halls, open editorial meetings, and not least gate-kept and curated written comments, opinions, and discussions by members following each published "article." So, without using what is normally understood as immersive technologies, for example, VR, *Zetland* expands the journalistic experience toward new formats and more multisensory experiences.

Zetland's biggest and, to many, most surprising success in terms of consumption is its audio formats. Less than two months after the medium had made all its written articles available as read-aloud recordings in summer 2018, the majority of its members" consumption was in audio form, and the audio format has continued to be much more popular than the written ones. From a consumer perspective, this changed *Zetland* from being mainly a written news medium to an audio news medium, as one of the founders said in an interview to a Danish magazine (Obitsø 2018). The audio long-read format is also known from *The Guardian*'s Audio Long Reads, which, however, only contains selected written articles. Not much academic literature exists on digital audio journalism (Lindgren 2016, McHugh 2016), and it is difficult to get access to numbers on the consumption of audio news since they are often an integral part of the general digital usage.

Although audio formats are not usually included in what we understand as immersive journalism, we would argue that sound in itself can afford immersive experiences – maybe not as an all-absorbed, first-person experience, but as a different kind of immersed experience associated with technology, journalistic storytelling, and the voice of another human being. In the book *Sounding New Media: Immersion and Embodiment in the Arts and Culture*, Frances Dyson compares the qualities of sound perception to the current media environment and refers to sound as the immersive medium par excellence:

> [...] new media reconstitute experiences characteristic of the aural, for sound is the immersive medium par excellence. Three-dimensional, interactive, and synesthetic, perceived in the here and now of an embodied space, sound returns to the listener the very same qualities that media mediates: that feeling of being here now, of experiencing oneself as engulfed, enveloped, absorbed, enmeshed, in short, immersed in an environment.
>
> (Dyson 2009, 3–4)

In sound studies, audio immersion usually refers to multichannel sound environments in cinemas and installation art. Adding to that, Dowling and Miller argue that podcasting must be included in immersive storytelling in digital publishing, not only as a factor of technology but also of journalistic storytelling through what they call the "thought-provoking documentary narrative, longform content known as deep-dives" (Dowling and Miller 2019 169).

We would like to add a third factor that has implications for the experience of immersion in audio news formats, namely the voice. Recent years' growth and popularity of audio media such as digital audiobooks and podcasts call attention to the importance of voice (Have and Stougaard Pedersen 2016, 2020, Heiselberg and Have). The presence of a human voice brings intimacy and authenticity and is able to generate first-person-like social attention. When wearing headphones, voices speak directly into the head of the listener.

Being there with the host, listening to recordings of real sound environments and actions in the world, and – maybe most importantly – sharing the experience here and now with the host generates another kind of immersing experiences, compared to VR.

Reaching out to journalism

To conclude, this chapter has introduced journalism and news communication to the discussion of changing forms of reading following the application of digital technologies. As the latest addition to a longer history of web journalism, digital journalism today seeks to engage readers in new ways that foreground, on the one hand, different sensory modes, and on the other, explore new ways of spreading journalistic content through new channels such as podcasts and other audio formats.

A distinctive quality of immersive technologies is presence or a sense of "being there." Thus, the competitive advantage of immersive storytelling in journalism lies in its ability to "create a sense of emotional connections to people, events and places," as Uskali et al. have put it (2021, 3). They continue: "[I]n the case of climate change deniers, for instance, the only way to change someone's mind is to put people in a position to directly experience something in order to "see the light"" (ibid.).

Immersive journalism may still be seen as an add-on to the long-form journalistic text that is modeled on the print newspaper, but such newer forms are growing in scope and importance and are already impacting the ways in which readers engage with journalistic content. The scientific report *Journalism, Media, and Technology Trends and Predictions 2022* concludes that AI and sound are among the most important areas of expansion in news publishing in 2022 (Newman 2022).

With this chapter, we have pointed out some digital reading tendencies within the journalistic field, and we agree both with the argument that digital immersive journalism does not undermine deep and serious journalistic content (Dowling and Miller 2019) and with the argument that the Internet is not just a place of distraction, and skimming and scanning is obsolete (Carr 2011). However, experiments with immersive journalistic formats intensify discussions of public knowledge and democracy in relation to reading, and the current debates on fake news and algorithmic journalism constitute a critical backdrop for these discussions. Digital multisensory reading is, in a news context, still underexplored, and we hope this book about the digital reading condition will be able to reach out to discussions on how we read with our senses within the field of journalism too.

References

Beech, Hannah. 2018. "Step inside the thai cave in augmented reality." *The New York Times*, July 21, 2018. https://www.nytimes.com/interactive/2018/07/21/world/asia/thai-cave-rescue-ar-ul.html.

Berg, F. S. A. 2021. "The value of authenticity and intimacy: A case study of the Danish independent podcast Fries before Guys' utilization of Instagram." *Radio Journal: International Studies in Broadcast & Audio Media* 19: 155–173. 10.1386/rjao_00039_1.

Biewen, John, and Dilworth, Alexa, eds. 2017. *Reality Radio: Telling Trues Stories in Sound*. Chapel Hill: University of North Carolina Press.

Carr, Nicholas. 2011. *The Shallows: What the Internet Is Doing to Our Brains*. New York: Norton.

Dowling, David O., and Miller, Kyle J. 2019. "Immersive audio storytelling: Podcasting and serial documentary in the digital publishing industry." *Journal of Radio & Audio Media* 26, no. 1: 167–184. 10.1080/19376529.2018.1509218.

De la Pena, N., et al. 2010. "Immersive journalism: Immersive virtual reality for the first-person experience of news." *Presence: Teleoperators & Virtual Environments*, August 2010. 10.1162/PRES_a_00005.

Dyson, Frances. 2009. *Sounding New Media: Immersion and Embodiment in the Arts and Culture*. Berkeley: University of California Press.

Heiselberg, Lene, and Have, Iben. In review 2022. "The Dream host: Conceptualising Listeners' Expectations for Podcast Hosts". *Journalism Studies*.

Have, Iben, and Stougaard Pedersen, Birgitte. 2016. *Digital Audiobooks. New Media, Users and Experiences*. New York: Routledge.

Have, Iben, and Stougaard Pedersen, Birgitte. 2020. "To read an audiobook." In *Beyond Media Borders: Intermedial Relations Among Multimodal Media*, vol. 1, edited by Lars Elleström, 197–216. London: Palgrave Macmillan.

Lindgren, Mia. 2016. "Personal narrative journalism and podcasting." *Radio Journal: International Studies in Broadcast & Audio Media* 14, no. 1: 23–41.

Lund, Erik. 2017. "Journalistik" (journalism). *Den Store Danske*. Accessed January 20, 2022. https://denstoredanske.lex.dk/journalistik.

Mottram, Christine. 2017. "Finding a pitch that resonates: An examination of gender and vocal authority in podcast." *Voice and Speech Review* 10, no. 1: 53–69. 10.1080/23268263.2017.1282683

McHugh, Siobhan. 2016. "How podcasting is changing the audio storytelling genre." *Radio Journal: International Studies in Broadcast and Audio Media* 14, no. 1: 65–82.

Newman, Nic. 2022. *Journalism, Media, and Technology Trends and Predictions 2022*. Digital News Project, Reuters Institute for the Study of Journalism.

N.n. 2016. "6x9: A virtual experiment of solitary confinement." *The Guardian*, April 27, 2016. https://www.theguardian.com/world/ng-interactive/2016/apr/27/6x9-a-virtual-experience-ofsolitary confinement.

Obitsø, Ole. 2018. "Podcast vokser markant:'Lyd er blevet en del af hjertet hos Zetland'." *Journalisten*, July 22, 2018. https://journalisten.dk/podcast-vokser-markant-lyd-er-blevet-en-del-af-hjertet-hos-zetland/.

Ofcom. 2021. *News Consumption Report 2021*. https://www.ofcom.org.uk/research-and-data/tv-radio-and-on-demand/news-media/news-consumption.

Roberts, Graham. 2018. "Augmented Reality: How We'll Bring the News Into Your Home." *The New York Times*, February 1, 2018. https://www.nytimes.com/interactive/2018/02/01/sports/olympics/nyt-ar-augmented-reality-ul.html.

Uskali, Turo, Gynnild, Astrid, Jones, Sarah, and Sirkkunen, Esa, eds. 2021. *Immersive Journalism as Storytelling. Ethics, Production, and Design*. Routledge.

Watson, Amy. 2021. "*New York Times* Company: Digital news subscribers Q1 2014-Q3 2021." https://www.statista.com/statistics/315041/new-york-times-company-digital-subscribers/.

8 Multisensory reading of digital audiobooks

Iben Have and Birgitte Stougaard Pedersen

Introduction

Listening to literature has a long historical tradition – even longer than literature itself, you might say. Long before written texts and printed books occurred, oral storytelling was practiced in different cultures around the world (Ong 2002, Cavallo and Chartier 1999, Saenger 2000). And both *The Iliad* and *The Odyssey* attributed to Homer and written down in the eighth century BC were meant to be orally performed, and so were William Shakespeare's plays almost 24 centuries later.

In ancient times, reading was usually oral, performed aloud in groups or individually through multiple forms of engagement and senses. But as Paul Saenger describes in his book *Space Between Word*, reading developed into a silent and solitary activity (2000). This development began in exclusive groups of erudites, but expanded concurrently with the emergence of printed books, and reading skills became more widespread among other classes. For centuries now, reading with your own eyes and with the body remaining relatively passive has been the predominant way of reading, but, as we argue in this book, the digital reading condition is challenging this "monopoly" and opening up other ways of reading, including mobile audio reading.

Academic attention to the materiality of the printed book is not new (e.g., Eisenstein 1996, Brügger 2003, Hayles 2004, Spence 2020). "Books are fundamentally multisensory objects," as Spence puts it, referring to the printed codex. And if we include the wide range of digital formats as well, this statement becomes even more true, and maybe this is even more obvious in relation to the digital audiobook. Because of the clear difference – both in relation to technology, materiality, usage, and perception – between audiobooks and book formats favoring the eye, audiobooks offer a fundamentally different perspective on multisensory reading. And with the worldwide popularity of internet-based audiobooks, it has become impossible to ignore this medium as an important player in the digital reading condition.

In this chapter, we suggest that listening to digital audiobooks can be discussed and analyzed as multisensory reading. Audio reading is often widely misunderstood as being mono-sensory; however, it decidedly affords

DOI: 10.4324/9781003211662-13

multisensory reading by setting the eyes and body free to move, so that tactile, kinesthetic, visual, and audio input can mutually affect one another and influence the reading experience. Audiobook reading is not always mobile, but the technology affords mobility, more so than book formats that require fixing your eyes on the words. Following anthropologist Steven Feld, motion draws upon the kinetic interplay of the tactile, sonic, and visual senses (2005). With his *acoustemological* approach to how we experience, navigate, know, and make sense of the world through sound, Feld is primarily interested in sounding matters of the world, though he includes the multisensory perspective in describing how sound accommodates bodily experiences. We find that Feld's *acoustemological* approach can be a productive path to describing audiobook reading as a mobile, multisensory experience of reading, always situated, embodied, and synaesthetically based.

Background and specifics of audio reading

Oral storytelling became recordable with the invention of audio recordings in the late 19th century with the phonograph attributed to Thomas Edison in 1877, and the gramophone developed in a race between Graham Bell and Edison through the 1880s (Sterne 2003). A few decades later, headphones made it possible to listen to recorded sound alone and in private. The first headphones were invented for telephone operators and weighed more than 10 pounds resting heavily on their shoulders. A lighter, portable version of audio headphones was invented by engineer Nathaniel Baldwin in 1910 and were like most new media technologies first adopted by the army. By then the technology was ready for the audiobook as we know it today, defined as an electronic recording of a printed, published book (Have and Stougaard Pedersen 2016). However, the term "audiobook" first appeared with the market penetration of the compact cassette tape in the 1980s.

What differentiates the technological materiality of the audiobook from other books is that it follows the development and logics of audio media. Digital audiobooks are like music recorded through microphones in studios, distributed as digital audio files, and played via apps in digital devices, usually through headphones or earbuds. With the digital audiobook, the whole body is set free to move around in space. So, there has never been much *bookish* materiality about audiobook technology, and that is partly what makes the sensory experience so fundamentally different from other kinds of reading practices. The sensing body is always present in all kinds of reading, whatever format is used, but the uniqueness of audiobooks is that hearing becomes the primary sense, setting the other senses free. The sense of hearing plays a vital role in the reading of audiobooks, but that does not mean that the other senses are turned off.

While the ancient Greeks listened to *The Iliad* in the amphitheaters, their sensing body was included in an audience, and with all senses potentially activated, the audience would register the rocky seat and the smell, sounds, and visual impressions of the surroundings. When reading became silent with the printed book, and something you do alone, vision became central and fixed while reading, the body at rest, and the attention to other senses like smell and touch typically withdrew to the background of the sensory reading experience. For people reading braille, it was the fingers and the sense of touch that were foregrounded, but the lack of mobility is comparable to printed book reading.

Naturally, attention, concentration, and engagement are often critically discussed in relation to audiobooks and audio reading, because this form of reading releases some of the attention to other activities (see Baron 2021, Sousa, Carriere, and Smilek 2013, Daniel and Woody 2010, Birkerts 1994, and Section III of this volume). However, these studies are interested in (and some of them lab-test) memorizing and learning differences between audio reading and traditional eye reading. Most of these studies disqualify audio reading compared to visual reading without taking into account the hundreds of years where human beings have practiced eye reading, which naturally makes us more familiar with that kind of reading. It is not surprising that we are not as experienced and trained in audio reading. Other studies are less critical and find no significant difference in comprehension memorability when comparing audiobook reading and printed book reading (see Spence 2020, Rogowsky et al. 2016). As Spence puts it, "when it comes to the multisensory imagery that is triggered while reading, there is far less evidence thus far for a convincing difference between formats. Differences in comprehension and memorability between formats, digital, audiobook, and traditional printed format also appear to be fairly modest" (2020, 217).

The broad understanding of the reading experience suggested in this book is not limited to comprehension and memory output, but more focused on embodiment, on *being present* in an engaging reading situation, where the materiality, technology, and the surroundings influence the reading experience. The aim of this book is to demonstrate how reading can be carried out through engagement with different formats, media technologies, and senses. While it has long been clear to reading historians that reading has always been carried out in various ways and with different senses, the radically different affordances of audiobooks may help us call attention to these different opportunities for reading. With a focus on various kinds of haptic and tactile experiences, we will in the following sections go into more detail with the different sensory aspects that, combined with hearing, constitute audiobook reading as a multisensory experience.

Haptics of technology

The physical *tactility* of audiobooks is connected to the handling of the technology before, after, and in between the listening act: you must turn on your loudspeakers and use your computer keyboard or the interactive touchscreen on your smartphone to access, play, stop, and regulate the volume, speed, etc. while reading. The interface looks like most audio media players with icons for "play," "stop," "rewind," and "fast forward," as well as an indication of the volume and sometimes a timer and a button for speed regulation. When you listen to audiobooks through headphones attached to your smartphone, other audio signals from the phone can be allowed to interrupt the reading. Small earbuds typically allow in more ambient sound than ear-covering headphones, and they may therefore be better suited to situations in which, for example, you want to be able to orientate yourself in traffic while listening to the audiobook. But more and more headphones and earbuds today include a noise-canceling function neutralizing the surrounding sounds, and with wireless earbuds you can control the playing of the audiobook by tabbing softly on the earbuds and relocate the *tactility* of navigation from the screen to the plastic pods in your ears. The haptic experience with buttons, glass, plastic, and metal is similar to most formats of digital books. The screens are smooth and cool, and the earbuds may pinch the ear, but the digital technology typically does not smell or taste of anything.

But in the handling of the audiobook, the materiality of the technology matters. And in the article "Reading Audiobooks" from 2021, we argue for the importance of taking at least four technological levels into account when studying digital audiobooks: (1) storage technologies (sound files as downloaded on a device or streamed from the Internet cloud), (2) medium of distribution (the Internet), (3) providers (libraries, bookshops, streaming services), and (4) playback media (computer, tablet, smartphone, loudspeakers, headphones, earbuds). Each of these four areas also include visual representations and functional structures: book covers (or thumb-nails linked to mp3 files), interfaces, functions, and organization of the providers' Internet sites or apps, and icons for using the playback medium (Stougaard Pedersen and Have 2021, 207). All these inputs are relevant to consider when analyzing the multisensory practice of reading digital audiobooks.

Mediated touch

In her book *Touch* (2008), Laura U. Marks draws the contours of a mediated sense of touch related to the experience of visual and audiovisual cultural artifacts. From a visual media paradigm, she develops a materialist theory as an alternative to the general understanding of digital media as virtual and immaterial. Marks generates the concept of touch as an embodied relationship we can experience while watching a movie or a video. Similar theories have been developed in relation to the experience of sound in audiovisual media. Music semiologist Philip Tagg introduces the term "tactile anaphones," describing how sound structures and expressivity semiotically signify a feeling of being touched. And Have (2008) presents – from a phenomenological and cognitive approach – a theory of the experience of sound structures and the materiality of sound as a synaesthetic, cross-sensory experience drawing on modal, embodied metaphorical experiences of objects, surfaces, forms, textures, temperatures, movement, and intensity – all of which contribute to a feeling of being touched by sound and music. Both Tagg's and Have's theories argue that sound is able to communicate some sensations of the missing haptic sense in audio and audiovisual media. With a specific focus on voices, Klausen and Have (2019) describe this haptic feeling of being touched by sound as "audio grooming."

Unlike visual, immaterial, mediated touch, sound is actually also perceived as haptic in a physical and material sense, since sound consists of physical impulses that hit our ears. In a much-cited text, R. Murray Schafer describes this physical experience of sound waves in relation to a metaphorical description of how sound "touches" the listener, and how sound can help to create a feeling of intimacy and bodily sociality independent of physical boundaries:

> Touch is the most personal of the senses. Hearing and touch meet where the lower frequencies of audible sound pass over to tactile vibrations (at about 20 hertz). Hearing is a way of touching at a distance and the intimacy of the first sense is fused with sociability whenever people gather together to hear something special.
> (Schafer 1993, 102)

Adriana Cavarero takes these physical aspects of sound and hearing a step further (or deeper) when she describes how the human organs producing and processing sound (the voice and the ear) are affording intimacy and a sense of a physical body.

> The sense of hearing, characterized as it is by organs that are internalized by highly sensitive passageways in the head, has its natural referent in a voice that also comes from internal passageways: the mouth, the throat, the network of the lungs. The play between vocal emission and acoustic perception necessarily involves the internal organs. It implicates a correspondence with the fleshy cavity that alludes to the deep body, the most bodily part of the body.
> (Cavarero 2012, 522)

Schafer also mentions in the quote above the social element of listening together. Listening to audiobooks is usually something you do alone, but in the following section, we will discuss how the audiobook voice can afford a social and intimate experience of being with someone, even if you are listening to it in solitude.

The intimate and social voice of audiobooks

The voice, whether human or artificially generated, is the medium of the digital audiobook per se. It is the voice, expressed through the medium of sound, which accentuates the distinctive feature of the audiobook. The voice of the performing narrator reading the text to a listener adds something to the reading experience, just as it removes something from the reading experience, as we know it from the printed book: it adds an interpretation, a controlled or fixed sense of temporality, a specific voice quality, diction and phrasing, and a rhythm of reading. But the voice of the narrator also deprives the reader of the flexibility of time, and it may create an annoying clash with the silent, implicit voice of the text itself and disturb the process of creating inner pictures while reading. However, some people also feel that the voice helps them create inner pictures, attach to the story, and immerse themselves in it. In a recent Swedish survey (Linkis and Plennert 2021), the voice as company was enhanced among the users as a positive feature of the digital audiobook, the quality of someone reading to you, someone to be with. This can be compared to Horton and Wohl's understanding of a *parasocial* relationship between TV viewer and host (Horton and Wohl 1997).

Thus, voice, as a mediated sounding medium, also creates a sense of intimacy and bodily sociality. The voice has for centuries, theoretically, been placed in the corner of essentialism: Romanticist ideas of the voice, representing the inner self, have often been connected to ideas of what Derrida has called *logocentrism*; the voice has been referred to as fundamentally essentialist, representing a self-presence that has had a hard time during the theoretical turns of the 20th century, for instance post-structuralist and deconstructive ideas of thought (Ree 1999, Derrida 1997).

The mediated voice of the digital era, as it appears in audiobooks, can be understood as a kind of distributed subjectivity, producing an *effect* of intimacy, not necessarily subscribing to the bodily and self-representative idea of voice itself. Norie Neumark, in the book *VOICE. Vocal Aesthetics in Digital Arts and Media* (2010), describes how the mediated voice and its sense of touch generate this effect of intimacy, or in other words, how the voice, digitally produced and distributed, appears as a kind of unembodied presence, still producing the sense of intimacy when touching the listener – an intimacy that can be experienced rather intensely when listening with in-ear headphones to the sound waves of the voice, which also in a physical sense directly touch the ear (cf. the quote by Schafer above). Especially a whispering voice and voices recorded closely to the microphone or with a binaural microphone have this pseudo-haptic effect on the body, as described by Klausen and Have (2019) in relation to ASMR (Autonomous Sensory Meridian Response) videos on YouTube.

Reading an audiobook performs a meeting between at least two voices: the physical voice of the performing narrator and the immaterial, implicit voice of the text. Sometimes the voice of the performing narrator belongs to a recognizable actor or actress, sometimes the author himself or herself (Have and Stougaard Pedersen 2016). In the latter case, there is a possible doubling of the voice of the text and the bodily voice speaking. When the text is an autobiographical novel, read by the author, the reader hears the autobiographical story told by the voice writing, and that adds an extra dimension to the experience. The text lends its voice to the performing narrator who embodies not only the text but also the referential contour of the world described. This is the case of the audiobook version of the novel *Det samme og noget helt andet* (2021, *The Same and Something Completely Different*) by the Danish author Katrine Marie Guldager (born 1966). Her autobiographical novel will be used as an example in the next section.

Voice as *orality* and *vocality*

The voice of the performing narrator, touching the ear, is both an instrument and a channel of communication. By making this distinction, we build on Adriana Cavarero and her ideas regarding the voice as fundamentally relational (2012). She creates a distinction between the voice as *vocality* and the voice as *orality*. As *vocality*, the voice is first and foremost experienced as a physical instrument. The voice produces the sound of the body – and flesh, referring to the previous quote of Cavarero – brought into vibration, tone, rhythm: it can be raspy, hoarse, treble, or something else entirely. These are haptic qualities of the voice as *vocality*. The voice as *orality* deals with how the voice carries and performs language as a channel of communication. From this perspective, the *relationality* or rhetoric of language is at stake. From Cavarero's double perspective, the performing narrator reading an audiobook can be experienced as a kind of sensory touch, a *relationality* that is activated by both vocal and oral qualities.

This can be exemplified by the audiobook by Katrine Marie Guldager (2021), where the author is the performing narrator of her own autobiographical novel. The vocal properties of the voice of Guldager, its material characteristics, are that of a deep, calm, and slightly hoarse voice. Regarding the oral perspective, her pronunciation of words is rather affected. In Danish, this becomes obvious when choosing a specific, open pronunciation of the vocal "a," signaling an upper-class dialect. The deliberate and slow reading tempo foregrounds the words' qualities – the listener can almost taste them in their own mouth – partly because the diction of Guldager's oral performance bears more similarity to poetry reading than to the reading style of most audiobook narrators. An observation supported by the fact that several readers at the audiobook streaming site Mofibo suggest listening to the book in a slightly raised tempo. The oral aspects of the voice thus create a mediated and embodied relation to the listener. This is the result of the affective diction of voice, which at times makes it hard to determine whether Guldager performs her own text with an ironic attitude toward the implicit narrator of the text.

Nevertheless, the style of writing and the voice performance strive toward creating a strong relational bond with the listener.

The protagonist invites the listener into an autobiographical and quiet private universe, and she does not make an effort to cover up her personal mistakes and insufficiencies, hereby producing an unreliable narrator position. The reading performance invites the listener uncritically to enter a contract of intimacy with the narrator of the novel, and the performing narrator seems to laugh both *with* and sometimes *behind the back* of the protagonist of this autobiographical novel.

In this example, and in the combination of oral and vocal aspects, the voice is experienced as a kind of social company. The voice reading to you expresses a *relationality* that creates both distance and intimacy or presence; in both cases, a rhetorical contract between performer and listener is exposed and developed. This *relationality* works as a kind of haptic quality or mediated touch, as described by Marks, here relocating her concept from the visual to the domain of the sound of a voice. The *vocality* of the voice touches the listener through the aesthetic relation to the sounding qualities of the voice itself, and the oral qualities of the voice handling language touch the listener through a rhetorical, mediated approach (Marks 2008).

Audiobook reading as a multisensory experience

In our investigation in this chapter of audiobook reading as multisensory, we have focused on different aspects of the haptic and tactile qualities of sound, voices, and audiobooks, downplaying other sensory impulses like the visual, olfactory, and taste (see Stougaard Pedersen and Have 2017 for an analysis of sound and smell in food commercials). Here, toward the end of the chapter, we would like to open up toward this wider spectrum of the multisensory experience by including the situations in which we read. As described in Chapter 12 of this volume, audiobook reading affords engagement in other activities while you listen (see also Have and Stougaard Pedersen 2016, 2020), and these activities influence and stimulate the multisensory reading experience – the smell of the forest or food cooking, the body moving through the landscape, the sensation of wind on your face, or the sun warming your cheeks while walking. It is a reciprocal relationship, or a symbiotic reading situation, you might say, where the story and voice in your ears influence how you sense and experience your surroundings, and vice versa. The analytic outline of this chapter, the mediated, haptic qualities of audio reading, exemplifies some of the aspects that make the audio reading activity in particular well suited for discussing reading not from a mono-, but from a multisensory perspective. We take part in the world through our body as a whole, but the mediated sound and voice in our ears support and intensify the reading experience as a sensory matter.

References

Baron, Naomi S. 2021. *How We Read Now: Strategic Choices for Print, Screen, and Audio*. New York: Oxford University Press.
Birkerts, Sven. 1994. *The Gutenberg Elegies: The Fate of Reading in an Electronic Age*. Boston: Faber and Faber.
Brügger, Niels. 2003."Bogen som medie – nedslag i bogobjektets historiske transformationer." *Passage* 48: 77–96.
Cavallo, Guglielmo, and Chartier, Roger, eds. 1999. *A history of reading in the West*. Oxford: Polity.
Cavarero, Adriana. 2012. "Multiple Voices." In *The Sound Studies Reader*, edited by Jonathan Sterne, 520–532. New York: Routledge.
Derrida, Jacques. 1997. *Stemmen og Fænomenet: Introduktion til Tegnproblematikken i Husserls Fænomenologi*. Copenhagen: Hans Reitzel.
Daniel, David B., and Woody, William Douglas. 2010. "They hear, but do not listen: Retention for podcasted material in a classroom context." *Teaching of Psychology* 37: 199–203.
Eisenstein, Elizabeth L. 1996 (1983). *The Printing Revolution in Early Modern Europe*. Canto: Cambridge University Press.
Feld, Steven. 2005. "Places sensed, senses placed – Towards a sensuous epistemology of environments. In *Empire of the Senses*, edited byDavid Howes, 179–191. Oxford: Berg.
Guldager, Katrine Marie. 2021. *Det Samme og Noget Helt Andet*. Copenhagen: Politikens Forlag.
Have, Iben, and Stougaard Pedersen, Birgitte. 2016. *Digital Audiobooks. New Media, Users and Experiences*. New York: Routledge.
Have, Iben, and Stougaard Pedersen, Birgitte. 2020. "To read an Audiobook". In *Beyond Media Borders: Intermedial Relations Among Multimodal Media*, edited byEllestrøm L. 197–216. Vol. 1, London Palgrave Macmillan.
Have, Iben, and Stougaard Pedersen, Birgitte. 2021. "To read an Audiobook." In *Beyond Media Borders: Intermedial Relations Among Multimodal Media*, vol. 1, edited by Lars Ellestrøm, 197–216. London: Palgrave Macmillan.
Hayles, N. Katherine. 2004. "Print is flat, code is deep. The importance of media specific analysis." *Poetics Today* 25, no. 1: 67–90.
Horton, Donald, and Wohl, Richard R. 1997 (1956). "Massekommunikation og parasocial interaktion: Et indlæg om intimitet på afstand." *MedieKultur. Journal of Media and Communication Research* 13, no. 26: 27–39.
Klausen, Helle Breth, and Have, Iben. 2019. " 'Today let's gently brush your ears': ASMR som mediekulturelt og lydligt fænomen." *MedieKultur – Journal of media and communication research* 66: 37–54.
Marks, Laura U. 2000. *The Skin of the Film: Intercultural Cinema, Embodiment, and the Senses*. Durham, North Carolina: Duke University Press.
Marks, Laura U. 2008. "Thinking Multisensory Culture." *Paragraph* 31, no. 2: 123–137.
Neumark, Norie. 2010. "Doing Things with Voices: Performativity and Voice." In *VOICE: Vocal Aesthetics in Digital Arts and Media*, edited byNorie Neumark, Ross Gibson, and Theo van Leeuwen. MIT Press.

Ong, Walter J. 2002 (1982). *Orality and Literacy. The Technologizing of the Word*. London and New York: Routledge.
Ree, Jonathan. 1999. *I See a Voice*. New York: Harper Collins.
Rogowsky, Beth A., Calhoun, Barbara M., and Tallal, Paula. 2016. "Does modality matter? The effects reading, listening and dual modality." *SAGE Open* 6, no. 3. 10.1177/2158244016669550.
Saenger, Paul. 2000. *Space Between Words: The Origins of Silent Reading*. Stanford University Press.
Schafer, R. Murray. 1993. *The Soundscape - Our Sonic Environment and the Tuning of the World*. Rochester: Destiny Books.
Sterne, Jonathan. 2003. *The Audible Past: Cultural Origins of Sound Reproduction*. Durham: Duke University Press.
Sousa, Trish L. Varao, Carriere, Jonathan S. A., and Smilek, Daniel. 2013. "The way we encounter reading material influences how frequently we mind wander." *Frontiers in Psychology* 4, 892. doi: 10.3389/fpsyg.2013.00892.
Spence, Charles. 2020. "The multisensory experience of handling and reading books." *Multisensory Research* 33, no. 8: 902–928.
Stougaard Pedersen, Birgitte, and Have, Iben. 2017. "Smørbar æstetisk kommunikation: En Lurpak-kampagne i et multisensorisk perspektiv." In *Kreativ markedskommunikation: Æstetik og deltagelse*, edited by Birgitte Stougaard Pedersen and Anne Marit Waade, 29–46. Aarhus, Denmark: Systime.
Tanderup Linkis, Sara, and Pennlert, Julia. 2021. "'It adds a dimension': Consumption Patterns among Swedish Audiobook Users." Conference paper, *Revolutions in Reading*, Stockholm June 24–26.

9 How to read a network, or the Internet as unfinished demo

Lori Emerson

If humanities-based disciplines teach us how to read content that appears on the surface of discrete media technologies (what I call a horizontal reading practice) and if materialist media studies teach us how to read individual media technologies by descending down through layers of hardware and software functionalities (what I call a vertical reading practice), what if we more explicitly combine both approaches to offer up accounts of complex, connected technologies such as networks? In this chapter, I experiment with developing a methodology for reading networks by focusing specifically on the Transmission Control Protocol/Internet Protocol – or TCP/IP – the engine that drives "the Internet," the term we use to refer to the largest internet in the world, and which consists of the TCP/IP. My reading treats TCP/IP as a kind of case study in reading networks insofar as I work both horizontally, moving freely across disciplines and across a wide range of documents on the protocol, and vertically, moving from the surface where these same documents reside down to the underlying technical specs of the protocol. My hope is that this demonstration of how to read TCP/IP both vertically and horizontally can be adapted to read any number of networks that may have preceded the internet or that currently exist on or outside of the internet. The alternative to not knowing how networks work or how to read them is that we too easily accept them as neutral or as technological structures that could not possibly be constructed otherwise.

Net neutrality ≠ neutrality of the net

February 8, 1996, was a watershed moment for the status of the internet in our cultural imaginary. The date marks the moment that John Perry Barlow published his "Declaration of the Independence of Cyberspace" as part of the online project *24 Hours in Cyberspace*. At the time, for Barlow, the net of the mid-1990s was "an act of nature" that "grows itself through our collective actions" (Barlow 1996). Continuing on in his attempts to position the internet as utterly unmoored from the messiness of material reality and politics, he declares, "We are creating a world that all may enter without privilege or prejudice accorded by race, economic power, military force, or

DOI: 10.4324/9781003211662-14

station of birth" (ibid.). Barlow's story was powerfully seductive as its rhetoric managed to overshadow the fact that while anyone could freely view *24 Hours in Cyberspace* the project as a whole cost as much as five million dollars, was funded by 50 mostly large computer companies, and raised 5.4 million dollars in venture capital for the Apple spinoff company NetObjects which provided infrastructural support (Maloney 1996, Halfhill 1996). Still, seemingly oblivious to how Barlow's "Declaration" and its parent project, *24 Hours in Cyberspace*, were buoyed up by a complex assemblage of economic power, privilege, and supporting infrastructure, the "Declaration" soon appeared on over 40,000 different websites as it became a canonical text for those on both the far left and the far right who wanted to believe the internet was a world beyond governments, nations, laws, cultural norms, social conventions, and even material reality itself (Frezza 1996, Turner 2006).

The publication and worldwide circulation of this document thus marks a point at which the internet became more of a story than a material reality as it floated free from its technological underpinnings. Only three years later, in 1999, Lawrence Lessig could describe the mythology of cyberspace firmly in place: "Cyberspace, the story went, could *only* be free. Freedom was its nature. But why was never made clear. That *cyberspace* was a place that governments could not control was an idea that I never quite got. The word itself speaks not of freedom but of control." (5. emphases in original). He then goes on to deftly trace the roots of "cyber" to cybernetics, first proposed in 1948 by Norbert Wiener as the study of control at a distance – arguably exactly what corporations have been doing with the Internet since the mid-1990s. Eerily speaking to ongoing attempts to repeal net neutrality in the U.S., over 20 years later from when Lessig was writing *Code and Other Laws of Cyberspace*, he also urges us to remember:

> Liberty in cyberspace will not come from the absence of the state. Liberty there, as anywhere, will come from a state of a certain kind. We build a world where freedom can flourish not by removing from society any self-conscious control; we build a world where freedom can flourish by setting it in a place where a particular kind of self-conscious control survives [...] I mean an architecture [...] that structures and constrains social and legal power. (1999, 5)

Lessig reminds us that the internet is an architecture – a material structure built by particular groups of people with partisan goals in mind – as well as a structure that requires careful, one might say nonpartisan government policies around maintenance and access. However, even this reminder that the internet is an architecture strangely ignores certain hard, material facts about this network's infrastructure which exist prior to any regulation or policy about usage or access. Thus, even for its good intentions, Lessig's critique inadvertently advocates for net neutrality at the cost of having readers understand the ways in which the net is anything but neutral.

However, if the notion of net neutrality along with the many recent critiques of surveillance and tracking online provide us with important horizontal readings of online content, revealing the extent of corporate control of the internet, what might an additional vertical reading of the internet look like? In other words, how do we build on these horizontal readings while moving away from the confusion wrought by the phrase "net neutrality" and toward uncovering the determinisms built into the architecture of the internet? One way to answer these questions is to complement documents or narratives about the internet with an analysis of TCP/IP – a suite of layered protocols for sending and receiving data communications across disparate networks. Happily, both Andrew Russell's (2014) work on network standardization and Nicole Starosielski's (2015) work on the internet's undersea cables provide us with a general outline of what such work looks like at the intersection of content- and materialist-oriented disciplines, with Alexander Galloway (2004) having already provided us with an initial reading of TCP/IP. However, there is still much more that can be written about TCP/IP in terms of both its functionalities and flaws as well as alternative internet protocols. The latter is crucial for getting us to think harder about alternative networks and network structures, rather than remaining focused on governmental or corporate policy about internet access or content.

Technical specs matter

Perhaps already daunted or bored by the acronyms and the technical language woven through any discussion of network protocols, one might reasonably ask: as long as the internet continues to work, what difference does it make whether we undertake this vertical reading or not? It matters because we have become so accustomed to the usual narratives about the internet that we are immune to seeing how this network of networks is actually not functioning effectively, beyond just matters of, again, content and access. Without knowing the basics of the internet's technical specs, we are left unthinkingly believing this is the only possible and accepting ideologically loaded statements made by corporations such as Google as statements of fact. Take Google's "Take Action" webpage as an example. Created in the wake of the U.S. Federal Communications Commission's 2014 decision to consider allowing Internet Service Providers to charge users for faster access to content and potentially put an end to net neutrality (reversed in 2015, but still repeatedly challenged, depending on the political party in control of the Federal Communications Commission), it is hard not to be seduced into head-nodding by its call-to-arms rhetoric. Google declares that "the internet was designed to be free and open [...] Internet policy should be like the Internet itself – open and inclusive. It was founded on principles of collaboration and transparency, and has always been an instrument of the people [...] the internet belongs to the people who build and use it" (Google n.d.). Setting aside for the moment that no one benefits more than Google from this so-called open network which allows them to track, index, and *algorithmize* every click and every bit of text "the people" enter into the network, TCP/IP was actually created more out of the desire to not interfere with the burgeoning computer industry than to build an open and inclusive network for the good of the people.

The internet emerged after years of heated international debate about the need for standardized hardware, software, and user interfaces in the computer industry that was reaching a pitch of urgency by 1982. Up to this point, buying a computer meant reading the hefty manual that came with your machine, for it was practically a guarantee that your Texas Instruments 99/4a operated differently than your Commodore 64 or your Atari 800. Even computer keyboards were not yet standardized. And if personal computers were not yet standardized, neither were there ways in which these computers communicated with each other, resulting in thousands of yet-to-be documented networks. For example, demonstrating early on their dedication to a single brand environment rather than the kind of abstraction and consolidation made possible by TCP/IP, Apple began to develop a local network called Apple Net, later renamed AppleTalk. Similar to the Ethernet, Apple Net would connect only Apple Lisa computers, though the company claimed to have distant plans to make it possible for non-Lisa computers to talk to one another.

Vinton Cerf and other developers recognized in the early 1970s or earlier the need for a standard protocol that would not endorse any one computer manufacturer because they believed the protocol should transcend the particularities of particular machines, thereby not interfering with the growth of the computer industry (Cerf et al. 1976). The way that TCP/IP acts as a kind of mechanism for abstraction, hiding differences between hardware/software particularities, does not make it an instrument of neutrality and therefore freedom from control. It makes TCP/IP a highly effective work-around to both the telecommunications monopoly maintained by the Postal, Telegraph, and Telephone service providers (PTTs) and the impossibility, at that time, of imposing standards on computer manufacturers from the ground up. Instead, the protocol suite imposes a series of hierarchical layers on top of individual data processes, thereby allowing the free market to settle the issue of hardware/software standardization. More, the decision to use this protocol rather than any of the other protocols that were discussed internationally in the 1970s and early 1980s was not one arrived at through broad and transparent collaboration. It was, instead, the result of intense political wrangling between entrenched communities of select engineers, industry workers, and representatives from PTTs from Canada, the U.S., and Europe. As Alexander Galloway (2004, 122) points out, "Like the philosophy of protocol itself, membership in this technocratic ruling class is open [...] But, to be sure, because of the technical sophistication needed to participate, this loose consortium of decision makers tends to fall into a relatively homogenous social class." Perhaps too obvious to mention, the majority of the participants in the early development of the internet were also men.

Gender aside, it is also true that decisions about the architecture of the internet were based largely on specific infrastructure constraints rather than on philosophical considerations about what constitutes an effective distribution of power to users or the importance of an open, democratic design. Rather, as Tim Wu (2010) states,

> The Internet's creators, mainly academics operating within and outside the government, lacked the power or ambition to create an information empire. They faced a world in which the wires were owned by AT&T and computing was a patchwork of fiefdoms centered on the gigantic mainframe computers, each with idiosyncratic protocols and systems [...] they did not have the resources to create an alternative infrastructure, to wire the world as Bell had spent generations and untold billions doing.

However, there are at least two other significant aspects of the telecommunications landscape in the early 1980s that Wu does not mention. For one, the example of Apple Net/AppleTalk above points to how computer companies were building networks for their own vendors, quite in contrast to his claim for AT&T's overwhelming control of the phone lines. For another, the well-funded and powerful DARPA (Defense Advanced Research Projects Agency, originally named ARPA and the creator of the ARPANET) decided to adopt TCP/IP in the early 1980s, not because the protocol was necessarily the only or even the best choice, but because it had, since the late 1970s, already invested substantial money and resources in converting its ARPANET machines from NCP to TCP and then finally to TCP/IP (McKenzie 2014). In short, we seem to have forgotten that standards such as the TCP/IP protocol were adopted because of "pure political and financial muscle" (Shuford 1983, 6).

That said, even though the political and financial struggle was effectively between the engineers and industry representatives on the one side and the telephone carriers on the other, this did not necessarily have to create an either/or situation in which the internet would have to be based on either distributed control (as I discuss below, an approach embodied by packet switching and datagrams) or centralized control (an approach embodied by virtual circuits). Even with the existing infrastructure, the internet architecture could in fact have been quite different – for example, it could have been a combination of both centralized and distributed modes of control, of packet switching and virtual circuits, potentially resulting in a more robust and reliable internet than the one we currently have. Thus, while it might appear as though American engineers did not have much choice in their

How to read a network, or the Internet as unfinished demo   103

design of what we could call "an Internet," there were other available options.

While I have pointed out some of the economic and political factors driving the creation and adoption of TCP/IP, what about the technical design of TCP/IP itself? If it is true that, as Eugene Thacker (2004, xi) puts it, "the technical specs matter, ontologically and politically," what are the technical specs of TCP/IP and, crucially, how can we attend to these technical specs and extrapolate some kind of broad-reaching meaning?

Layers, interfaces, and black boxes

Consisting most importantly of the Transmission Control Protocol and the Internet Protocol, TCP/IP is the engine that drives "the Internet," the word we now use (misleadingly) to refer to the largest internet in the world. Figure 9.1 is a standard representation of the layers comprising TCP/IP and the corresponding protocols for each layer.

It is important to first point out that the internet consists of packet-switching networks that function by breaking communication messages into datagrams which are, according to the Internet memo Request for Comments 1594 (Malkin et al. 1994), "self-contained, independent [entities] of data carrying sufficient information to be routed from the source to the destination computer without reliance on earlier exchanges between this source and destination computer and the transporting network." Thus, IP is one of the protocols for the lower internet layer. This layer and its respective protocol are responsible for providing an address for the data packet's destination and for relaying the packets from host to destination; but since the data packets are sent across the network in no particular order, IP is considered unreliable. TCP, however, is a higher transport layer

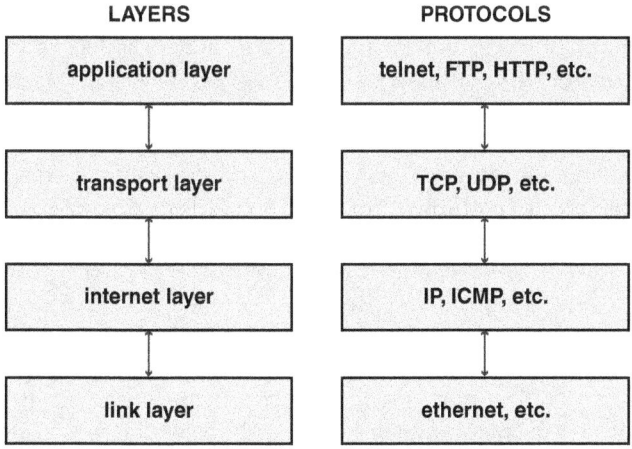

Figure 9.1 TCP/IP overview.

responsible for providing the reliability between processes that IP does not provide. TCP detects errors at the Internet layer, helps with what is called "flow control" (or the means to control the speed of transmission from sender to receiver so that the latter is not potentially overwhelmed with data from the former), correctly orders data packets, and passes on data to the upper layer.

Second, I mentioned earlier that TCP/IP evolved out of TCP and it did so because engineers believed the protocol would only be successful if it fully implemented the concept of layers that had been developed in the late 1960s for operating systems by the Dutch computer scientist Edsger Dijkstra. In "The Structure of the 'THE'-Multiprogramming System," Dijkstra (1968) put forward a ground-breaking proposal for an operating system that worked according to a strict, hierarchical system of layers in which higher layers abstract information from lower levels. The notion of layering then became so fundamental to the design of computer systems that engineers applied the same principle of layering to networks. However, while it might at first seem odd to apply the concept of layers to networks, as networks are utterly different from operating systems, the critical error was not the importation of the model of layers, but the way in which the layers were conceived. As John Day clarified in an email to me (October 6, 2014):

> [T]he primary reason for layers in networks is that in networks we have "a loci of distributed shared state of different scopes." […] Where we (and Dykstra) went wrong was the idea that the layers had different functions. What I figured out (and we were very close to seeing in the mid-70s before the politics took over) was that all layers have the same functions, they just operate on a different range of the problem. That led me to also see that OSs showed the same pattern. Dykstra missed it because machines were so small in 1968.

To clarify: the problem with using layers in networks has to do with an original misperception of the way layers ought to be structured that can be traced back to its implementation in operating systems. On the one hand, layering allows for, as Lydia Parziale et al. (2006) put it, "division of labor, ease of implementation and code testing, and the ability to develop alternative layer implementation." However, higher layers make use of services provided by lower levels through interfaces that black box each layer; thus, the layers are not only separated from each other, but the processes that define each layer happen independently of each other. Although black boxing layers is one way the designers wanted to "future proof" the Internet so that one can update certain layers without affecting the whole system, it also "hides most of the problems from those who use the Net. Only a relatively few people have to deal with the underlying issues; the vast majority are given the illusion that it simply works" (Day 2008). Martin Geddes (2014) succinctly states the problem:

What lies behind the Internet is an unconscious belief that networks deliver packets between computers. This is obvious, right? The problem is, it sees networking as a mechanistic activity, and fails to capture its true nature as a form of *distributed computing* that is all about moving information between *computing processes*, not network interfaces. You can see this play out in the way IP only partially delivers data, as it addresses network interfaces, not the true destination application process. (n.n emphasis in original)

This weakness in IP, the way in which it addresses, comes out of a flawed method of layering that broke up the earlier TCP into TCP and IP. Thus, to return to the question I posed early on in this piece, of whether it matters that we know how the Internet works as long as it continues to work, it turns out that, in fact, the Internet is already not working in some respects and will likely continue to not work well in the coming years.

The Internet as an unfinished demo

The way IP creates addresses is only one of many problems with TCP/IP that prevent the Internet from functioning better and that have led John Day (2008) to declare that "the Internet is an unfinished demo." For example, in addition to the flaws of IP, our modern-day Internet also lacks any kind of security architecture, a design flaw that can be traced back to the ARPANET. In other words, while the backbone of the supposedly "open" Internet is built on a protocol suite modeled not on networking but on the closed layers of abstraction comprising operating systems, so too is the Internet built on an experimental network that was never meant to be the driving engine for most of the modern world.

However, researchers have proposed alternative network architectures that could solve many of the problems of TCP/IP. RINA, or the Recursive Internet Network Architecture, is an alternative network architecture being developed by Day along with a team of faculty and students at Boston University. RINA is, as they describe it, a "clean-slate internet architecture that builds on a very basic premise, yet fresh perspective that networking is not a layered set of different functions but rather a single layer of distributed Inter-Process Communication (IPC) that repeats over different scopes" (RINA 2010). Thus, the architecture is "scalable," comes with its own complete naming and addressing architecture, and includes "security by design," among other features (Grasa et al. 2011). Unfortunately, even though it seems inevitable that a new architecture for the Internet needs to be implemented, given the money and resources already invested in the current Internet architecture, it is very unlikely that RINA will be adopted any time soon. Still, RINA does help us see the Internet that has given birth to a rhetoric about itself that habitually celebrates its supposed neutrality, inherent independence, freedom, and openness at the cost of seeing its limitations and foreclosures.

But, as I have demonstrated throughout this piece, once we implement both a horizontal and a vertical reading of the Internet – its surface-level content combined with a reading of its underlying material layers and technical specs – it becomes clear that the Internet cannot be a neutral tool and inherently good at the same time. The Internet could have been and could still be quite otherwise.

Acknowledgments

This piece was significantly improved from feedback by Nick Briz, John Day, Paul Eberhart, Sarah Melton, Jussi Parikka, Benjamin Robertson, and several anonymous commenters. My sincere thanks for these individuals' time, energy, and generosity.

References

Barlow, John Perry. 1996. "Declaration of the independence of cyberspace." Electronic Frontier Foundation.
Cadwalladr, Carole. 2018. " 'I made Steve Bannon's psychological warfare tool': Meet the data war whistleblower." *The Guardian*, March 18, 2018.
Cerf, Vinton, McKenzie, Alexander A., Scantlebury, R. A., and Zimmermann, Hubert. 1976. "Proposal for an international end to end protocol." *SIGCOMM Computer Communication Review* 6, no. 1: 63–89.
Day, John. 2008. *Patterns in Network Architecture: A Return to Fundamentals*. Upper Saddle River, New Jersey: Pearson Education.
Dijkstra, Edsger. 1968. "The structure of the 'THE'-multiprogramming system." https://www.eecs.ucf.edu/~eurip/papers/dijkstra-the68.pdf.
Frezza, Bill. 1996. "Can public network computing save democracy." *Network Computing*, November 1, 1996, 35.
Galloway, Alexander. 2004. *Protocol: How Control Exists After Decentralization*. Cambridge, Massachusetts: MIT Press.
Google. n.d. "Take action." https://google.com/takeaction/.
Geddes, Martin. 2014. "Network architecture research: TCP/IP vs RINA." *Geddes: Fresh Thinking*.
Grasa, Eduard, Trouva, Eleni, Phelan, Patrick, de Leon, Miguel Ponce, Day, John, Matta, Ibrahim, Chitkushev, Lubomir T., and Bunch, Steve. 2011. "Design principles of the Recursive InterNetwork Architecture (RINA)."
Grassegger, Hannes, and Krogerus, Mikael. 2017. "The data that turned the world upside down." *Motherboard*, January 28, 2017.
Halfhill, Tom R. 1996. "Inside the ultimate web site." *BYTE Magazine*, December 20, 1996.
Lessig, Lawrence. 1999. *Code and Other Laws of Cyberspace*. New York: Basic Books.
Malkin, Gary S., Marine, April, and Reynolds, Joyce K. 1994. "FYI on questions and answers – answers to commonly asked 'new internet user' questions." *Request for Comments 1594*.

Maloney, Janice. 1996. "Netobjects publishing software." *Fortune Magazine*, July 8, 1996.

McKenzie, Alex. 2014. "INWG and the conception of the internet: An eyewitness account." *Alex McKenzie*.

Parziale, Lydia, Britt, David T., Davis, Chuck, Forrester, Jason, Liu, Wei, Matthews, Carolyn, and Rosselot, Nicolas. 2006. "TCP/IP tutorial and technical overview." IBM RedBooks.

RINA. 2010. "About." http://csr.bu.edu/rina/about.html.

Russell, Andrew L. 2014. *Open Standards and the Digital Age: History, Ideology, and Networks*. New York: Cambridge University Press.

Shuford, Richard. 1983. "Standards: The love/hate relationship." Editorial. *Byte* 8, 2.

Starosielski, Nicole. 2015. *The Undersea Network*. Durham, North Carolina: Duke University Press.

Thacker, Eugene. 2004. "Preface." In *Protocol: How Control Exists After Decentralization*, edited by Alexander Galloway, xi. Cambridge, Massachusetts: MIT Press.

Turner, Fred. 2006. *From Counterculture to Cyberculture: Stewart Brand, the Whole Earth Network, and the Rise of Digital Utopianism*. Chicago, Illinois: Chicago University Press.

Wu, Tim. 2010. *The Master Switch: The Rise and Fall of Information Empires*. New York: Alfred A. Knopf.

Section III
Reading Engagement: Aspects of Digital Reading

Introduction to Section III

Building on Section II, this section explores new ways of engaging with different digital book formats. The section addresses how so-called "deep-reading" experiences have been theorized and how such concepts have an implicit or explicit bias toward a particular medium or engagement in a text. Immersed or deeply engaged reading experiences do not by default belong to reading printed books, and both immersed and distracted reading practices change and take on different shapes because of their mediation. In the chapters of this section, concepts like intensity and immersion will be renegotiated and nuanced to be able to capture the digital reading condition of today, and the general approach is that reading engagement is not just a question of comprehension and memory output, but must also include sensory and social experiences of embodiment and being present in a specific situation in an interplay with materiality and technology. The experience and intensity of reading a piece of literature will differ depending on whether you read it as a printed book, as a digital audiobook, or as an interactive app, and whether you read it in school, in your bedroom, or while taking a walk in the forest.

The chapters suggest that reading with the ears and reading through touch, alongside other sensory input, are different kinds of reading flows that support and intensify the relation between reader, interface, content, and the world. This includes social settings and activities framing the reading situation. What you do while you read is an important factor when studying engaging reading experiences.

A main premise in this section is the fact that the digital reading condition affords possibilities of reading on new terms. When you explore sensory and personal engagement in digital audio or app reading, you need other scholarly approaches than you do for studying printed text reading. We need to adjust and revisit conventional conceptions of reading as well as critically discuss the ideas of close and deep versus distant and distracted reading, as suggested by N. Katherine Hayles (2010), Franco Moretti (2013), and Naomi Baron (2021). The chapters in this section in different ways confront ideas of "good and proper" reading and "bad and pernicious" reading often associated with digital media by giving empirical examples of different forms of reading engagement in the digital age.

In the first chapter, "Deep, focused, and critical reading between media," Birgitte Stougaard Pedersen and Maria Engberg engage in the general discussions of deep, focused, and critical reading traditionally associated with the printed book and a certain kind of literature. They confront the widespread idea that digital reading is distracted, superficial, hyper, and even detrimental to our ability to focus and engage deeply. The chapter suggests that other aspects of engagement in digital reading must be introduced and not be inextricably linked to a particular medium or genre.

Following the theoretical discussions of engaged digital reading in Chapter 10, Ayoe Quist Henkel and Birgitte Stougaard Pedersen in Chapter 11, "Reading digital interfaces and audiobooks: media-specific and multisensory aspects of immersion," discuss multisensory aspects of immersion in relation to different kinds of reading in an everyday school context. In a comparative study of eighth-grade students in Denmark who read the graphic novel *NORD* in three different formats – a hardback book, a digital audiobook, and a browser-based born-digital story – the chapter demonstrates how the students' sensory engagement and immersion take on different forms when they interact with the different media and texts.

In the last chapter, "Motivations for audiobook reading in modern everyday lives," Iben Have continues the empirical approach by referring to existing studies of multitasking as a motivating and engaging aspect of audio reading. The chapter focuses on social and practical aspects of reading audiobooks in modern, busy everyday lives. Being able to audio-read while you do other not cognitively demanding activities can lead to deeply engaged and embodied reading experiences and a feeling of autonomy and dynamic in the reading situation. Thus, the chapter challenges cultural values and negative prejudices usually related to audiobooks by emphasizing them as positive aspects of audio reading.

References

Baron, Naomi S. 2021. *How We Read Now: Strategic Choices for Print, Screen, and Audio*. New York: Oxford University Press.

Hayles, N. Katherine. 2010. How We Read: Close, hyper, Machine. *ADE Bulletin* 150: 62–79.

Moretti, Franco. 2013. *Distant Reading*. Verso Books: London and Brooklyn.

10 Deep, focused, and critical reading between media

Maria Engberg and
Birgitte Stougaard Pedersen

In 2019, Brad Wages, a copywriter, published a six-minute read story on Medium.com entitled "The Art of Deep Reading." With some surprise and consternation, Wages recounts how he tried to give his friends a recap of an important book that he had read (the book is, interestingly, *Wired for Story: The Writer's Guide to Using Brain Science to Hook Readers from the Very First Sentence* by Lisa Cron). He could not recall much. The experience led him to go back to the book and develop a set of strategies to not only read but study the book, with the aim of improving his recall. And here is where Wages's account becomes fascinating: the step-by-step guide to deep reading starts with the following list of must-haves: "An Amazon Account, so you can access Kindle Cloud Reader. The book you want to deep read, you need in Kindle form. The Bookcision app to make accessing your highlights easy. Optional, but highly recommended: The Libby App for free library ebooks" (Wages 2019). If this list did not already highlight how enmeshed with digital culture Wages's notion of deep reading is, his insistence in what followed does: "When you come across a book that looks interesting, borrow or buy it in Kindle form. This is important – for the Deep Reading method, the book needs to be in electronic form because you're going to be doing a lot of copying and pasting." The deep reading practice that Wages supports is of course a well-worn tactic of reading, writing, note-taking, and re-reading in a continuous loop until the most important content is memorized. Only, in Wages's description, deep reading occurs in a decidedly digital, multichannel fashion.

The picture of a reading and learning situation that Wages presents is in stark contrast to the account of another, equally poly-mediated reading situation by *The New York Times* bestselling author Nicholas Carr:

> Over the last few years I've had an uncomfortable sense that someone, or something, has been tinkering with my brain, remapping the neural circuitry, reprogramming the memory. My mind isn't going – so far as I can tell – but it's changing. I'm not thinking the way I used to think. I feel it most strongly when I'm reading. I used to find it easy to immerse myself in a book or a lengthy article. My mind would get caught up in

DOI: 10.4324/9781003211662-17

> the twists of the narrative or the turns of the argument, and I'd spend hours strolling through long stretches of prose. That's rarely the case anymore. Now my concentration starts to drift after a page or two. I get fidgety, lose the thread, begin looking for something else to do. I feel like I'm always dragging my wayward brain back to the text. The deep reading that used to come naturally has become a struggle.
>
> (Carr 2010)

Carr identifies his increasing, and often very useful, time spent online on the web as the culprit. As he queries his own changed reading patterns and that of three bloggers, all men with a keen interest in writing, researching, and reading, a common thread seems to emerge. They no longer read as they used to. "I have very little patience for long, drawn-out, nuanced arguments," says one of them (Carr 2010, locations 200), and a college student states, "Sitting down and going through a book from cover to cover doesn't make sense" (ibid. locations 217). Carr's vignettes about the state of reading among these men presumably date from just before the book's publication date in 2010. Over 10 years later, these descriptions of reading digitally will arguably be recognizable to an even wider group of readers. Of course, it is also notable that what counts as valuable reading is "long stretches of prose," and Carr's account includes mentions of classical literature and more theoretical fare, such as "recently published scholarly history or a two-hundred-year-old Victorian novel" (ibid., locations 1790). In Carr's account, and in much of the research and the many reports about reading that have appeared since 2010, the definition of a loss of reading in the age of the Internet and the web seems largely to concern so-called serious, or canonical, literature, rather than, say, historical textbooks or popular non-fiction.

There is, and possibly always will be, an intensity to the discussions of what reading constitutes and what kinds of reading are more useful, critical, pleasurable, or neurologically sound for us – from the continued research into literacy and reading competencies in educational research fields (for instance by the New London Group) to propositions, fears, and hopes about, and, less frequently, research into the effects of digitally mediated reading formats. This chapter continues the exploration of the digital reading condition by discussing various propositions of what constitutes a deep, focused, and critical reading, as they relate to the mediation and materiality of that which is read. Conversely, there are other modes of reading that have been associated particularly with digital technologies – hyper reading and distant reading, for instance – and which are interesting to investigate as facets of how affordances and expectations about technologies as material contexts for reading are perceived.

To read deeply, focused, and/or critically, as the title of this chapter states, suggests various value statements about reading that are culturally and historically linked to a particular time and specific practices and attitudes toward reading. Focused and sustained reading, for instance, is often argued to be preferred over quick or cursory reading, especially when dealing with longer or more complex texts. Implicitly or explicitly, the assumption is often that this reading requires traditionally printed texts, and that conversely digital technologies are unsuited for this kind of reading (see for instance Chapter 1).

This was not always the case. Historically, some attitudes toward reading included panic, once contemporaneous commentator felt that too many people were becoming readers. Frank Furedi (2015) reminds us of thinkers who suggested that their contemporaries were in the grips of "book madness" and "reading mania" in an expanding reading public in the 18th and 19th centuries. During the Enlightenment, the objection was not to reading as such by a broader reading public, but to popular fiction and "inferior" reading material that would "estrange people from the fine words of their educated superiors" (ibid. 40). At the time, the novel was vilified for what was seen as baser pleasures (ibid. 41). There was an elitist concern about how to control the reading masses, and reading as the foundation of education, learning, and enlightenment took hold. However, as Furedi notes, Western cultures still found it difficult to value "all readers and all forms of reading" (ibid. 42), a sentiment that remains. Similar long-standing concerns about education and not enough reading of "the right kind of material" are now cast in a debate about the material and embodied practices of reading as they play out in various printed and digital forms.

A discussion of the values and types of reading means engaging with perceived qualities and paces of reading: slow, fast, skipping, skimming, and so on. We are interested in how technologies – or what Daniel Bell described as "intellectual technologies" (1999) – configure digital reading conditions and how we might articulate more specific reading conditions rather than seek to define a particular digital or print mode of reading. Bell's insights are still valid for understanding not only what technologies are, but how they influence our intellectual endeavors. Computers were of course central to Bell's description of a move from mechanical to intellectual technologies, so not surprisingly do we find algorithms and programming on his list. But he also includes linguistics and describes various kinds of mathematical techniques as part of the intellectual technology that forms that basis of post-industrial society (Bell 1999, 188). We discuss the details of material and technological affordances for the digital condition of reading in Chapters 2 and 3; here, the focus is on how computers and digital formats reshape or challenge the way in which different reading practices are named and understood.

Close reading or reading closely?

In academia, reading is also a method of sorts – a practice of various flavors and styles that allows the academic to explore scholarly ideas and trace patterns and arguments throughout texts of various kinds. Reading practices have functioned as heterogeneous and not-always-clearly-elucidated methods: The close reading of New Criticism in the 1920s and 1930s proposed bracketing off insights about authors' biography or historical contexts so as to focus on the words of the individual work (Smith 2016). Guillory named the more expanded understanding of close reading to pay close attention to a text as "reading closely" (2010). More recent terms such as "deep reading" (Birkerts 1994) remind us of such activities: focused, slow, and attentive reading (Baron and Mangen 2021). According to Birkerts, the activity of "deep reading" corresponds to an element of tempo, namely slow reading. Slow reading is closely connected to the importance of the paper book, and the book has through centuries been associated with the opportunity for "slow reading" (Kukkonen 2021, 175). The general activities connected to "close reading" are still assigned to classrooms throughout the Western world by for instance identifying the narrator, the voices of the narrator and characters, searching for stylistic choices and the overall structure of texts (ibid.). The ideas of close reading are historically tied to the role of New Criticism, and both in the writings of Birkerts and Baron and Mangen do we witness an underlying idea that paper book reading is deeper and more attentive than digital reading. This reliance on the materiality of the medium is also a historical offshoot of for instance Benjamin's ideas of the loss of cultural aura of the artwork in the age of reproduction. In its most simplified versions, such overemphasis on a particular material can lead to binary or reductive thinking regarding what print versus digital can offer for literary reading, which is being challenged by several scholars; here we refer to Kukkonen. Later in the chapter, we will unfold the idea about temporality and compression as complex positions that need to be nuanced when linked to the discussion of close reading (Koepnick 2021, Stougaard Pedersen et al. 2021).

It could be argued that slower, more attentive reading, or an emphasis on focused reading of long and complicated texts, are put in opposition to the seemingly pervasive modes of reading that digital technologies foreground: quick modes of perusal, scanning over texts, looking at other readers' highlights, and clicking on links to jump to another text, or, as Carr described, abandoning the text altogether to go searching for information online, or, worse, to check one's email or social media feed. In scholarship interested in digital literary texts and digital humanities scholarly methods, counterpoints have been proposed to close and careful reading of individual texts. N. Katherine Hayles has suggested that we engage in hyper reading, repurposing James Sosnoski's term, which he defined as "reader-directed, screen-based, computer-assisted reading" (1999, 167). As Hayles points out, this includes search queries, filtering by keywords, skimming, hyperlinking, "pecking" (pulling out a few items from a longer text), and fragmenting (Hayles 2010, 66, Sosnoski 1999, 163–72). Hayles continues to add to these modes with examples from a distinctly digital screen reading, such as switching between windows, and suggests, "There is considerable evidence that hyperreading differs significantly from typical print reading, and moreover that hyperreading stimulates different brain functions than print reading" (2010, 66). While Hayles agrees with Carr's assertions that hyper reading has cognitive effects, she instead argues that our reading strategies have expanded to include more modes that can function side-by-side: "[There are] interrelations between the components of an expanded repertoire of reading strategies that includes close, hyper, and machine reading. The overlaps between them are as revealing as the differences. Close and hyperreading operate synergistically when hyperreading is used to identify passages or to home in on a few texts of interest, whereupon close reading takes over" (ibid. 74).

In a different way of engaging texts in a "hyper mode," to follow Hayles' thinking, scholars such as Franco Moretti propose "distant reading," which instead of deepening the scholar's understanding of individual texts should go searching for other questions and insights by taking on large data sets of texts – large enough that only a distanced means of analysis and visually presenting networks, relationships, and correlations across a multitude of texts would work. A methodological approach more than a mode of reading for, say, pleasure, distant reading is facilitated by technologies. Computational technologies are particularly suitable to aid the scholar in this kind of reading. In the interstices between the detailed and the macro-levels of literary studies, Moretti argues that we can find new approaches to scholarly questions:

> [C]lose reading will not do it. It's not designed to do it, it's designed to do the opposite. At bottom, it's a theological exercise – very solemn treatment of very texts taken very seriously – whereas what we really need is a little pact with the devil: we know how to read texts, now let's learn how not to read them. Distant reading: where distance, let me repeat it, is a condition of knowledge: it allows to focus on units that are much smaller or much larger than the text: devices, themes, tropes – or genres and systems. And if, between the very small and the very large, the text itself disappears, well, it is one of those cases when one can justifiably say, Less is more.
> (Moretti 2010, 57–8)

In the field now known as digital humanities, we can find many similar ways of approaching reading as deciphering or even detecting patterns or exploring queries across large data sets whose answers can only be found by computer code.

Distant reading as a method, whether conducted by machines or human readers, to detect correlations, patterns, and unseen links, becomes spatial in its characteristics and visual output. Early in the scholarship of digital *textualities*, in the era focused on hypertext and hypermedia, different kinds of spatial characteristics of digitally mediated texts were foregrounded. When contemplating the writing software Storyspace that he co-developed with Jay David Bolter, Michael Joyce wrote that "any novelist's accustomed sense of developing motif structures and recurrences now had a visual, seemingly tactical, metatextual representation, a performative space in [Johanna] Drucker's sense" (2011, 23). Further, both Bolter and Joyce wrote of the spatial properties of both print and digital writing, in Bolter's case a writing space: "Each writing space is a material and visual field, whose properties are determined by a writing technology and the uses to which that technology is put by a culture of readers and writers. A writing space is generated by the interaction of material properties and cultural choices and practices" (Bolter 2001, 12). This still holds true, even as the properties and practices evolve and change. More recently, Scott Rettberg foregrounds that the process of reading digital literary works is part of how a reader meets them:

> The first question asked by beginning readers of electronic literature – and even experienced readers encountering a new text – is "how do I read this?" For electronic literature, this question is not only hermeneutic – it refers not simply to how readers might encounter the meaning, style, themes, and language of the work but also to how readers can operate the text-machine itself. (2019, 16)

The assumption is that we already know how to operate the printed "text-machine," a statement that we have seen in Chapters 2 and 5, and which textual scholars such as Chartier and McGann would disagree with, to a degree at least.

The reading of a piece of digital (or electronic) fiction or poetry demands, in the words of Espen Aarseth, non-trivial work. So, a novel such as Michael Joyce's *afternoon: a story* (1987, published by Eastgate systems in 1990) requires deliberate choices of where to go from one text to another, from one screen of reading to the next. Those choices are driven not only by the computational affordances of hypertext, but by the narrative as well. Choosing to click on a word means making a choice in a narrative that is forked into different paths in the narrative. The experience is similar and yet sensorily quite different from reading on a printed page: reading Joyce's classic hyper fiction or the more recent and decidedly more multisensory experience which Tenderclaws' *Pry* or Kate Pullinger's *Inanimate Alice* fiction series (with Andy Campbell, Chris Joseph, Mez Breeze, Lorri Hopping among the collaborators) offer, filled as they are with text, images, video snippets, interactions that go beyond clicking on words. In this and other chapters of the present book, we would challenge the notion that these digital works, *a priori*, can be described as distracted, or that they do not offer a more complex reading experience.

Deep reading

Maryanne Wolf and Mirit Barzillai explore the shift in reading as we transition from a print-based to a digital culture. Evoking the Aristotelian three lives: the life of enjoyment, the life of activity and productivity, and the life of contemplation, Wolf and Barzillai argue that digital reading may not be compatible with the latter. Deep reading, they argue, is vital for a contemplative life: slower and contemplative cognitive processes (Wolf and Barzillai 2009, 33). They continue: "By deep reading, we mean the array of sophisticated processes that propel comprehension and that include inferential and deductive reasoning, analogical skills, critical analysis, reflection, and insight" (ibid.).

Leaning both on cognitive views on the brain while reading, and on historical and philosophical accounts of reading, Wolf and Barzillai paint a rather bleak picture of what might happen with our abilities to contemplate and reflect if we were to lose the ability and the intellectual technological support for what they call deep reading. Digital technologies, they maintain, emphasize other kinds of properties: "pervasive emphases on immediacy, information loading, and a media-driven cognitive set that embraces speed and can discourage deliberation in both our reading and our thinking" (Wolf and Barzillai 2009, 33). The solution is to develop a "biliteracy" (Wolf 2018), and, as Wolf explains in *Reader, Come Home* (2018), "[t]he ultimate goal [...] is the development of a truly biliterate brain with the capacity to allocate time and attention to deep-reading skills regardless of medium" (ibid., 178). Wolf and Barzillai are not alone in understanding digital reading situations in this manner. In Naomi Baron's work, too, we can see a fascination with the nascent cognitive research into how reading literature affects our brains (2015).

This emphasis on cognitive abilities is not surprising. Scholarship on digital reading that is focused on building literacy, comprehension, and retention of information puts memory in the center: a reading should not introduce distractions or put anything in the way of the aim of remembering. However, what we are proposing throughout this book are the ways in which other dimensions of experience and intention come to the fore in other modes of reading, and how these change and shift in interesting ways by way of digital technologies. The inclusion of sensory input in what might in a learning situation feel distracting can become a heightened moment in a reading session with other intentions than retaining and comprehending information. As Ryan James and Leon de Kock have shown (2013), the age and level of media literacy and media experience of readers are as important, if not more important, to take into consideration when understanding digital reading as the technology supporting the reading.

Fast, slow, reading compression

Lutz Koepnick shares this need for acknowledging and supporting developments of reading flexibility. In "Reading in the age of compression," he states that "readers able to scan, skim, and surf textual material at unprecedented speeds do not just coexist with readers willing to pause, ponder, or even procrastinate; twenty-first-century readers may in fact perform all these different registers of reading flexibility at any given moment" (2021, 204).

Koepnick's article deals with – and critically discusses – the idea of compression as an imagined "royal road to process data" (ibid. 193). By enhancing both the PDF format (Gitelman 2014) as well as the reading technology SPRITZ, Koepnick states that the perspective of compression often overlooks the multilayered temporalities of reading as well as the role of embodiment while reading.

For both Kukkonen and Koepnick, digital reading is not defined as synonymous with fast reading, and conversely, literary reading is not synonymous with slow reading. Kukkonen refers to findings in cognitive investigations of readers which suggest that we read fiction faster than non-fiction (Kukkonen 2021, 179), enhancing that the reading tempo is not identical to the reading experience. Being critical toward the ideas of a generally accelerating culture of late capitalist society (Rosa 2013), Koepnick also points to the problem with ideas about faster and more efficient reading, performed by primary school systems worldwide. He questions the notion that reading is a run that we can actually win, arguing that "dogmatic binaries between analog and digital reading are as useless and simplistic as any effort to claim that all reading in our contemporary moment is forced to live up to the demands of self-optimized and speedy textual processing" (2021, 204). It seems to be a paradox that our educational system on the one hand seems to demand and reward reading by speed and on the other hand continuously seeks for and mourns the loss of students' close reading skills, often blaming the digital reading condition (Baron and Mangen 2021). Like Koepnick, we want to point to the multilayered aspects and multiple skills that digital reading affords, especially when we include an understanding/analysis of the embodied and sensory aspects of reading experiences. These embodied digital reading skills need to be supported and developed by acquiring a language that reflects aspects of embodied, digital reading as well as by exploring how we treat and are treated by digital technologies.

Polyreading – understanding the multisensory

We can turn to digital media studies to find insights into how technologies work upon us, directly and indirectly, when we make everyday life choices about which technologies to use and how. Studies of media use, although not primarily concerned with reading, can provide elucidating insights into how we engage with digital technologies and how they in turn change our practices. In their ethnographic study of the consequences of the choices of digital media in the context of interpersonal communication, Madianou and Miller propose what they call a "theory of polymedia" (2012). Although over a decade old, and digital communication channels and tools have developed continuously during this time, their study shows how users actively and deliberately choose communication technology to suit their needs for particular kinds of experiences, carefully balancing what Madianou and Miller call a new relationship between the social and the technological. Similarly, we are drawing on notions of the multiple, of choices that can be made to link technology with the social, or the cultural. What we encounter in the multimedia and multisensory digital environments today can be called "polyaesthetic" (Engberg 2014), and we apply this concept to understand how a different relationship between the aesthetic and the technological is forged in each instance of digital materialized reading experience. Fueled by intricate circuits of digital affordances, reading context and situation, the intentions and imagination of the author(s), and the individual choices of the reader, reading digitally calls for an understanding of the multisensory. A *polyaesthetically* driven reading can switch between modes of reading depending on what the work itself calls for, go from reading text to clicking on it, looking at images to allow the mouse pointer to hover over or click on them or in other ways explore the space of the digital text. What we would call a multisensory appeal is often foregrounded, as digital texts easily can go from text-only to highly interactive and multi-mediated reading experiences. By invoking concepts such as polymedia and the *polyaesthetic*, we suggest that the digital reading condition relies simultaneously on the materiality of the reading/writing technology and the embodied experience, apprehended by the human reader.

Concepts such as deep, focused, or "critical" reading implicitly or explicitly invoke or rely on an unquestioned and universalizing definition of printed text that through various material properties – differently described depending on the author or scholar's point of view – elicits certain kinds of engagement. Although research has shown that these embodied and cognitive processes are affected by the specific instantiations of the reading situation, we would argue that beyond scientifically proven impact, there is a lot of nostalgia, fears, and hopes that surround both print and digital technologies, which in turn color and shape both research questions and research designs. And it also colors the value of concepts like fast, slow, deep, and hyper, as this chapter has shown, concepts that are being reshaped and must be rediscussed in terms of technological developments of contemporary text and reading practices. Readers in what we have named the "digital reading condition" deal with various differentiated reading practices and registers using multiple technologies which make the unquestioned and universalizing definition of printed texts appear as increasingly obsolete.

References

Baron, Naomi S., and Mangen, Anne. 2021. "Doing the reading: The decline of long long-form reading in higher education." *Poetics Today* 42, no. 2: 253–279. 10.1215/03335372-8883248.

Bell, Daniel. 1999. *The Coming of the Post-Industrial Society*, New York, Basic Books.

Birkerts, Sven. 1994. The Gutenberg Elegies: The Fate of Reading in an Electronic Age. Boston, MA: Faber & Faber.

Bjørnsten, Thomas B. 2018. "Mellen medie og format." *Litteratur mellem medier*. Aarhus, Denmark: Aarhus University Press.

Bolter, J. D. 2001. *Writing Space: Computers, Hypertext, and the Remediation of Print*, 2nd ed. Lawrence Erlbaum Associates.

Carr, Nicholas. 2010. *The Shallows: How the Internet is Changing the Way We Think, Read and Remember*. New York: WW Norton & Co.

Engberg, Maria. 2014. "Polyaesthetic sights and sounds: Media aesthetics in The Fantastic flying books of Mr. Morris Lessmore, upgrade soul and the vampyre of time and memory." *SoundEffects - An Interdisciplinary Journal of Sound and Sound Experience* 4, no. 1. 10.7146/se.v4i1.20370.

Felski, Rita. 2008. *Uses of Literature*. Malden, Massachusetts, and Oxford, United Kingdom: Blackwell.

Furedi, Frank. 2015. *Power of Reading: From Socrates to Twitter*. London: Bloomsbury.

Gitelman, Lisa. 2014. *Paper Knowledge – Toward a Media History of Documents*. Durham, North Carolina: Duke University Press.

Guillory, John. 2010. "Close reading: Prologue and epilogue." *ADE Bulletin 149*, no. 7: 8–14.

Hayles, N. Katherine. 2010. "How we read: Close, hyper, machine." *ADE Bulletin* 150, no. 18: 62–79.

James, Ryan, and Leon de Kock. 2013. "Deepening the 'Shallows': The fate of reading in an electronic age, revisited." *Current Writing: Text and Reception in Southern Africa* 25, no. 1:4–19. 10.1080/1013929X.2013.795744.

Joyce, Michael. 2011. "Liquid fictions: 'between electronic and paper fiction'." *Revue Française d'Etudes Américaines* 128, no. 2. 10.3917/rfea.128.0015.

Kaplan, Nancy. 2008. "To read, responsibly." *Public Library Quarterly* 27, no. 3: 193–201. 10.1080/01616840802229297.

Koepnick, Lutz. 2016. *Reading in the Digital Era*. Oxford University Press. 10.1 093/acrefore/9780190201098.013.2.

Koepnick, Lutz. 2021. "Reading in the age of compression." *Poetics Today – Modes of Reading* 42, no. 2: 193–206.

Kukkonen, Karin. 2021. "Reading, fast and slow." *Poetics Today – Modes of Reading* 42, no. 2: 173–191.

Madianou, Mirca, and Miller, Daniel. 2012. "Polymedia: Towards a new theory of digital media in interpersonal communication." *International Journal of Cultural Studies*. 10.1177/1367877912452486.

Moretti, Franco. 2010. "Conjectures on world literature." *New Left Review* January/February 2000 4, no. 1: 54–68.

Pedersen, Birgitte Stougaard, Maria Engberg, Iben Have, Ayoe Quist Henkel, Sarah Mygind, and Helle Bundgaard Svendsen. 2021. "To move, to touch, to listen - multisensory aspects of the digital reading condition." *Poetics Today* 42 (2). 10.1215/03335372-8883262.

Rettberg, Scott. 2019. *Electronic Literature*. Cambridge, Massachusetts, USA: Polity.

Rosa, Harmut. 2013. *Social Acceleration: A New Theory of Modernity*. New York: Columbia University Press.
Seaboyer, Judith, and Barnett, Tully. 2019. "New perspectives on reading and writing across the disciplines." *Higher Education Research & Development* 38, no. 1: 1–10. 10.1080/07294360.2019.1544111.
Smith, Barbara Herrnstein. 2016. "What was 'close reading'? A century of method in literary studies." *The Minnesota Review* 2016, no. 87: 57–75. 10.1215/00265 667-3630844.
Sosnoski, James. 1999. "Hyper-readers and their reading-engines." In *Passions, Politics, and 21st Century Technologies*, edited by Gail E. Hawisher and Cynthia L. Selfe, 161–177. Urbana: Utah State Unversity Press.
Wages, Brad. 2019. "The art of deep reading." Blog. Medium. June 28, 2019. https://medium.com/@BradWages/the-art-of-deep-reading-c1287c9a9333.
Wolf, Maryanne. 2018. *Reader, Come Home: The Reading Brain in a Digital World*. Harper Collins.
Wolf, Maryanne, and Barzillai, Mirit. 2009. "The importance of deep reading." *Educational Leadership* 66, no. 6: 32–37.
Wolf, Maryanne, and Gottwald, Stephanie. 2016. *Tales of Literacy for the 21st Century*. Oxford University Press.
Zacher-Sørensen, Mette-Marie. Forthcoming 2022. "Modes of instant reading in the ages of attention." Submitted to *Language, Culture and Society*.

11 Reading digital interfaces and audiobooks: media-specific and multisensory aspects of immersion

Birgitte Stougaard Pedersen and Ayoe Quist Henkel

Reading with the senses up front – multisensory reading

Digital reading is rapidly and profoundly changing our reading habits as well as the reading landscape. Though we still read printed books, we also read on smartphone, tablet, and computer screens as well we listen to texts via digital audiobooks or text-to-speech technologies on our smartphones. As a consequence, reading practices very often become a mixture of modalities, combining eye reading, listening, and touching. We refer to and investigate these reading habits as multisensory reading, as we unfold it throughout this volume. This chapter will outline the experience of immersion in concrete reading practices in a school context. Exemplified by audio reading and web-based digital literary reading experiences, the chapter points to a need for investigating the distribution of immersion as media-specific aspects of reading experiences, as they make us take part in literary atmospheres under new conditions. The chapter builds on qualitative data investigating the digital reading habits of students and collected as part of the Danish collective research project Reading Between Media funded by the Novo Nordisk Foundation (2019–2023). The research project has been engaged in outlining and qualifying knowledge on the impact of the sensorial modes through which reading takes place in the current literary media landscape. How reading both includes listening, seeing, touching, and interactively engaging with digital texts, and how this might change the act of reading itself and at least challenge us to rethink how we should understand and define reading as a mediated and multisensory practice (Stougaard Pedersen et al., 2021) and explore how different types of sensory activities can be included in a concept of reading. In so doing, we adopt the definition of reading outlined in Rita Felski's book *The Limits of Critique* (2015), where she enhances the relation between being attentive and being bodily and sensory attached while reading:

> Reading […] is not just a cognitive activity but an embodied mode of attentiveness that involves us in acts of sensing, perceiving, feeling,

DOI: 10.4324/9781003211662-18

registering, and engaging. [...] In the act of reading, we encounter fresh ways of rapprochement and distancing, relaxation and suspense, movement and hesitation.

(Felski 2015, 176)

An embodied mode of attentiveness that helps create a flow in the reading activity, as pointed out by Felski, is also at stake when Hans Ulrich Gumbrecht in the volume *The Production of Presence – What Meaning Cannot Convey* (2004) formulates a critique, similar to Felski's, of the paradigm of hermeneutics. This critique deals with hermeneutic reading as primarily focusing on interpreting thematic and structural aspects of meaning, building on the idea that a text in some respects can reveal a "true" reading. Instead, Gumbrecht describes reading as a variation between "presence effects and meaning effects," hereby reconfiguring the ideas of meaning production to also include presence (Gumbrecht 2004). This presence is a way of feeling immersed in the text, as it unfolds, instead of solely reading for plot, for character analysis, for themes. Places, worlds, and spaces are created by the sounds of language, by rhythms, and by sensorial interplays.

In enhancing and investigating the possibility of immersed reading experiences in digital and audio formats, we challenge the research positions regarding digital reading that foreground the possibly damaging effect screen reading has on our ability to read in a focused and immersed way and to read longer texts (Baron and Mangen 2021).

Media-sensitive analysis

Pointing to reading as a bodily, embodied practice not only relates to the mental activity of reading but also includes the materiality by which the reading takes place. This aspect is also central to the writings of N. Katherine Hayles. In order to broaden the concept and the notion of reading, we need to take media specificity as well as materiality into account. As stated previously in this volume, Hayles (2002, 2004) has pointed to how reading in a digital landscape intensifies the need for what she has called media-specific analyses for both print reading and digital reading practices. By also stressing the aspects of immersion and distraction as situated and related to specific media practices in time and space, we outline the need for developing dynamic analytic models of multisensory reading.

With the aspect of materiality, we build on N. Kathrine Hayles's focus on the material aspects of literature and the field of tension between literature and technology in particular. She develops a notion of media specificity of texts (Hayles 2002, 2004, 2008) and media-specific analysis (Hayles 2002, 6), which is a triangulation between form, content, and media (ibid. 31, Hayles 2004).

This media-specific approach that Hayles develops as a tool for understanding literary texts, we bring into dialogue with the qualitative analysis of how 14- to 15-year-old students interact with the same story in two different media formats, a digital story and an audiobook version, respectively. The qualitative data collected in our ongoing collective research project focuses on students' interactions and experiences with the various literary media works and on how they each integrate and differ in their sensory appeals (Quist Henkel et al. 2021). Specifically, in this chapter, we investigate how the students experience immersion when reading the story in a digital interface or via an audiobook. It is our thesis that by enhancing the multisensory aspect of the reading situation – combined with the aspect of materiality – the singular meeting between student, interface, and situation creates different versions of immersion, which we will exemplify in the following.

In 2019, we conducted a study among an entire year group (60 eighth-grade students) in a school in the municipality of Silkeborg in Denmark. We investigated their reading of the same story (*NORD* by Camilla Hübbe and Rasmus Meisler 2018) in a printed book, as a born-digital work, and as a digital audiobook, respectively, and focused in our inquiries, on the one hand, on the similarities and differences between audiobook reading, paper book reading, and the reading of born-digital works and, on the other hand, on the interaction between the student and the interface – as a multisensory reception process (Quist Henkel et al. 2021, see also Chapter 14).[1]

In the processes of analysis, we developed the following codes through several joint coding sessions, and they will be used as guidelines in the following discussion of theoretical concepts of immersion which emerged from our interviews with the students. The codes are: "Being absorbed or immersed", "Voice," and "Atmosphere/moods/presence." Via this joint iterative process of analysis, the codes emerged through both theory and the data (Quist Henkel et al. 2021).

Aspects of immersion

Before moving on to how immersion did affect the students' reading, we will address the concept of immersion from different scholarly perspectives. Immersion designates a mental stage that can be triggered in different ways by different media and materialities as well as by different sensory inputs. Generally, the concept of immersion in audiovisual environments deals with "a state of deep mental involvement in which the individual may experience disassociation from the awareness of the physical world due to a shift in their attentional state" (Agrewal et al. 2020). Both film, sound, and computer game studies deal with the concept in different terms, and as we have highlighted the material perspective above, scholarly concepts have also developed versions of the concept that take into account the aspect of materiality and culture of each media.

In game studies, immersion is often related to flow, and we see a general focus on attentiveness and the senses, as discussed in for instance Michailidis et al. (2018). These insights are also discussed and debated in relation to how virtual reality can create a mediated sense of immersion and presence, already presented in 1997 by Lombard and Ditton. Scholars like Mark Grimshaw focusing on audiovisual media point to how the aspect of sound in gaming situations can intensify the immersive experience (Grimshaw 2016). In film studies, audiovisual immersion deals with emotional responses – how being in the cinematic room leads you to focus on auditory as well as visual aspects of the experience combined with feeling immersed in the narration. Immersion is also discussed in relation to journalism, for example in debates on whether journalism can support the emergence of empathy (Sánchez Laws 2017).

Altogether, a picture emerges where different theoretical fields such as game studies, film studies, sonic studies, and reading studies subscribe to differentiated, yet related understandings of immersion. Generally, one can distinguish between immersion in the place of the reading and immersion in the narrative. Marie-Laure Ryan makes this distinction in her studies of narrative experiences that encompass reading, watching, and playing. She distinguishes between phenomenological immersion "as a sense of being-in-the-world" and immersion that presupposes an imaginative relationship to a *"world projected by a text"* (Ryan 2015, 9, original emphasis). She emphasizes that immersion entails not only a shift of attention toward a fictional world but also the construction of a mental representation of that world. Also, she distinguishes between three different forms of immersion: *spatial immersion* in the setting, where the reader develops a sense of place or of being on the scene of the narrated events; *temporal immersion*, where the reader is caught up in narrative suspense, eager to know what happens next; and *emotional immersion*, where the reader develops a personal attachment to the characters and a sense of participating in their human experience (Ryan 2015, 85–114).

Being absorbed or immersed

Whereas Ryan researches immersion in narratives across media and technologies and draws on analytic points from many different studies, our focus is on the way students express their immersion based on the previously described phenomenological and materiality-based understanding of the reading experience following Felski, Gumbrecht, and Hayles. Spatial, temporal, and emotional immersion in particular are involved in the students' verbalizations of their reading experiences. For example, a student listening to the audiobook says:

> I was sitting with my earbuds [...] so if anyone was saying something I would not be able to hear them before they had called out five times or

had come to grab me [...] also because it was an exciting book. So I was very immersed in it. And because there were no pictures, I needed to use more energy to imagine myself, so I could just listen and that was … it is probably the best way if you have to make pictures yourself.

Here spatial immersion converges with temporal immersion: the student invests herself in the story and experiences narrative suspense. She finds that the audio world creates a kind of bubble, where she needs to use her imagination, intensely creating inner pictures. Her immersion is also a result of the reading situation: the student is reading through earbuds and therefore is not disturbed by the school context. Thus, she experiences immersion in the place as well as in the story (cf. Ryan's distinction), in this case, prompted by the mono-modality of the audiobook. The earbud-based listening situation facilitates the merging of the outer and inner listening/reading spaces. However, a similar reaction can be observed among students who read the digital story, which is narrated through text, pictures, sounds, and simple animations, and the reader moves through the story by finding and touching interactive stones that make text boxes appear. The text is read aloud, though this function can be disabled. One student says:

I believe you get very caught by it because there are sound effects and because there is someone reading it to you, and you look at the pictures that in a way move. So I get very absorbed by it and just want to go on reading.

Here the combination of audio, visuals, and interaction in the digital version is foregrounded as elements that support the sense of immersion in a multisensory way, and the student highlights the spatial immersion, which is echoed by one of her classmates:

I believe it is good because [...] with sound effects and things like that helps you to feel that you are in the place where things happen. So I believe that it is like really good and easy to get absorbed in.

Again, the spatial dimension is prominent since the student experiences a high degree of presence in fictional space, and this immersion is supported by sensory elements like the sound universe. Likewise, another student stresses interactivity.

To find the stones, and they are sometimes easier to find that at other times, because you need to move the picture around and then, when you have found the stones then you can hear a car motor or something that is running in the background where it nearly merges with the sound that is being read aloud. So, sometimes you have to listen carefully.

Here the audio universe converges with the haptic – touching the stones and moving the pictures – making the student listen very attentively. In all three cases, immersion arises from the correlation between a subject willing to be immersed and conditions in the narrative as well as media-specific conditions such as interactivity and the specific address to the reader in the form of pictures, sounds, and voices. Throughout the study, voice is mentioned as an element that supports immersion in both the digital and the audio version.

Voice

The audiobook listening/reading experience takes place in and negotiates the experiences of time and space when reading on new conditions. Adults reading digital audiobooks often highlight the mobility of the audiobook reading experience as one of the preferred affordances hereof. Due to the school context, the students were unable to move around while listening. However, one aspect highlighted by a number of the students, and by listeners in general, is the importance of the voice of the performing narrator (Have and Stougaard Pedersen 2016).

The voice is often described as the primary medium of the digital audiobook (Have and Stougaard Pedersen 2016, see also Chapter 8), interpreting the text and addressing the reader in a vocal representation. The voice of the performing narrator reads in a specific manner: tone, diction, rhythm, voice quality, and gender are all aspects of the materiality of this expression.

Thus, the media-specific conditions of the voice, such as intonation, intensity, and credibility, contribute to creating a state of immersion. Where Ryan talks about emotional immersion in relation to empathy and attachment to the characters, the students mention a kind of emotional immersion in relation to the speaker's voice. The students enter into a kind of intimacy contract with the voice, a point also often raised in relation to present-day podcast culture, where the mode of in-ear earbuds gives you a close sense of the voice right next to your ears, and where the podcast speaker often makes use of soft and potentially cuddly vocal aesthetics (Dann and Spinelli 2019. The voice of the audiobook is a digitally produced audio track; however, it still performs and can create – a feeling of intimacy (Neumark 2010) that helps the listener feel engaged in the story, especially if the voice is experienced as resonant of the story and of the listener's vocal preferences. The voice also acts as a companion in the reading experience.

The voice in the digital version of *NORD* is a typical old woman's voice, whereas the voice in the audio version is that of a young woman who could be 14-year-old Nord, the protagonist. Thus, the levels of resonance will be very different in the two versions.

Even though the students have difficulties describing the voice as such, there is no doubt that the voice is important to their experience of being immersed. The voice can carry and support the sense of an atmosphere:

> It is her that reads aloud. She is very calm but also [...] it is not a happy atmosphere. It is like [...] that what happens is not good.
>
> For instance [...] when she talks a bit more gloomy the atmosphere becomes a bit scary [...] and intense.

The voice can add to the comprehension of the text, just as it can support the creation of inner pictures:

> She is pretty good at stressing the things that she wants us to remember. So the things that she puts pressure on I start to imagine.

A number of the students experience transports between sensory inputs, and they feel that the voice can help create a mood or an atmosphere when reading digital interfaces. In that sense, their reading becomes multisensory – both in the concrete interface, the website's audiovisual expression, and the interface of the audiobook, but also in their sensory experience and comprehension of the text.

Atmosphere, moods, presence

These concepts are related to the overall idea of multisensory reading and play a key role both in our understanding of the text and in the intensity of the reading experience. Gernot Böhme, with the concept of atmospheres, outlines a phenomenological approach that describes and conceptualizes how we connect to moods around us. An atmosphere exists only as relation, constituting a non-linguistic dimension of expression that can arise in various reading experiences. The experience can create a specific mood as we become immersed in a story, for instance by creating a sense of presence (Böhme 2001, Gumbrecht 2004).

Describing the experience of atmospheres, two students reading the digital interface work explain:

> This is for instance when you are sitting, reading and it rains and you get a bit [...] you can sense the atmosphere and then you know, you feel that you are present where things happen [...] because there are rain effects and things like that.
>
> There is a dark tone and there is a lot of suspense [...] We also experience the story, it is gloomy and it is also a bit scary. But in a way also odd.

And from the group reading the audiobook:

> It is just because – there is sometimes a very dark-like atmosphere.

An interesting observation is how several students refer to colors and thus make synesthetic transports between mood and colors:

> The atmosphere is kind of dark green (audiobook reader).

> The atmosphere is more like dark blue or dark green (digital interface reader).

> The colors are like very gloomy and dark, I believe (digital interface reader).

The students' synesthetic registrations suggest that experiencing a story through sound and visuals can initiate sensory emotions related to colors – a kind of synesthetic transport from one sense to another. What is experienced through sound, for instance the mood and tone of a voice, can compensate for or enhance the impressions in a different expression.

This is also the case when we study audiovisual experiences in a context. For instance, listening to music while moving around in an urban space can perceptually change the environment (Gram 2012). The music can amplify the listener's sense perception and have an intensifying effect. Maybe the same goes for a reading experience where we deal with synesthetic listening or experiencing? The digital reading experience can create an embodiment which, together with the audiovisual input, supports immersion, and sound can contribute to making the reader immersed or absorbed – here creating experiences of colors.

Multisensory reading in context

Our examples have shown how digital texts can draw in the body and the senses of the reader when they interact with texts in new ways. And to read with the senses up front creates new experiences of time and space – embodied ways of being attentive, in the words of Felski.

In this way, we seek to nuance the critical perspective on screen reading as distracted, as argued by both Anne Mangen (2013) and Naomi Baron (2015).

Anne Mangen, in her text "Putting the body back in to reading" (2013), claims that reading is embodied in new terms in a digital landscape of texts. In continuation of the digital reading condition, she argues that we need to rethink the concept of reading by looking into, for instance, the role of the body in combination with the cognitive processes of reading. She discusses how the reading technology corresponds to being able to "deep read", how the reading technology supports the phenomenological immersion (ibid. 22). Her analyses show that the haptic, tactile, and audio-visual feedback of the digital formats is very different from the feeling of reading a printed book and cannot necessarily satisfy the haptic and sensorial feeling of interacting with a paper book. Her impetus for bringing the embodiment aspect forward thus appears to be a strong focus on how, in negative terms, screen reading affects the chances of deep reading.

This article has shown, by bringing forward the students' sensory experiences of digital and audio reading, respectively, that engagement and immersion can take a number of different forms, and that the interactive elements as well as the role of the voice in relation to the creation of intimacy, rhythm, and tone can contribute to immersed reading experiences. Hereby, the chapter challenges the idea of deep reading as something that mainly has to do with reading primarily for structures, characters, and plot. That a more atmosphere-based reading experience of digital formats can lead to immersed experiences that offer knowledge of the literary universe, just as sound, audiovisuality, and digital aspects can support and produce engagement in reading processes.

Based on the empirical statements of the students presented in this chapter, the children actually experienced reading as intense and immersive – and they reflected on the fact that the different reading experiences required the same amount of mental work – but on different levels:

> I believe that, it is like equal labor you put in to them. Just on different levels, yes.

Thus, a one-to-one translation of digital reading to screen reading seems far too narrow and generally produces notions of screen reading as a poorer alternative to the book page. The idea of immersed reading as primarily connected to the book as a medium has thus been challenged. As our empirical examples have shown, the experience of audible and digital interfaces can contribute productively to creating immersed digital reading experiences. The chapter has projected and discussed how the digital reading condition in new ways orchestrates, choreographs, and potentially intensifies immersion when reading.

Note

1 In the study, the class was split into three homogeneous groups: One group read the graphic novel *NORD* as a hardback book, one group read *NORD* as a digital audiobook using eReolen (streaming service), and one group read *NORD* as a browser-based born digital story using their laptops. Over the course of two weeks, we organized and observed 12 reading lessons at the school, and over the weekend the students were asked to read as homework.

References

Agrewal, Sarvesh, Simon, Adèle Maryse Danièle, Bech, Søren, Bærentsen, Klaus B., and Forchammer, Søren. 2020. "Defining immersion: Literature review and implications for research on audiovisual experiences." *Journal of the Audio Engineering Society* 68, no. 6. https://vbn.aau.dk/en/publications/defining-immersion-literature-review-and-implications-for-researc-3.

Baron, Naomi S. 2015. *Words Onscreen: The Fate of Reading in a Digital World*. New York: Oxford University Press.

Baron, Naomi S., and Mangen, Anne. 2021. "Doing the reading: The decline of long long-form reading in higher education. *Poetics Today* 42, no. 2: 253–279.

Bolter, Jay David. 1991. *Writing Space: The Computer, Hypertext, and the History of Writing*. Hillsdale, New Jersey: L. Erlbaum Associates.

Böhme, Gernot. 2001. *Aisthetik: Vorlesungen über Ästhetik als allgemeine Wahrnehmungslehre*. Munich: Wilhelm Fink.

Bull, Michael. 2007. *Sound Moves: iPod Culture and Urban Experience*. New York: Routledge.

Carr, Nicholas. 2010. *The Shallows. How the Internet Is Changing the Way We Think, Read and Remember*. London: Atlantic Books.

Dann, Lance, and Spinelli, Martin. 2019. *Podcasting, The Audio Media Revolution*. London: Bloomsbury Publishing.

Drucker, Johanna. 2013b. "Performative materiality and theoretical approaches to interface." *DHQ: Digital Humanities Quarterly* 7, no. 1. https://dhq-static.digitalhumanities.org/pdf/000143.pdf

Felski, Rita. 2015. *The Limits of Critique*. Chicago: University of Chicago Press.

Gram, Nina. 2012. "Når musikken virker," PhD diss., Aarhus University.

Grimshaw, Mark. 2016. "Computer game sound: From diegesis to immersion to sonic emotioneering." In *Sound as Popular Culture: A Research Companion*. MIT Press.

Gumbrecht, Hans Ulrich. 2004. *Production of Presence – What Meaning Cannot Convey*. California: Stanford University Press.

Have, Iben, and Stougaard Pedersen, Birgitte. 2016. *Digital Audiobooks: New Media, Users, and Experiences*. New York: Routledge.

Hayles, N. Katherine. 2002. *Writing Machines*. Cambridge: MIT Press.

Hayles, N. Katherine. 2004. "Print is flat, code is deep: The importance of media-specific analysis." *Poetics Today* 25, no. 1: 67–90.

Hayles, N. Katherine. 2007. "Hyper and deep attention: The generational divide in cognitive modes". *Profession*: 187–199.

Hayles, N. Katherine. 2008. *Electronic Literature. New Horizons for the Literary*. University of Notre Dame Press.

Hübbe, Camilla, and Meisler, Rasmus. 2018. NORD. https://fortell.dk/nord/.

Lombard, Matthew, and Ditton, Theresa. 1997. "At the heart of it all: The concept of presence." *Journal of Computer Mediated Communication* 3, no. 2.

Mangen, Anne. 2013. "Putting the body back in to reading." In *Pædagogisk neurovidenskab*, edited by Theresa Schilhab. Aarhus University.

McGann, Jerome. 1991. *The Textual Condition*. Princeton, New Jersey: Princeton University Press.

Michailidis, Lazaros, Balaguer-Ballester, Emili, and He, Xun. 2018. "Flow and immersion in video games: The aftermath of a conceptual challenge." *Frontiers in Psychology* 9, no. 1682. 10.3389/fpsyg.2018.01682. https://www.frontiersin.org/article/10.3389/fpsyg.2018.01682.

Neumark, Norie. 2010. "Doing things with voices: Performativity and voice." In *VOICE – Vocal Aesthetics in Digital Arts and Media*, edited by Norie Neumark, Ross Gibson and Theo van Leeuwen. Massachusetts and London: The MIT Press.

Nielsen, Anne Maj. 2018. "Artikulationsanalyse i fænomenologisk perspektiv: Kontemplativ undervisning som eksempel." In *Kvalitative analyseprocesser med eksempler fra det pædagogiske psykologiske felt*, edited by Louise Bøttcher, Dorte Kousholt, and Ditte Winther-Lindqvist. Samfundslitteratur.

Quist Henkel, Ayoe, Mygind, Sarah, and Bundgaard Svendsen, Helle. 2021. "Exploring reading experiences in three media versions: Danish 8th grade students reading the story Nord." *L1-Educational Studies in Language and Literature*, special issue: Working with Literature in Nordic Secondary Education.

Ree, Jonathan. 1999. *I See a Voice*. Great Britain: Harper Collins.

Ryan, Marie-Laure. 2015. *Narrative as Virtual Reality 2. Revisiting Immersion and Interactivity in Literature and Electronic Media*. Baltimore: Johns Hopkins University Press.

Sánchez Laws, Ana Luisa. 2017. "Can immersive journalism enhance empathy?" *Digital Journalism* 8, no. 2: 213–228. 10.1080/21670811.2017.1389286.

Stougaard Pedersen, Birgitte, Engberg, Maria, Have, Iben, Quist Henkel, Ayoe, Mygind, Sarah, and Bundgaard Svendsen, Helle. 2021. "To move, to touch, to listen: Multisensory aspects of the digital reading condition." *Poetics today* 42, no. 2.

12 Motivations for audiobook reading in modern everyday lives

Iben Have

Andy, who calls himself an avid audiobook user, writes on his blog *Please Read it to Me*: "Listening to audiobooks makes even the dirty work less tedious [...] and rush hour traffic more bearable" (Please Read it to Me 2020). Many audiobook readers share this experience.

This chapter will discuss the motivations behind listening to audiobooks related to pleasure, habits, and perceived efficiency. Audio reading affords a flexible and mobile reading situation, where the body and the eyes are set free, which enables the reader to engage in other tasks while reading. Depending on the character of the task, this does not necessarily result in a distracted way of reading, which is a common conception of audio reading (Baron 2021, Have and Stougaard Pedersen 2016, Kozloff 1995). Being able to audio-read while you are engaged in other not cognitively demanding activities can also lead to deeply engaged and embodied reading experiences and a feeling of autonomy, dynamic, and flow in the reading situation.

Listening to audiobooks is not isolated to privileged societies, but is practiced in cultures all over the world as smartphones and Internet access are globally widespread. Some of the points in this chapter will apply to this general global audiobook reader. However, people in different parts of the world live very different everyday lives with different resources and technological infrastructure, and their motivation for listening to audiobooks as accompanying everyday tasks is also very different, both on the individual and cultural level. That said, the chapter will present and discuss patterns of audio reading drawing on existing studies, statistics, and literature on the topic limited to Northern European and North American contexts. Most examples will be Danish and Scandinavian.

For busy people in modern societies, reading a book voluntarily (and not as a chore) in their spare time is often associated with an isolated withdrawal from a hectic everyday life – in bed at night, in weekends, or on holidays. Having time to read is a luxury, a self-indulgence that may cause postponement of duties and obligations, and as a consequence, a feeling of guilty conscience depending on your everyday life situation. This reading situation certainly has qualities of its own, precious to many readers. But this condition is also one of the reasons why so many readers have taken the

DOI: 10.4324/9781003211662-19

digital audiobook to heart because it radically expands the situations where you can read and enjoy literature and enables you to read while doing the chores. The top answers in surveys studying the use of audiobooks and why people audio-read are typically different variations of "because I can do other things while I am reading," or "because it enables multitasking" (Audio Publishers Association 2020; eReolen 2019; Have and Stougaard Pedersen 2016). In a Danish survey of the Danish National Library's streaming service *eReolen*, this category got 8,200 answers (n = 9,305, multiple-answer question),[1] which is more than twice as many as the second most popular answer.

There is evidence that audiobooks are enhancing the general consumption of literature. So, there is no need to fear that the convenience of audio reading will parasite traditional visual reading. It is not a zero-sum game, and the audio reader is typically a dedicated visual reader as well. In keeping with other studies of audiobook reading (e.g., Have and Stougaard Pedersen 2016), the latest yearly survey from the American Audio Publishers Association (2020) shows that 56% of audio readers say they are making "new" time to listen to audiobooks. And recently, a German Bookwire consumer survey with the title *Battle for attention* (2020) focusing on only three media concluded: "Ebooks, audiobooks, and podcasts hardly cannibalize each other at all [...] A maximum of 14% of users said that they use e-books, audiobooks, or podcasts at the expense of one of the other two media" (Klingelhöfer and Ruhrmann 2020).

Part of the reason for the overwhelming popularity of digital audio reading is that it offers fundamentally different reading situations allowing "wasted" time (waiting for the bus, commuting, etc.) to become quality time. Efficiency and productivity are for good and for bad a condition in modern societies permeating all aspects of our lives. In a critical perspective, audio reading is feeding into the ever-demanding accelerating society (Rosa 2015) by offering a motivation for being even more productive and not wasting a second. However, in a more positive light, audio reading can also make dull daily duties and routines more meaningful adding to them a literary layer of experience – in other words, turning the *must-dos* of our lives into *enjoy-dos* – as the quote by Andy above illustrates.

Not only is the audiobook able to create immersion in a story world that you can literally carry around with you (unlike printed and e-books), audiobooks at the same time set the eyes and body free to do other things while reading, which creates a unique opportunity to engage in multitasking, compared to other reading situations. Some of the tasks you can do are not unique to audiobooks – reading while sitting in a train for instance or sunbathing. But reading a book while vacuuming (with noise-canceling headphones on), weeding in the garden, cooking, driving, or doing fitness are activities only afforded by audiobooks, compared to reading other formats.

Chapter 8 in this volume discusses how audiobooks afford multisensorial reading experiences. Compared to Chapter 8, the aim of this chapter is to move the perspective from perception to practical doings, or from an aesthetic approach to a more sociological one by focusing on the affordance of multitasking in relation to audio reading. The chapter deliberately takes a non-normative and non-critical approach to the many downsides of the performance culture and accelerating modern society, focusing instead on the value of audio reading in many people's everyday lives. As a consequence, the chapter seeks to challenge the negative cultural values and media hierarchies usually related to audiobooks (see Chapters 2 and 3).

From wax to web: the technological development

The distinctive affordances of audiobooks such as mobility, flexibility, and multitasking originate from their roots in audio media technology not traditionally associated with books, publishing, and reading practices. Historically, the audiobook has shared technology – both in relation to production, distribution, and reception – with other audio media like music or radio, and that technology has over the years become more flexible and more mobile. Until the introduction of audio cassettes in the 1970s, and with them also the term "audiobook" (Rubery 2011, 8), the primary medium for recording of spoken words was wax cylinders and later vinyl records. In fact, Edison's invention of the phonograph in 1877 was for the purpose of recording speech and not music, which later became the most widespread content of vinyl records (Rubery 2011, 3).

With the Walkman and the integrated tape decks in most cars, audio cassettes really made the audiobook mobile. In the 1980s, the Walkman was replaced by the Discman, though without changing the flexibility and mobility much. That happened from 2002 onwards, when the digital audiobook became available directly from the Internet as downloads or streaming through compressed digital formats such as the MP3 file. The audiobook now became weightless, mobile, and flexible in fundamentally new ways and converged with other digital media in the smartphone, which most people always have handy (Have and Stougaard Pedersen 2016).

The smartphone technology has made audiobooks more accessible and user-friendly than ever before, which also explains the enormous and, to many, surprising success of digital audiobooks worldwide (Have and Stougaard Pedersen, 2016, 2019) creating headlines in public media like "The Audiobook Boom" and "The Audiobook Revolution" (Have and Stougaard Pedersen 2019). With the help of technological development, the audiobook has developed from a medium supporting people with reading or vision disabilities to a medium for everyone and in its own right.

This technological kinship with the development of audio media affords fundamentally different ways of consuming literature, which until the past decade has not been acknowledged (see also Chapter 8). Audio reading is far from what publishers, scholars, critics, librarians, and the general public have historically acknowledged as "publishing," "a book," "literature," "reading," and that is probably the reason why so many still find it difficult to say that we *read* audiobooks or maybe even recognize the audiobook as a literary format at all. Nevertheless, users around the world have embraced this format, challenging and loosening the structures and normative discourses of the audiobook.[2]

Listening to audio media like radio or music recordings is often described as "secondary" listening – something you listen to in the background of other activities (Berland 1990, Hendy 2000, Dubber 2014). These claims are often anchored in the fallacy that you cannot listen attentively if you are doing other activities simultaneously. However, this depends on the nature of the activities in question and how much cognitive attention they demand. You can take a walk in the forest, weed in the garden, or sit on the subway and still pay deep attention to what you are listening to, making that your "primary" activity (Have 2018). The following sections will discuss audio reading in combination with other activities, which seems to be one of the most motivating factors for choosing the audiobook over other book formats.

Multitasking and mood management

The above-mentioned survey conducted by the Danish National Library (2018) investigating users who were streaming or downloading digital audiobooks from the library's digital platform *eReolen* also asked the question: "When do you listen to audiobooks?" The two most popular answers with more than 3,500 hits each were: "During transport (bus, car, cycle)" and "Doing practical things at home" (*n* = 9,305, it was possible to tick up to three categories).

The three Cs "commuting," "cleaning," and "cooking" are repeated in most studies of the use of audiobook among adults. The user patterns found in the Danish library survey were confirmed by the latest yearly survey from the American Audio Publishers Association (2020).[3] Whereas Denmark is known as a nation of cyclists, in North America the car was not surprisingly the main listening locale for audiobooks in 2019, with 74% of respondents (*n* = 1,044) answering that they listen to audiobooks while driving. The second most popular venue for audiobook reading, 68%, was the home. As the literary critic Leah Price has playfully stated, the car should actually be included as one of the most important technologies for audiobook reading (Price 2009, 1) – at least, I should add, in cultures with such a distinct tradition for driving like the American. The growing amount of time spent commuting or fitness training is, together with the technological development, an important part of the answer to why the audiobook has become so popular (Have and Stougaard Pedersen 2016). And the COVID-19 pandemic isolating people and generating more time at home and time for outdoor exercising boosted the usage of audiobooks in 2020. Danes streamed 58% more audiobooks from *eReolen* in spring 2020 compared to spring 2019. In April 2021, the audiobook streaming service *Mofibo* published a survey showing that 31% of Danes[4] increased their use of audiobooks during the COVID-19 lockdown, while 39% said that their general consumption of literature increased in 2020 as a consequence hereof (Ørregaard Andersen 2021).

Podcast is a medium very similar to audiobooks regarding production and use. From a Uses and Gratifications study based on five focus groups of podcast listeners, the media and communication scholars Perks and Turner conclude that multitasking is the primary motivation for listening to podcasts.[5] Inspired by previous studies, they define multitasking as "engaging in at least one more activity at the same time," and add that "[m]ultitasking can be motivated by several factors, including perceived efficiency, enjoyment, and habit" (Perks and Turner 2018, 105). An interesting finding in this study is the link between multitasking and arousal regulation and mood adjustment:

> We call this multitasking mood management "mood balancing" because the nature of the podcast is complementary to the nature of the work. For folks doing boring tasks, the podcast was an engaging arousal boost. For those at work who perhaps liked background noise but still needed mental space to think, the podcast was more of an arousal moderator.
>
> (Perks and Turner 2018, 106)

They introduce the term "temptation bundling" in relation to this kind of mood-balancing multitasking. Temptation bundling means that you couple instantly gratifying "want" activities like podcast or audiobook listening with engagement in a "should" activity like cleaning, commuting, etc. You simply make the boring more enjoyable by "putting on an engaging story or learning something new about the world" (ibid. 107).

The meaningful connection between audio media and multitasking and the benefits of temptation bundling also seem to have reached the audiobook providers. Music streaming services like Spotify have supplemented traditional genre categories like jazz, hip-hop, or electronica with categories focusing on mood or activity (Krogh 2020). The same development is found in audiobook streaming services offering categories that focus on supplementing other activities, such as audiobooks for the beach, audiobooks for relaxing, audiobooks for walking, etc. Thus, the market for audio media is utilizing the sales promotion of multitasking and customized reading experiences.

This illustrates how a meaningful reading experience can also be found outside traditional communication models describing the transmission of meaning from a sender to a receiver. Audio reading becomes meaningful not only for its literary value, but also by way of the social and cultural activities you can do while consuming literature. Some may see this as "noise" that disturbs a deep, focused reading, but it can just as well enhance an immersed reading experience – a state of flow, where you forget time and space and what you are doing because you are absorbed in a narrative and a story world.

Forgetting time and space

The experience of mood-balancing multitasking has some similarities with Hungarian-American psychologist Mihaly Csikszentmihalyi's term "flow." Csikszentmihalyi's term has been widely used (and misused) in positive psychology and the motley field of coaching and management and describes an attractive state of mind that can be compared to a feeling of happiness and meaningfulness (Csikszentmihalyi 1990). When we are in the right stimulation zones, we forget time and place, perform best and are at ease. Flow occurs when there is no resistance in what we do, experience, and think, and we can direct our full attention to a task that matches our abilities in a balance of stimuli, routine, and challenge. If the task is either too hard or too easy for us, we either get anxious/nervous or bored resulting in an unfocused restlessness, and then you find yourself outside the "flow" channel.

The tasks mentioned in the surveys mentioned above are routine tasks that would normally result in boredom if we put all our attention into that task. Audiobook reading can challenge us cognitively, so we do not get bored running on a treadmill or peeling potatoes. It adds a layer of cognitive input to the routine, non-demanding activity resulting a perfect total flow of stimuli. One could, with reason, object that audio reading in such cases prevents free thoughts from emerging, and that boredom is a value that we need to strive for in modern, busy societies, but that is another discussion.

The experience of being in a perfect flow of stimuli is related to the experience of immersion that has been widely discussed especially in relation to a computer game and VR studies – and in Chapter 7 of this volume. Wearing headphones while you audio read, maybe even with the noise-canceling function switched on, you can ignore the sounds of your physical surroundings and let yourself be absorbed and immersed in a story world that you can literally carry around with you while your body is performing different kinds of tasks.

It is a main argument in this volume that multisensorial reading can afford immersion (see Chapters 7 and 8). This chapter would like to add that so can multitasking. Being able to audio read while you do other activities is not per default stealing attention from the literary content resulting in distracted reading. Depending on what you do, it can also lead to deeply engaged and embodied reading experiences and a feeling of autonomy and dynamic in the reading situation.

The paradox of multitasking

In the current digital reading condition, audio reading has infiltrated users" daily routines. As this chapter has documented through results from different empirical studies, a key motivation for choosing audiobooks over other book formats is anchored in the shared technology with other audio media, affording a mobility and flexibility which enables the audio reader to multitask. Audio reading is often combined with commuting or duties at home such as gardening, cleaning, cooking, etc. While this kind of reading situation is considered, by critics, as distracted and a degradation of the true literary experience, the chapter has tried to acknowledge the value this form of reading can add to daily routines by turning chore time into quality time.

Digital audio reading is not just something that accompanies tasks that you would have done anyway, but is the very motivating factor for doing these tasks – or as Andy puts it, it "makes the dirty work less tedious and rush hour traffic more bearable". Under the right circumstances in the right balance between your skills, cognitive capacity, the practical activity, and the complexity of the narrative you are listening to, you may even reach an immersed state of flow in the company of a captivating narrator.

Having acknowledged these positive sides of audio reading, one must not ignore that behind multitasking and strategic "temptation bundling" is a wish to optimize your daily performance and be more productive and efficient. This is a paradox that may not be visible to the individual audio reader, or in the surveys presented in this chapter, but may feed into an unhealthy accelerating society, as diagnosed by Hartmut Rosa (2015). The ambivalence of modern audiobook readers is that on the one hand multitasking and "temptation bundling" feed the acceleration of society and everyday life, making our lives even more stressful, while on the other hand, they add a meaningful layer of literary experience as well as a feeling of qualifying our time and various tasks.

Notes

1 This number has roughly been read from a bar chart and given here as the nearest hundred. I have not been able to get the exact number from *eReolen*.
2 For an analysis of how the digital audiobook is changing the publishing industry see Colbjørnsen (2013) and Have and Stougaard Pedersen (2019).
3 The study made by Edison Research is a national survey of Americans aged 18 years and older who have at least once listened to a complete audiobook. Edison Research completed 1,044 online interviews in January/February 2020.
4 Population of approximately six million, $n = 1,141$.
5 Two focus groups were conducted in person on a college campus, and three focus groups were conducted online, $n = 23$ (14 women and 9 men).

References

Audio Publishers Association. 2020. *2020 Consumer & 2019 Sales Surveys Announcement*. Press release. https://www.audiopub.org/uploads/pdf/2020-Consumer-Survey-and-2019-Sales-Survey-Press-Release-FINAL.pdf.

Baron, Naomi S. 2021. *How We Read Now: Strategic Choices for Print, Screen, and Audio*. Oxford Scholarship Online.

Berland, Jody. 1990. "Radio space and industrial time: Music formats, local narratives and technological mediation." *Popular Music* 9, no. 2: 179–192.

Colbjørnsen, Terje. 2013. "Continuity in change: Case studies of digitization and innovation in the Norwegian book industry 2008-2012." PhD diss., University of Oslo, Norway.

Csikszentmihalyi, Mihaly. 1990. *Flow: The Psychology of Optimal Experience*. Harper & Row Publishers.

Dubber, Andrew. 2014. *Radio in the Digital Age*. Cambridge: Polity.

eReolen. 2019. *Overview of Audiobook User Study*. Based on a survey for internal use. Danish National Library.

Have, Iben. 2018. "The lost link between music and hosts. The development of a morning music-radio show." In *Tunes for All. Music in Danish Radio*, edited by Morten Michelsen, Steen Kaargaard Nielsen, Mads Krogh, and Iben Have, 131–162. Aarhus, Denmark: Aarhus University Press.

Have, Iben, and Stougaard Pedersen, Birgitte. 2016. *Digital Audiobooks: New Media, Users, and Experiences*. New York: Taylor & Francis.

Have, Iben, and Stougaard Pedersen, Birgitte. 2019. "The audiobook circuit in digital publishing: Voicing the silent revolution." *New Media and Society* 22, no. 3: 409–428. https://journals.sagepub.com/doi/10.1177/1461444819863407.

Have, Iben, and Stougaard Pedersen, Birgitte. 2020. "Reading Audiobooks." In *Beyond Media Borders: Intermedial Relations among Multimodal Media*, vol. 1, edited by Lars Elleström, 197–2016. London: Palgrave Macmillan.

Hendy, David. 2000. *Radio in the Global Age*. Oxford: Polity Press.

Klingelhöfer, Jens, and Ruhrmann, John. 2020. *Listen & Read: The Battle for Attention*. Frankfurt: Bookwire GmbH.

Kozloff, Sarah. 1995. "Audiobooks in a visual culture." *Journal of American Culture* 18, no. 4: 83–95.

Krogh, Mads. 2020. "Context is the new genre: Abstraktion og singularisering i digital musikformidling." *Norsk Medietidsskrift* 27, no. 3: 1–15.

Madsen, Søren Anker. 2021. "Når Danmark lukker ned, lytter vi til lydbøger," *Bogmagasinet Bog.dk*, February 29, 2021. https://bog.dk/nar-danmark-lukker-ned-lytter-vi-til-lydboger/.

Ørregaard Andersen, Stina. 2021. "Lydbøger får litteraturforbruget til at stige." *Kristeligt Dagblad*, April 14, 2021.

Perks, Lisa Glebatis. 2015. *Media Marathoning: Immersions in Morality*. London: Lexington Books.

Perks, Lisa Glebatis, and Turner, Jacob S. 2018. "Podcasts and productivity: A qualitative uses and gratifications study." *Mass Communication and Society* 22, no. 1: 96–116.

Please Read it to Me. 2020. "Can you really listen to an audiobook and multi-task?" https://www.pleasereadittome.com/home/can-you-really-listen-to-an-audiobook-and-multi-task.

Price, Leah. 2009. "Reading as if for life." *Bookishness: The New Fate of Reading in the Digital Age. Michigan Quarterly Review* XLVIII, no. 4. Michigan Publishing, University of Michigan Library.

Rosa, Hartmut. 2015 (2013). *Social Acceleration: A New Theory of Modernity.* Columbia University Press.

Rubery, Matthew, ed. 2011. *Audiobooks, Literature, and Sound Studies.* New York and London: Routledge.

Section IV
Young Readers Between Media

Introduction to Section IV

How do young people interact with audio and digital interfaces when reading? And how do the digital and transmedial aspects of texts affect education in the classroom as well as in students' spare time? This section of the volume deals with aspects of reading that are not comprehensive for the volume as such. The section focuses on a younger target group, upper-secondary school students and young people reading transmedial story worlds in their spare time, respectively. We address aspects of the digital reading condition of young people in relation to existing socio-cognitive perspectives on reading from a didactic and transmedial point of view. The chapters address multisensory reading in a school context, underlining the importance of a sensitivity toward investigating and understanding reading in specific contexts. Young people read intensively across several media, also including the web, e-books, audiobooks, podcasts, computer games, YouTube, and other social media platforms. The chapters show how we must discuss screen reading as well as website reading and audio reading on new conditions or at least take the *materiality* of media as well as the reading context into consideration when discussing young readers' practices of reading between media.

The target group affects the way we pose questions regarding reading in this section: what is special for young people's reading experiences regarding reading engagement, interests, maintenance of reading habits, and a general interest in how one can support the development of a love of reading? One of the arguments that can be followed across the empirically based chapters of the section is that these aspects need to be developed, regarding the school context, in close cooperation with didactic strategies. Three out of four chapters thus address how we can use didactic formats to support engagement and love of reading across media in the classroom. All chapters share a common multisensory, phenomenologically based approach to digital reading.

Nikolaj Elf in the chapter "Digital reading in education: a situated disciplinary literacies perspective" examines connections between literacy and technology in language arts or L1 teaching and relates the aspect of literacy to digital reading. Based on multi-case fieldwork, it is documented, from a first-person perspective, how teachers and students experience and express qualities of inquiry-based literature teaching when using resources in specific teaching situations. What happens when we need more technical tools and competencies to read literature? In this development the reading experience is changing, and therefore we need to methodologically rethink and possibly redefine ways of teaching.

In the chapter "Different modes of reading: eighth-grade students' interaction with a digital narrative" by Signe Hjort Nielsen and Ayoe Quist Henkel, the phenomenological interest in the multisensory reading situation is pursued in a study of digital reading related to game spaces and interactive story worlds. The chapter investigates reading of a digital novel resembling navigation in game spaces. The students' interactions are studies between expressions of form such as text, picture, and sound, with a focus on their bodily being-in-the-world and interaction with the digital interface. Also, the aesthetic interplay between text and reader/player is investigated with a focus on their aesthetic response.

Method is important in Susana Tosca's chapter "Transmedial reading," which explores the category of transmedial reading, referring to reception experiences that go beyond a single text and are related to bigger fictional universes. Through an empirical reading case of a comic book, the chapter argues that reading in transmedial environments is always multiple. Readers interpret the text in relation to a whole ecology of related media products set in the same fictional world. How does the new text fit the *worldness* that readers have built through their previous engagement? What kinds of relations are established, and how is the reader's own affect activated in relation to a set of personal memories? The chapter proposes a transmedial reading interview method based on the author's own theoretical framework investigating transmedial environments across media; a kind of ecology of related media is qualitatively proposed.

The last chapter in this section, by Ayoe Quist Henkel, "Readers between media: sixth-grade students tuning in on literature in different formats/media versions," analyzes the reading experiences of sixth-grade students in their meeting, in a school context, with a fantasy story which they read as either an illustrated print novel, an audiobook, or a digital narrative. The chapter takes a cognitive-sensory approach, inspired by Rita Felski's ideas of attunement in the recent volume *Hooked* (2020), dealing with how children attune to audio and digital literature. What designates a multisensory reading experience among 11- to 12-year-old students across media? How do they feel connected to or engaged by reading?

13 Digital reading in education: a situated disciplinary literacies perspective

Nikolaj Elf

A situated literacies perspective

Recent decades' rapid development of digital communication technologies across the world has led to educational and curricular debates about the relationship between technology and the teaching and learning of reading and writing, that is, of *literacy*. There are no simple answers in this debate. Rather, as prominent literacy researcher James Paul Gee has put it, the relation between digital media and literacy is an emerging area (Gee 2010, 14). Gee's point is that digital media and literacy learning is a field that is difficult to grasp from only one theoretical perspective; instead, it calls for transdisciplinary work due to:

> an age of convergent media, production, participation, fluid group formation, and cognitive, social, and linguistic complexity – all embedded in contemporary popular culture. Digital tools help create and sustain these features of 'modern times,' but they do not stand alone and cannot be studied in isolation from these features.
>
> (Gee 2010, 4)

Following Gee, I will argue that there is a call for a pluralistic understanding of literacy and indeed for a rethinking of digital reading in education. We must reject what Brian Street once characterized as an "autonomous understanding of literacy" (Street 1984) – still very much dominating in education and in the public – which assumes that reading is the decontextualized ability to decode information units in verbal language. Instead, like many others within the so-called New Literacy Studies movement, I claim that literacy can and should be understood from a much broader, semiotically rich, and situated perspective. Literacy comprises multiple contextual practices of perceiving and producing meaning with different technologies and in different forms of multimodal representation and communication. Hence, decontextualized literacy becomes situated literacies. This point will be illustrated in the following by focusing on a disciplinary, subject-specific case.

DOI: 10.4324/9781003211662-22

A disciplinary literacies perspective

If we acknowledge that digital reading is situated, we should then ask from an educational perspective: *what* does digital reading refer to in practice in educational settings, and *where*, *how*, and by *whom* does digital reading take place?

One obvious approach to these questions that will be pursued in this chapter is that digital reading takes place in *school subjects* taught every day in schools in different countries and localities around the world. Subjects are basically about teaching and learning "disciplinary literacies" (Shanahan and Shanahan 2008). However, little attention has been given to digital literacy practices that are becoming part and parcel of school subjects and the disciplinary literacies that define them.

In this chapter, I will explore how digital disciplinary literacies are emerging in one subject: the so-called *language arts* subject, or what is internationally – and in this chapter – referred to as *L1*. Specifically, I focus on Danish as a school subject within a broader Nordic and global L1 context. L1 is highlighted, among other reasons, because it is one of the prominent school subjects responsible for literacy learning in school, including learning to read digital texts. What does this mean from a historical and a contemporary perspective?

In the first part of the chapter, I offer a brief mapping of how digital reading has been enabled and constrained technologically and institutionally in a Nordic educational context. I then focus on L1, offering an archeology of how digital reading practices in L1 in Denmark have been sanctioned in the curriculum, and how they have been practiced broadly. In the second part, drawing on ethnographic research from a Danish upper-secondary education context and focusing on Danish as a school subject, I highlight findings from an empirical research project, the so-called Hans Christian Andersen case study, which illuminates some of the situated and disciplinary characteristics of digital reading in L1 education.

One main finding is that teachers and students take up and engage with digital reading in quite diverse ways, which co-shape what digital reading is or rather *becomes* in practice, for individuals. For discussion, I argue that what is regarded as digital reading in L1 is what counts as disciplinary literacy practices within the school subject; and what counts as digital reading in a subject like L1 is limited and should be contested. While some of the potential of digital reading has been realized in the Danish L1 classroom, much remains to be seen. This is the case not only in Denmark, but across the globe.

Digital reading in a Nordic context

In the Nordic countries, digital technologies have catalyzed curricular reforms prescribing practices that allow students not only to read but also to produce digital texts. A basic prerequisite for this development is the fact that Nordic schools have invested large sums in giving students access to digital hardware. This has led to the current situation, where 98% of students in the Nordic countries have access to a laptop at home and in school and full access to Wi-Fi in school.

However, this does not necessarily imply that access is granted or exploited for teaching. Empirical research of the actual accessibility and use of learning resources suggests that the use of digital technologies is constrained and that students read digital resources in remarkably different ways and with different levels of proficiency.

On an institutional level, it is not unusual that banning and lockdown practices of Wi-Fi computer use at school management levels are implemented, justified as a way to avoid distraction and ensure effective learning (Tække and Paulsen 2022). Often, students' counter-strategy is to go under the radar and engage in closed microsites, such as Facebook groups, that will include some peers and segregate others, while teachers are more or less unaware of what is going on. Alternatively, teachers allow digital technologies such as smartphones to be part of classroom practices, with the potential problematic consequence that a few students are actively participating in productive classroom dialog, while the majority is not; instead, their focus is elsewhere on the Internet (Sahlström et al. 2019). As such, the implementation and integration of digital technologies and reading in Nordic classrooms is rather heterogeneous and ambiguous in its realizations.

Digital reading in L1

Focusing on L1, reviews of classroom research of L1 teaching experimenting with digital and/or multimodal resources find that it is difficult for teachers to integrate digital technologies in meaningful curricular ways, not least in relation to reading and writing practices, including literary reading. A Nordic review of the use of technology in L1 covering studies from 1992 to 2014 found a dominant "hesitation and uncertainty" toward new multimodal digital media amongst teachers and even some students: both teachers and students find it hard to *justify* why they should teach digital technologies and teach *with* digital technologies, and they do not see how digitization and reading would fit together (Elf et al. 2015). These findings are linked to the technology culture at schools more broadly, as sketched above.

Focusing on digital *reading* in L1 in a Danish context from a contemporary programmatic, *curricular* perspective, the national curriculum for L1 on primary and secondary levels expresses so-called "Skills and knowledge areas and goals" within the broader competence area of "Reading" that include the area "Finding text." Within this area, explicit goals are listed and expand from grade two, through grades four and six, to grade nine. For example, at the end of grade two, students should know about websites' structure and be able to "navigate from what they want to search for on websites adequate for their age;" and at the end of grade nine, the student "has knowledge about the producers and genres on the Internet," and "they know how to plan and realize different phases of information searchers on the Internet" (Ministry of Children and Education 2015, my translation). On upper-secondary school level, at the end of grade 12, "students should be able to navigate, select and act critically and analytically in relation to information in all media and participate reflexively in and contribute to digital communities" (Ministry of Children and Education 2017, my translation).

In this way, digital reading in Danish L1 education is indeed framed discursively, progressively, and programmatically. As one may note, *navigation on the Internet* is emphasized. Interestingly, navigation is precisely the metaphor highlighted in a study by Norwegian scholar Tove Stjern Frønes that explored students' reading patterns in the PISA Digital test (a test that simulated how students would read an authentic website) (Stjern Frønes 2017). Frønes is an advocate of the navigating metaphor for understanding the characteristics of Internet reading and fostering digital reading skills, but found that students' Internet reading patterns differed substantially. She argues that L1 should focus much more on the teaching of reading-as-navigation, drawing on well-known strategies applied in the teaching of "normal" analog reading, while supplementing them with strategies that reflect the affordances of the Internet.

An archeology of digital reading in Danish L1

However, digital reading practices in Danish L1 education should be understood not only from a contemporary prescriptive perspective. Rather, it should be stressed that digital reading practices vary in time and space and are a product of a long and complex history of technology and education in which *some* aspects of digital reading have been enacted, and *some have not*, due to multiple translocal conditions. A brief archeology of technology[1] in the language arts/L1 curriculum would highlight at least four important discursive changes, which research suggests have had an impact on and in practice:

I In the late 1960s and early 1970s, the Danish curriculum introduced the so-called "expanded notion of texts" concept. This concept, which was inspired by a communicative turn in the humanities as well as a democratization of schooling, would include "reading" popular media such as comics. Within language arts research we refer to this development as a "communicative paradigm shift" that was introduced in many Western L1 subjects during the 1960s. I would argue that this communicative paradigm has paved the way, at least to some extent, for digital reading in L1 in Denmark and other Nordic countries.

II The late 1970s and 1980s would introduce media pedagogy in different variants. This would include advertising and media subcultures as a source for teaching and learning. Inspiration came from both semiotics, critical sociological, and cultural studies and catalyzed, in classrooms, analyses of a rich variety of media, from graffiti to MTV culture. It also led to experiments with film production and later digital video production practices that involve digital reading.

III From the late 1980s into the 1990s and onwards, the personal computer and other digital devices were introduced and increasingly used in L1 teaching. The Internet and World Wide Web started to become integrated in both the prescribed and enacted curricula, introducing the development of skills for searching for and reading Internet texts in classrooms and requiring teaching and even testing of students' digital reading abilities as "information literacy." As such, the interest in technology shifted, to some extent, from technology as mediated culture that students should learn to "read" to a more skills-oriented approach. This development is also linked to a more paradigmatic "utilitarian" development in L1 education, which would stress the importance of learning goals, student output, and effective learning. This utilitarian discourse, developed within the OECD and other global policy organizations, affected our understanding of the "whats, hows and whys" of digital reading in school and continues to do so today (Elf and Troelsen 2021).

IV From the late 1990s into this century, one fundamental change is that resources for learning to read became increasingly networked and available 24/7. For example, the literary canon started to be digitized, including for example the work of Hans Christian Andersen (www.adl.dk) – which is a case I will return to below. Furthermore, publishers' learning platforms and local municipalities started to take control over resources for teachers, providing explicit goals, outputs, and linkage to the curriculum. Research on big publishers' "platformification" of resources (Selwyn et al. 2018) – a phenomenon observed not only in Nordic countries, but globally – finds that this digitization development in L1 has, somewhat paradoxically, led to a *narrow* text choice and a standardization of the school subject's literacy practices (Bundsgaard et al. 2020). On the other hand, the technological literacy trend, which is unfolding globally and locally, is currently *broadening* the conceptualization of Danish L1 and all other subjects in the Danish curriculum.

As should be clear from this brief archeology, the development of teaching practices meant to enable students' digital reading practices in school in general and in L1 specifically is complex and not progressing in any simple linear way. Rather, they are trends on a macro level that overlap to a lesser or higher degree with many local practices. In other words, such historically embedded characteristics overlap with, complement, contest, recalibrate, or are ignored by local agents' previous understanding and practice of technology and education, as demonstrated in multiple examples of empirical research, including my own. In the next section, I offer findings from a case study conducted in 2007–2009 which illuminate these points close to practice. Subsequently, I discuss the study's implications from a contemporary and a future perspective.

The Hans Christian Andersen case study on digital reading in L1

The Hans Christian Andersen case study applied a technology-rich approach to the teaching of world-famous – and highly *medialized* – author Hans Christian Andersen, exploring how and why Andersen fairy tales could be taught in school in ways that reflect 21st-century networked, digital, and popular culture (Elf 2009). Empirically, I cooperated with teachers in upper-secondary school (age group 16–19) experimenting with digital and multimodal resources for reading and interpreting Andersen fairy tales in new ways and reflecting on the implications for L1 disciplinary literacies. Theoretically, the study was informed by a theory bricolage including media pedagogy, social semiotic theory, and John Dewey's understanding of teaching and learning as "doing knowledge" (Dewey 1997) as well as the New London Group's theory on multiple literacies (Cope and Kalantzis 2000, Kress 2000). Based on this framework, a design model for teaching the multiple modes and media of Andersen's work was presented (Figure 13.1):

Note that "the digital" is not highlighted as such; rather, the digital is regarded as an aspect of a broad semiotic framework, represented in the model as a portfolio of "knowledge-making" resources. These resources are made available to students through inquiry-oriented design processes (marked by a question mark and four iterative phases) that could lead to a student portfolio of "knowing," including material produced digitally and/or analogically by students.

The model was used to design four experiments addressing different modes and media of Andersen's work – including *digitized*, *oral*, *illustrated*, and *animated* versions of Andersen fairy tales, which were the material starting points, so to speak, of the four experiments, respectively. The overarching research question was whether such experiments would push the limits of the L1 teaching rationale while still being regarded as meaningful L1 disciplinary literacy practices that would "count as knowledge" from the teachers' and the students' points of view. Methodologically, the four experiments comprised an intervention that took place over the course of one school year, 2007–2008, in four Danish upper-secondary classes involving four teachers and around 100 students, a qualitatively analyzed

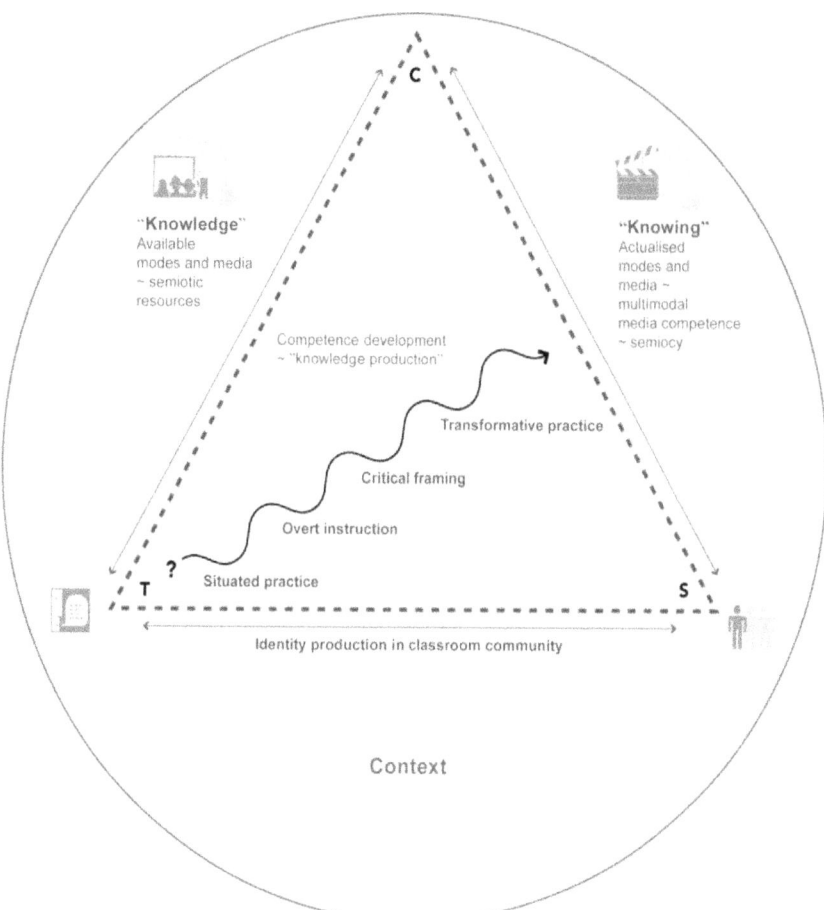

Figure 13.1 A design model for inquiry-oriented teaching of modes and media of Hans Christian Andersen.

intervention. What happened, then, in situated classroom settings? Findings from two of the experiments will be highlighted in what follows.

As hinted at, the first experiment exploited teaching potentials of offering access to digitized Andersen fairy tales and contemporary 19th-century reviews curated on the Internet by the Danish National Library (adl.dk). I hypothesized that this resource would, in engaging ways, offer students the opportunity to search and select for themselves the fairy tales and reviews they wanted to focus on and read. The task-driven purpose of engaging in these reading practices, it was explained in an assignment, was for the students to write their own reviews of a fairy tale in a genre, on a platform, and in a historical time and space of their choice. However, what I found when observing the students' designing processes, was a striking inability amongst the students to navigate websites unfamiliar to them. I also found a relatively low degree of engagement, at least to begin with. Clearly, the students were not digital natives, at least not in the way some digital literacy scholars at the time, including Marc Prensky, imagined it in the advent of the Internet. Rather, teachers and available learning resources had to *scaffold* the students' search processes. Teachers were not surprised by this outcome; rather, it confirmed their general impression of the students' engagement and proficiency when it came to *disciplinary* digital work, as compared to digital literacy practices not linked to school and school subjects. This finding backs the finding made in later research that students lack digital navigation reading proficiency. Having said that, it should also be noted that when the students *did* manage to search, find, and select resources, they appreciated the increased agency they were offered in the reading and writing processes. As Gee has pointed out, among others, *choice* is a motivation *generator* for student literacy engagement, and choice can be designed, pedagogically, as a *digital choice* of canonical work afforded by available Internet archives.

In the fourth experiment, we focused on "animated fairy tales," introducing students to available animated Andersen resources on the Internet – including Walt Disney's Oscar-winning *The Ugly Duckling* (1938) found on YouTube – that would help them design their own new pre-productions of the fairy tales. Among other "knowledge" resources, they were prompted to "read" or rather navigate in and appropriate online step-by-step learning resources that would teach them what an animation is, how it works, and how they could design one quite easily. On the positive side, this stimulated engaged collaborative participation and complex cognitive and often quite creative work that reflected the identities and engagements of the students. Eventually, this led to rather unique "knowing" redesigns, some of which combined several fairy tales in intertextual ways while at the same time integrating aspects of the students' lives in contemporary popular culture (see also Tosca in this volume). For example, one group pitched an animated fairy tale based on "The Princess on the Pea," which would include a contemporary gallery involving a bodyguard and Oprah Winfrey![2] As Gee points out, pop culture is indeed prevalent and used in remixing ways. Perhaps most interestingly, I observed how students' interpretative reading of verbal fairy tales became a premise for student creativity – or to put it the other way around, I found that creativity required high-order analytical reading processes. On the more negative side, I also found that both teachers participating in the study and some students were somewhat reluctant toward this design approach due to the curricular obligations and the traditional ways of reading and teaching the canonical writer within Danish as a school subject. They feared, for good reasons, that reading and producing digital multimodal media in new popular ways did not really count as knowledge.[3]

It should be noted, however, that this data dates back to 2005–2006. The intervention might turn out differently today due to changes in the curriculum that call for creativity and multimodal expression, and also due to changes in students' experience with and participation in digital culture outside school. On the other hand, examination practices have not changed dramatically, and teachers tend to "teach to the test." Testing has a "washback effect" on everyday teaching practices. In other words, a change in reading practices within L1 requires an alteration of the regime of reading, writing, and testing in practice.

Reflecting on the potential implications of the Hans Christian Andersen case study, I argued that if L1 was to develop into a situation where an inquiry-based semiotically rich approach to Andersen's fairy tales – or any other canonical digitized author across the globe – was regarded as knowledgeable knowledge within L1, this would require a shift in the rationale of L1 – moving from a narrow cultural heritage understanding of literary literacy as the main goal to an expanded and pluralistic semiotic understanding of literacy in plural – literacies.

In order to address such an expanded notion of situated literacies within L1, new theoretical and conceptual work is required, among other aspects, helping us to imagine and practice a changed school subject. For this purpose, I coined a new term – *semiocy* – based on the Hans Christian Andersen case study. *Semiocy* is my name for the competency goal of L1 teaching that would reflect "modern times," in the words of Gee; or what I think of as a techno-semiotic rationale in which boundaries between the analog and the digital, and between high and low culture, become blurred. Rather, they merge into popular participatory, remixing culture, which children and adolescents engage in in diverse ways, and which teachers and schools should help them master even better critically and creatively for the sake of personal development and the good of society, as pointed out by the New London Group.

Digital reading in future education – a critical discussion

From a situated and disciplinary literacies perspective, this chapter has explored what characterizes digital reading in education. Generally, current public debates on technology in education seem to suffer from historical amnesia. Working against this tendency, I have tried to demonstrate, from a historical viewpoint, how digital reading in education is embedded in the complex technological archeology of a school subject. Zooming in on L1 in a Danish-Nordic context, I find that the understanding and practice of reading has expanded historically, both in the prescribing programmatic curriculum and in the enacted curriculum now including the reading and writing of digital texts in diverse ways.

The highlighted case study demonstrates that teachers and students take up and engage with digital reading in quite diverse ways, which co-shape what digital reading is or rather *becomes* in practice. Teachers and students do not necessarily embrace and identify with digital literacy practices. On the contrary. Later studies focusing on how technology co-shapes students' writing development have shown that some students may in fact oppose or resist digital reading and writing. They go analog! (Elf 2019). Such resistance suggests that digital reading in L1 practice is co-shaped by students' and teachers' identification with disciplinary literacies, which are again co-shaped by individual, institutional, and cultural trajectories and practices that enable and constrain digital reading within the school subject. Different uptakes and realizations of the potentials of digital technologies reflect that many different stakeholders – including politicians, school leaders, teachers, opinion makers, parents, and scholars like myself – explore, negotiate, cultivate, and try to act on the increasingly technologically and digitally mediated society we live in. It is, indeed, situated.

On a more critical note, I would argue that what is regarded as digital reading in L1 is what counts as disciplinary literacy practices within the school subject; and what counts as digital reading in a subject like L1 is historically constructed, limited, and should be contested. Making my own position more explicit, I have argued not only for a situated but also a disciplinary approach to digital reading in education. While many digital literacy scholars argue broadly for the integration of digital reading in education, I find it important to try to grasp the emerging area of digital media of learning from a school subject-specific perspective. In that sense, I both agree and disagree with David Buckingham, when he echoes Gee and the New London Group in an often-cited article, at least in a Nordic context:

> The increasing convergence of contemporary media means that we need to be addressing the skills and competencies – the multiple literacies – that are required by the whole range of contemporary forms of communication. Rather than simply adding media or digital literacy to the curriculum menu or hiving off information and communication technology into a separate school subject, we need a much broader reconceptualisation of what we mean by literacy in a world that is increasingly dominated by electronic media.
>
> (Buckingham 2015)

I agree that reconceptualization is needed, and that digital reading should not be a superficial add-on in the curriculum. Nonetheless, my Hans Christian Andersen case study, as well as many other studies focusing on digital literacies in L1 and other school subjects, demonstrates that a subject-specific disciplinary approach is needed if we are to better understand what digital reading is and could become in education. The main reason is that the epistemological interests of school subjects differ substantially and thus co-shape the forms, contents, and justifications – that is, the *hows*, *whats*, and *whys* – of integrating digital technology.

Reflecting on the many strong debates on technology and education around the globe, I would like to stress that education should be wary of any kind of techno-determinism, and that there is nothing self-evident or universal in the development of technology in disciplinary educational practices, such as L1. Together with L1 research colleagues from Greece and Australia, I have argued that research and development in the role of digital reading in a school subject like L1 must be approached in critical, contextualizing, and constructive ways, on the one hand, challenging the naturalization of literacy technologies in a given epoch, while at the same time acknowledging complex historical, technological, social, cultural, material, and local dynamics of the school subject. We think of technology within L1 as a translocal dynamic and have coined the term the "ongoing technocultural production of teaching and learning" for understanding this dynamic (Elf et al. 2020). The term implies that the integration of technology in education is something that is *done*; it is produced discursively and practically by more or less visible actors based on particular values, ideologies, and practices.

Thus, more emphasis on digital reading in any local L1 context is not necessarily advisable or preferable. In any case, any change in pedagogy should ideally depend on a democratic process involving local agents – from politicians, school leaders, teachers, and parents to individual students – who should all have a say in the shaping and definition of disciplinary literacies. Unfortunately, studies of the *platformication* of educational resources show that such processes are not always governed democratically. Rather, they are controlled by invisible market actors. Having said that, I will end on a positive note, suggesting, together with my colleagues, Bulfin and Koutsogiannis, that "a paradigmatic shift is needed in conceptualizing digital media in L1 and language teaching – a shift that has at the centre the spirit of the economic, social and cultural reality of the new capitalism, broadly understood" (Elf et al. 2020, 229).

Notes

1 For reflections on archeologies of technology, see also Jay David Bolter's chapter in this volume.
2 For an elaborated presentation of this and other student groups' work, see Elf (2018, 88).
3 For other studies that discuss cultural values related to reading books, see also Chapters 4 and 8 in this volume.

References

Buckingham, David. 2015. "Defining digital literacy: What do young people need to know about digital media?" *Nordic Journal of Digital Literacy* 4: 33. 10.18261/ ISSN1891-943X-2006-04-03.

Bundsgaard, Jeppe, Skov Fougt, Simon, and Buch, Bettina. 2020. "Danish L1 according to the learning materials used – a quantitative study." In *L1 –*

Educational Studies in Language and Literature 20, Special Issue: Danish as L1 in a Learning Materials Perspective, edited by Jesper Bremholm, Simon Skov Fougt, and Bettina Buch, 1–23. 10.17239/L1ESLL-2020.20.02.04.
Cope, Bill, and Kalantzis, Mary eds. 2000. *Multiliteracies. Literacy, Learning and the Design of Social Futures.* London and New York: Routledge.
Dewey, John. 1997 (1916). *Democracy and Education: An Introduction to the Philosophy of Education.* New York: The Free Press.
Elf, Nikolaj. 2009. *Towards Semiocy? Exploring a New Rationale for Teaching Modes and Media of Hans Christian Andersen Fairytales in Four Commercial Upper-Secondary "Danish" Classes: A Design-Based Educational Intervention.* Odense: University of Southern Denmark.
Elf, Nikolaj. 2018. "Teaching and learning modes and media of H.C. Andersen Fairy Tales." *Forum for World Literature Studies* 10, no. 1, special issue edited by Karin Esmann Knudsen: 88.
Elf, Nikolaj. 2019. "Enabling and constraining: Digital technology in students' writing and writer development." In *Understanding Young People's Writing Development: Identity, Disciplinarity, and Education*, edited by Ellen Krogh and Karen Sonne Jakobsen. London: Routledge.
Elf, Nikolaj, Bulfin, Scott, and Koutsogiannis, Dimitrios. 2020. "The ongoing technocultural production of L1: Current practices and future prospects." In *Rethinking L1 Education in a Global Era: Understanding the (Post-)National L1 Subjects in New and Difficult Times*, edited by Bill Green and Per-Olof Erixon. Cham: Springer.
Elf, Nikolaj, and Troelsen, Solveig. 2021. "Between joyride and high-stakes examination: Writing development in denmark." In *International Perspectives on Writing Curricula and Development: A Cross-Case Comparison*, edited by Jill V. Jeffery and Judy M. Parr, 169–191. London and New York: Routledge.
Elf, Nikolaj Frydensbjerg, Hanghøj, Thorkild, Erixon, Per-Olof, and Skaar, Håvard. 2015. "Technology in L1: A review of empirical research projects in Scandinavia 1992–2014." In *L1 – Educational Studies in Language and Literature, Special Issue: Paradoxes and negotiations in Scandinavian L1 research in languages, literatures and literacies*, edited by guest editors Ellen Krogh and Sylvi Penne, 1–88. http://l1.publication-archive.com/publication/1/1534.
Gee, James Paul. 2010. *New Digital Media and Learning as an Emerging Area and "Worked Examples" as One Way Forward.* Cambridge, Massachusetts: MIT Press.
Kress, Gunther. 2000. "A curriculum for the future." *Cambridge Journal of Education* 30, no. 1.
Ministry of Children and Education. 2015. *Dansk – Fælles Mål, Læseplan og Vejledning.* www.emu.dk.
Ministry of Children and Education. 2017. *Dansk a – Stx, August 2017.* www.emu.dk.
Sahlström, Frithof, Tanner, Marie, and Olin-Scheller, Christina. 2019. "Smartphones in classrooms: reading, writing and talking in rapidly changing educational spaces." *Learning, Culture and Social Interation* 22 (2019): 1–5.
Selwyn, Neil, Nemorin, Selena, Bulfin, Scott, and Johnson, Nicola F. 2018. *Everyday Schooling in the Digital Age: High School, High Tech?* London: Routledge.

Shanahan, Timothy, and Shanahan, Cynthia. 2008. "Teaching disciplinary literacy to adolescents: Rethinking content-area literacy." *Harvard Educational Review* 78, no. 1: 40–61. https://dpi.wi.gov/sites/default/files/imce/cal/pdf/teaching-dl.pdf.

Stjern Frønes, Tove. 2017. "Å Lese Og Navigere På Nettet. En Studie Av Elevers Navigasjonsstrategier." PhD diss., University of Oslo.

Street, Brian. 1984. *Literacy in Theory and Practice*. New York: Cambridge University Press.

Tække, Jesper, and Paulsen, Michael. 2022. *A New Perspective on Education in the Digital Age: Teaching, Media and Bildung*. London and New York: Bloomsbury Academic. 10.5040/9781350175426.

14 Different modes of reading – eighth-grade students' interaction with a digital narrative

Ayoe Quist Henkel and Signe Hjort Nielsen

Introduction

How do 14- to 15-year-olds experience, read, and interact physically, sensory, and verbally with a digital narrative? This question will be the focal point of the chapter that is based on a case study of students' navigation and aesthetic interplay with the digital narrative *NORD*. The basic theoretical understanding and qualitative method of the study is a phenomenological approach based on the analytical scope of the study which focuses on the students' interaction with the digital narrative and especially their bodily and sensory exchange with the narrative. Therefore, the analysis will focus on two aspects of the students' interaction: first, their navigation in the game spaces and between expressions of form such as text, picture, and sound with a focus on their bodily being-in-the-world and interaction with the digital interface (Keogh 2018, Walther 2005, Walther and Larsen 2019, Hayles 2002, 2008); and second, the aesthetic interplay between text and reader/player with a focus on their aesthetic response and immersion (Baumgarten 2012, Felski 2008, 2020).

The framework for the study of students' interaction with *NORD*

The chapter is based on case studies of four 13- to 14-year-old students' interaction with the digitally born young adult story *NORD* by Hübbe et al. (2018). *NORD* is told through text, picture, sound, and simple animations, and the reader moves forward in the story by finding and touching interactive stones, making text boxes pop up. The students navigated in the digital interface using the computer mouse, and one student used "gamer keys" for a while, that is WASD. The text is read out loud when a stone is activated, but this function can be omitted, and several languages can be selected (Danish, Norwegian, Swedish, Islandic, and English). In *NORD*, the 14-year-old girl Nord sets out to find her mother who has been abducted by the businessman Sejr who is building an empire in Iceland and wants to build a spaceship so that he can conquer the universe. On her way, Nord meets the squirrel boy

DOI: 10.4324/9781003211662-23

Different modes of reading 163

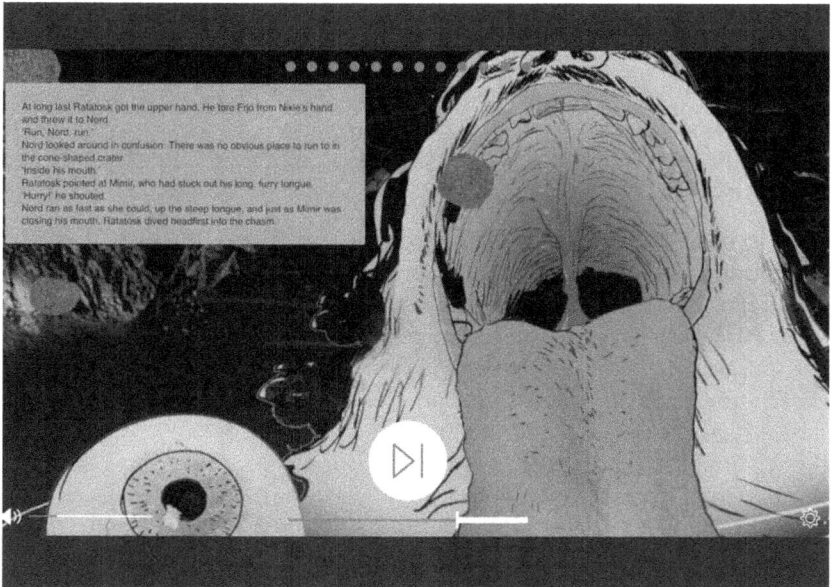

Figure 14.1 Screenshot from Hübbe et al. (2018), chapter 29.

Ratatoskr, the three *norns* Urd, Skuld, and Verdante, and the hair-raising monster Nidhug, who is gnawing at the roots of the tree of life deep down in Nifelheim. Gradually, Nord realizes that a new *Ragnarok* is underway, and that she has been chosen to save not only her mother but the whole world from destruction. By combining writing, picture, sound, and interaction in a simultaneous perception, *NORD* is also an example of intermedial children's literature (Henkel 2021) (Figure 14.1).

In order to focus on the students' interaction and aesthetic exchange with the digital story, we arranged the study as case studies. The class teacher chose the students based on their different personal interests and engagement in literature teaching. Two students were very interested in computers and computer games, and they, therefore, knew the architecture and dynamics of the game space. According to the teacher, they were less motivated for literature teaching, though. The other two students were in varying degrees engaged in literature teaching, while one of them read many books in her spare time and liked to become absorbed in literature. These four students read *NORD* individually in the course of four to five hours, only interrupted by two breaks to allow us to gain insight into their immediate experience of and interaction with the text. Each reading was videotaped, just as we made observations and entered into dialog with the students during the reading. After the reading, each student participated in an open, structured interview based on observations of how they had interacted physically and emotionally during the reading. The aim of using these different forms of data and data triangulation was to catch verbal as well as nonverbal aspects of the students' interaction. The collection of data and the first analyses were carried out by Signe Hjort Nielsen (2020).

Understanding interaction with the digital story as a bodily and aesthetic exchange

To understand the students' reading of the digital story as a bodily and sensory interplay we draw on conceptions and perspectives developed in video game theory, literary materialism, and theory on aesthetic engagement with literature. We employ the phenomenological approach to video games, seeing the video game experience as a *"play of bodies* that flickers between present and absent, corporeal and incorporeal, immanent and transcendent, actual and virtual, 'me' and 'not me'" (Keogh 2018, 13, original emphasis). From the video game approach, we also emphasize the concepts of different game spaces and game-aesthetic mechanisms and means (Keogh 2018, Crick 2011, Walther 2005, Walther and Larsen 2019) in order to analyze and comprehend the students' bodily and multisensory reading of the digital story. In other words, we carry out media-sensitive analyses (Hayles 2002, 2004) of the young people's interaction with the digital narrative. This media-specific approach and the idea of textual embodiment from Hayles correspond with the understanding of the sensory and special bodily appeal of texts which is shared also by computer game theoreticians like Keogh. Where Hayles analyzes the materiality of texts, including their embodiment, we analyze four eighth-grade students' different interactions with the "body" of the digital narrative.

In order to analyze and understand the students' aesthetic exchange and engagement with the digital narrative, we include Rita Felski's theory and thoughts on the reader's empathy, identification, and way of attachment to the text through attunement and presence, seeing this as essential for an aesthetic experience of literature and art in general (Felski 2008, 2020). According to Felski, we ought to rethink the arguments for reading and teaching literature, and she points to four reasons or so-called "aesthetic responses" that ordinary readers and researchers share: recognition, enchantment, knowledge, and shock (Felski 2008). The aesthetic response focuses on the dialog that taking place when the reader meets different elements or phenomena in the literary text and reacts or responds. This exchange is aesthetic as the reading is a sensory process, and it is dialogic as it is based on the exchange between text and reader. Highlighting the sensory focus and starting point draws on aesthetic theory. Baumgarten defined aesthetics as the science of sensory knowledge, and he claimed that "sensations, fantasy images, fables, waves of emotion, etc. [are a] great part of human recognition" (2012, 30). In this chapter, we recognize that aesthetic experiences are historical and socioculturally contingent but here we focus on aesthetic experiences from a phenomenological perspective as essential for imagination, empathy, and absorption. In the following chapter, we pay special attention to the students' aesthetic exchange with the digital narrative, including whether they express empathy, imagination, or sensitivity, and whether they create knowledge and meaning and/or experience for no purpose other than the experience itself. By combining theory on the students' navigation and bodily being in the game space, the materiality of texts, and the aesthetic exchange and attachment with the digital narrative, this chapter aims to draw a picture of different ways of being in a digital reading space.

A phenomenological approach and concepts for analysis

Our research interest here is what characterizes the interaction strategies employed by the four students. From the phenomenological approach, man is seen as a sentient being who is an active co-creator of his world, and his bodily being-in-the-world is seen as vital for recognition, just as body and mind are seen as inseparable (Merleau-Ponty 1962). An essential point for Merleau-Ponty is that conscience, body, world, and language are interwoven, and that human conscience and perception are bodily embedded. He states: "The perceived world is the always presupposed foundation of all rationality, all value and all existence" (ibid. 13). As theory and qualitative method, phenomenology makes it possible to address human existence, "[w]here the subject is seen as a bodily, socially and culturally situated in-the-world-being" (Zahavi 2018, 117). We employ the phenomenological approach in order to come close to the phenomenon: the students' interaction with the digital narrative.

The study is organized as a series of case studies, since this method is especially relevant for the phenomenological approach when studying contextual relations without expecting definite answers (Flyvbjerg 2006). To get close to the students' interaction with the digital story, we therefore apply the phenomenological understanding of interaction with computer games also shared by Keogh, since *NORD* as a digital narrative invites horizontal and vertical movements, shifts in perspective, and first-person eyes, creating space, atmosphere, and intensity through *tactility* and *auditivity*, just as *interactivity* allows for bodily and sensory incidents which may create the immersion known from computer games. In the following analyses of the students' interaction, we, therefore, pay special attention to the game-aesthetic means such as animation, visual and auditory elements, and time-space relations. Moreover, inspired by Walther and Larsen (2019), we distinguish between the following game spaces: the geometric game space which concerns the architecture of the game room, the narrative game room which concerns the piecing together of the underlying narrative, the phenomenological game room which concerns the experience of being present in the game, and the semiotic game room which concerns the understanding of the signs and connecting them to fulfill the mission (Walther 2005, Walther and Larsen 2019).

From Felski's theory about aesthetic response, we use the following concepts for our analysis: *Recognition* is about identifying with ideas, thoughts, feelings, sympathies, and antipathies in the text in ways that allow for identification with the literary characters. *Enchantment* is about total attachment and absorption in a text, about the reader forgetting time and place and disappearing into the literary universe. *Knowledge* is about the way texts offer us fundamental knowledge of the world as it is or can be, not as a copy of the world, but through critical reflection on the world. The knowledge offered by literature is knowledge of the world outside ourselves. Finally, the fourth reason for reading, according to Felski, is *shock*, in the sense that literature has the power to disturb the reader; it can be a "slap-in-the-face," or it can engage us deeply emotionally (Felski 2008). Thus, in our analysis of a students' interaction with *NORD* we focus especially on how and to which extent the interplay between writing, picture, sound compositions, the voice of the reader, animations, and interactivity can create recognition, enchantment, knowledge, and shock. Altogether, the above-mentioned concepts define in various ways the different reading and sensory experiences of the digital narrative, creating a basis for the following analysis of the four cases of navigation and bodily being-in-the-world during reading.

Case 1: The navigation challenges and motivates at the same time – determined and interpreting interaction

This student is active and attentive during literature teaching but does not read a lot in her spare time. Her interaction with *NORD* is characterized by a strong desire to find the stones in the game room in order to move forward in the story and obtain new information about the characters and the relationships between them. She interprets while reading and is motivated by a desire to evaluate and assess her interpretative perspectives so it is clear that the primary focus is the reading of the text boxes. Therefore, the student's navigation strategies are mostly in the narrative game room with a special focus on sorting out the narrative. Her movements in the game room are quick and determined, though somewhat influenced by music and sounds. These change the character of the navigation, which becomes slower and creates room for more sensory interaction. The different forms of expression – written text, picture, and sound – and the interplay between them affect the interaction – also in an aesthetic perspective, qualifying the otherwise text-directed focus. The student explains the significance of the pictures and the visual aspect: "The relationship between them all [the literary characters] can be difficult to show in a book, but you can do this with pictures."

This quotation is one of many that clearly shows that the student's attention to the visual aspect of *NORD* intends to link information and create connection and meaning. During the first half of the reading, she has difficulties finding the interactive stones and does not immediately try to change her navigation strategy and explore the game room any further, since she sees the navigation from stone to stone as an incentive: "[I]t was like a task. Where are they? And you have to pay attention and so on. I also liked that you could see at the top how many [interactive stones] there were, and how much time you had left at the bottom. It motivated me to continue reading." So the student uses determined navigation strategies and pays close attention to the sounds of the story, but has little interest in investigating objects and details in the game room and is less bodily and sensory receptive to the expression forms and their intrinsic aesthetic potential. Her aesthetic interplay is characterized by recognition and knowledge; she interprets while reading and becomes absorbed by a feeling of recognition and empathy in her meeting with the different characters and their development through the story, as the following quotation shows: "He probably has a profound need to love and like somebody, but every time he contradicts himself and says to himself, 'Ah, I don't need it anyway' – I would imagine." The student creates knowledge and connection through the interpretation of the character Sejr. The interaction is not particularly characterized by much sensory or bodily openness, but carries aesthetic potential in the student's commitment to navigating the game room in terms of immersion and interpretation.

On the one hand, the student's aesthetic interplay is motivated by a wish to piece together the parts of the narrative, and, on the other hand, it is characterized by an aesthetic response, that is, recognition through interpretation of the characters and the interplay between them, because the student is concerned with topics such as love and friendship in the interaction, trying to gain coherence and meaning. The problem with the student's interaction strategies, from an aesthetic and material perspective, is in particular her lack of interest in experiencing for no other purpose than the experience itself or in reflecting carefully on something intangible and sensory, just as the student shows no sensitive reflection on feelings, sensations, and ideas.

Case 2: Navigational game competencies with an eye for detail – investigative interaction

This student plays computer games in his spare time and is not especially interested in literature or literature teaching. In his interaction with *NORD*, the student moves slowly and investigatively around the game room. He pays attention to details in the game room and often clicks on objects, and he explores the possibilities for movement in the geometrical game room and quickly becomes familiar with the limits hereof. The student's navigation strategies are characterized by knowledge of the architecture of the game room, which clearly supports a flow in navigation from stone to stone. The time-space relation is therefore central to the way the student navigates; he is curious to learn how he can move around the game room and does so slowly and investigatively:

I: "You mentioned – being able to move about in the story – how does that feel?"
M: "Uh, well, it was actually quite cool that you could choose the pace, and it was sort of deliberate. So if you wanted to take a closer look at something, then you did not have to move on immediately."

The student wants to set his own pace, making the possibility of dwelling in the game room particularly important for his interaction and motivation. The student explores the possibilities of the geometrical game room which enables a bodily being and presence, where he experiences himself as part of the game room, but with a special focus on investigating details and interacting with objects. The student experiences the game room by navigating and interacting with the narrative. This type of interaction is promoted by increased awareness of the different expression forms:

M: "I think it is exciting; it is different. It is not something you have done before. […] it is great […] that there are illustrations. It is not so often you have books with illustrations. You can see what is going on."
I: "What did you look at most?"
M: "I think it was a mix between reading the text and looking at the pictures. Because when they were in the forest, then there were eyes, sort of like … animals or something, which looked at them. You would not have known this if you had only read the text, but in the pictures you could see that someone was watching them."

This student verbalizes, as the only one, an attention to the eyes in the forest, and in the following interview he reflects on the interplay of the expression forms and the significance of these eyes. The case presents an example of the way navigational game competencies can come into play in the interaction with *NORD*, but also an example of the ability to pay attention to several sign systems at the same time, thereby placing the reader in the semiotic game room. This student has less bodily focus in the meeting with the interactive stones, which are placed close together and at long text boxes, and this promotes his own reflections on the navigation where control of pace in movements and exploration of the game room constitute a significant motivation factor. He is suspended in between the phenomenological game room and the semiotic one.

Owing to his game competencies the student has an advantage in the navigation with *NORD*, and he uses this advantage to investigate many details in the visual universe especially. On the basis of these navigation strategies, he shows special attention to the interplay between expression

Different modes of reading 169

forms, thereby creating meaning, connections, and knowledge in an open and investigating way. He shows less bodily and sensory empathy in the aesthetic means, which may be due to his familiarity with computer games. However, by responding mainly to the visual universe, he does become engaged in exploring the game room, and he has the aesthetic potential of experiencing the universe for no other purpose than the experience in itself and the sensitive use of imagination.

Case 3: Being present in the game room – experiencing and sensory interaction

This student plays computer games and is not particularly engaged in reading literature in his spare time or in literature teaching at school. The student investigates and explores the limits of the geometrical game room, but makes quicker movements than the student in case 2. The student is concerned with details and objects in the game room, but not as much as the student in case 2, which is evident from the quicker movements. The student's navigation strategies differ from case 2 as he does not direct a bodily focus on the text boxes but rather navigates in the game room by listening to the reading. The student moves in the game room with quick and attentive movements, as if he were part of it. This observation is confirmed and unfolded in the following interview: "[W]ell sometimes I read along, but it was primarily that voice, and then looking at what was there." The student says that his attention in the game room is less tied to the text, whereas he orients himself in the visual universe while listening to the narrator's voice. This places his navigation strategies mainly in the phenomenological game room. When looking for the next stone, the student navigates by the "compass arrow" at the top of the screen. This strategy, combined with good structural skills and a good understanding of the dynamics and architecture of the geometrical game room, increases the flow, making his navigation strategies very "flexible," while the quick and investigating movements in the game room do not prevent him from pausing in order to listen to music or sounds. Just like the student in case 2, he loses bodily focus at the long and repeated text boxes, which accentuates the motivation for more phenomenological navigation strategies. The student in this case is therefore different from cases 1 and 2 because he prefers navigation strategies that support a more bodily and sensory interaction with NORD. In the interview, he reflects on this:" [I]t is also really cool that you can relate to it when there is something to listen to, so that you become sort of, like get into the same mood as in the book."

In the quotation above, it is interesting that he uses the word "mood" and verbalizes listening and relating to a mood as something positive for the interaction; this exemplifies an interaction where sensation is central, and where the navigation strategies employed are important for the possibility of an interaction with a more bodily and sensory scope. In the interview, the student expresses increased engagement and interest in the character Sejr. He feels addressed and involves himself in the description of Sejr. Sejr's character and actions create the feeling of something identifiable, a feeling which can be clarified by the concept of recognition.

Case 3 has an interest in playing computer games, which is evident in his navigational game competencies. The student's attention in the game room is aimed at being present in the game room, which is driven by immediacy since the student responds to what he experiences and is motivated by. This is expressed through the feeling of something recognizable and identifiable and immediate reactions to the game aesthetic means. The student enjoys being present in the game room for no other purpose than the experience itself, and he is able to become absorbed and show a receptive presence through his phenomenological being in the game room and an interaction that is only minimally tied to the written text. He becomes absorbed in the digital narrative, especially because of the navigation possibilities in the game room and the visual universe.

Case 4: Concentration and reflection pauses – experiencing and sensory interaction

This student reads a lot in her spare time but is not especially interested in literature teaching. The observation of the student's interaction with *NORD* shows challenges with navigation, and she faces these challenges by adopting slow movements in her search for the stones. Particularly distinctive in her reading and efforts to drive the story on is the navigation with short breaks in the time-space relation. In the following interview, the student reflects on her reading experience: "But it was fun, because it was not just reading and reading. Then there was a break in the middle of the story. That meant you could breathe, and then you could concentrate just as much when you were to hear the next part. I could concentrate more easily, and I was caught all the time. Because when you read a book, then I think you read and read and read, and there are no breaks for just a second or so." The student is motivated to navigate in *NORD*, and the interplay between forms of expression and their appeal contributes to keeping her concentrated. She explains: "[Y]ou had to find your own way, and there were video clips, something behind, and you also had a voice reading, then I think you could concentrate on coming up with ideas yourself. What is going to happen now? And then seeing what happens." She links the experience of increased focus and concentration to the more active role which the navigation from stone to stone requires, and this can be compared to the reflections of the student in case 1.

Altogether, the student's navigation is characterized by a rhythm in the form of the temporal navigation from stone to stone with her chosen pauses which offer time for reflection on the narrative. Adding to this, she mentions the expression forms as being important for the interaction. She navigates while reading, and her bodily focus is on the text boxes, which entails a special attention to the written text and the narrative plot. However, this attention diminishes at sudden sound effects and animations, where she decidedly responds verbally with shock sounds such as "HUH" and "OH," while showing a body language that confirms the verbalization, for example withdrawing from the screen. The student experiences her own interaction as tied to the text, but also recounts how a focus on the visual effects affects her ability to create immersion and coherence. Therefore, the student's own reflections on the applied navigation strategies position her in the narrative game room. But the reflections do not express the more bodily reactions exemplified by the outbursts, which confirm a bodily and sensory presence in the game room as part of the interaction. These reactions point toward a more phenomenological approach to navigating and being in the game room, shifting the navigation between the narrative and the phenomenological game room. This aesthetic interplay is characterized by immediacy and a personal and bodily engagement in the story. The student's capacity for empathy and immersion is seen as a strong response to the game aesthetic means, just as she includes personal experiences, linking the aesthetic responses to recognition and shock. The student's interaction strategies are predominantly experiencing but also sensory interaction types, as she wants to reveal parts of the narrative and, at the same time, dwell at them and pause to make room for empathy and immersion.

Different modes of reading a digital story

As showed in the four cases, there are many different ways of experiencing, reading, and interacting with a digital narrative. There are many nuances in the students' navigation strategies and their bodily and sensory sensitivity, which are revealed in their different ways of interacting with *NORD*, and which result in different aesthetic responses. The students' interactions and readings are different, often depending on their previous experiences with and preferences for computer games and literature. However, even the two students with game experience "read" in different ways. The differences are marked because of the media specificity of the digital narrative: it is a combination of different art and expression forms, and it prompts independent navigation and interaction depending on the way the reader interacts with the interface. Hayles labels this form of electronic literature a "hopeful monster [...] composed of parts taken from diverse traditions that may not always fit neatly together. Hybrid by nature, it comprises a 'trading zone' [...] in which different vocabularies, expertises, and expectations come together to see what might emerge from their intercourse" (Hayles 2008, 4). In this case study, *NORD* is the blended and hopeful "monster" and the students' reading becomes a "trading zone," where it makes no sense to draw up absolute divisions between reading, listening, seeing, and navigating, and where the bodily and sensory interplay becomes an essential part of the digital reading condition.

References

Baumgarten, Alexander Gottlieb. 2012 (1750). "Fra Æstetikken." In *Sansning og erkendelse*, edited by Jørn Erslev Andersen. Aarhus: Aarhus University Press.
Crick, Timothy. 2011. "The game body: Toward a phenomenology of contemporary video gaming." *Games and Culture* 6, no. 3: 259–269. 10.1177/1555412010364980.
Felski, Rita. 2008. *Uses of Literature*. Malden, Massachusetts, and Oxford: Blackwell Publishing.
Felski, Rita. 2020. *Hooked. Art and Attachment*. Chicago and London: University of Chicago Press.
Flyvbjerg, Bent. 2006. "Five misunderstandings about case-study research." *Qualitative Inquiry* 12, no. 2: 219. 10.1177/1077800405284363.
Hayles, N. Katherine. 2002. *Writing Machines*. Cambridge, Massachusetts: MIT Press.
Hayles, N. Katherine. 2004. "Print is flat, code is deep: The importance of media-specific analysis." *Poetics Today* 25, no. 1: 67–90. 10.1215/03335372-25-1-67.
Hayles, N. Katherine. 2008. *Electronic Literature. New Horizons for the Literary*. Indiana: University of Notre Dame Press.
Henkel, Ayoe Quist. (2021). In-Between. Intermedial understanding and analysis of children's literature. Exemplified by the digital story NORD (2018). *Barnelitterært forskningstidsskrift*, 12(1), 1–15. 10.18261/issn.2000-7493-3031-01-03.
Hübbe, Camilla, Meisler, Rasmus, and Olsen, Roar Skau. 2018. *NORD*. Copenhagen. Publishing House Nord. https://fortell.dk/nord/.
Keogh, Brendan. 2018. *A Play of Bodies: How We Perceive Videogames*. Cambridge and London: MIT Press.
Merleau-Ponty, Maurice. 1962. *Phenomenology of Perception*. Routledge.
Nielsen, Signe Hjort. 2020. "Den digitale fortælling i litteraturundervisningen – elevernes interaktionsstrategier i et æstetisk perspektiv." MA diss., Aarhus University, Denmark.
Walther, Bo Kampmann. 2005. *Konvergens og nye Medier*. Aarhus, Denmark: Academica.
Walther, Bo Kampmann, and Larsen, Lasse Juel 2019. "Bicycle kicks and camp sites. Towards a phenomenological theory of game feel with special attention towards 'rhythm'." *Convergence* 26, no. 5–6: 1248–1268. 10.1177/1354856519885033.
Zahavi, Dan 2018. *Fænomenologi. En introduktion*. Frederiksberg, Denmark: Samfundslitteratur.

15 Transmedial reading

Susana Tosca

Introduction

In our digital times, it is a widespread idea that we are reading less than before and losing our ability to interpret complex texts. However, many contemporary readers of popular fiction are used to juggling vast amounts of information as they navigate networks of related stories known as "transmedial worlds" or "transmedia storytelling." The word "transmedia" was coined by Marsha Kinder (1991) as a way to designate clusters of related popular media texts that exploit the same fictional universe. Kinder was intrigued by children's strong emotional responses to the universe of *The Teenage Mutant Ninja Turtles*. This affective dimension will be pivotal to this chapter.

The interest in stories that are told across platforms has only grown in media studies, spawning a whole field of research, as recent compilation works demonstrate (Freeman and Gambarato 2018). A transmedial world example could be *Harry Potter*, whose story is told across all the books, films, games, comic books, websites, and merchandise. When confronted with a new product belonging to the fictional universe, say, the book *Harry Potter and the Cursed Child*, a reader engages in a twofold (transmedia) reception process. On the one hand, they have to interpret the text in front of them according to its specific aesthetic code (and media affordances). On the other, they must pay attention to the role that said text plays in relation to others belonging to the same transmedia universe. This is the meta-level that I will be focusing on in this chapter, the transmedial reading level that happens *beyond* the individual work. Here, the text is understood broadly, because transmedial reading is most often multimodal reading, as we consume stories and plots belonging to different media platforms. Moreover, there is a wide range of transmedial experiences, as the meta-level can be equally activated by reading our second or our fiftieth text belonging to the same fictional universe. Of course, the more texts that are known by a reader (in reader response terms, the bigger their repertoire is), the more complex the interaction. This relational aspect shares some qualities with the kind of intertextual operations present in the reception of

DOI: 10.4324/9781003211662-24

adapted media products, for example when we watch a movie after having read the book it is based on. However, adaptation is about conveying the essence of the same single text through another medium, while *transmediality* is about expanding universes, where every new text contributes to filling a different gap, introducing for instance new characters, new timelines, new subplots, and stories that all fit the overarching *worldness* (Klastrup and Tosca 2004). We could say that adaptation has a story focus, and *transmediality* a world focus. Transmedia reception often unfolds over long periods of time, as the same fictional worlds are revisited over and over again. That is, transmedial reading is about re-reading, and even re-writing, as the core *worldness* of the fictional universe that we keep alive in our imagination shifts with every new addition, in an interactive process that is often entangled with emotions and our own personal biographies, as we will see later.

In previous work, I have developed a model of transmedial experience (described in detail in Tosca 2017) based on McCarthy and Wright to illustrate an experience-centric approach to the study of user engagement across media. In their view, any human activity is at the same time sensual, emotional, and intellectual, even more intensely so in the case of aesthetic experiences. Temporal situatedness is also crucial as lived experience is a culmination of past events, present circumstances, and future expectations. McCarthy and Wright's model is centered on the individual, so I added a social dimension at its center because the interpretive communities around transmedial worlds are very important for reception (Figure 15.1).

The model tries to illustrate the complexity of the meeting of an individual with the world through two kinds of categories: the "experiential threads"

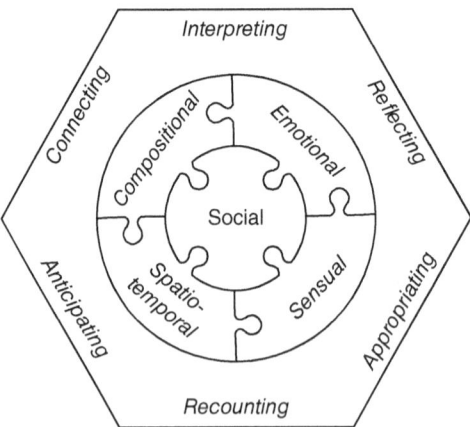

Figure 15.1 A transmedial experience model (Tosca 2017, based on McCarthy and Wright).[1]

and the "cognitive operations." The "threads" in the central circle (emotional, compositional, spatio-temporal, sensual, and my addition, social) refer to the different kinds of dimensions of any situation. Maybe the reader is settling in for a free evening on a soft sofa, in front of a warm fire, with a storm raging outside, feelings of coziness creating a specific mood for the reading experience. The "cognitive operations" in the six sides of the hexagon (anticipating, connecting, interpreting, reflecting, appropriating, and recounting) define the activities that users engage in when making sense of an experience. Maybe the book is the long-awaited continuation of a beloved series, and the reader has a set of specific expectations about what they are about to encounter. In an aesthetic experience, the work of art emerges in the situated meeting of reader and work. This is very much in sync with classical literary reception theories, although it goes beyond cognition to also incorporate the sensual, affective, and material worlds framing the situated experience. In this respect, the position I take here can be considered a phenomenological approach to reading, where it "is understood as a course of sense making within daily life," as Heap has proposed (1977, 104).

The case study introduced below applies the transmedial experience model deductively, both in order to elicit a response from my interviewees and also as a heuristic tool to analyze their reception experience. This serves a double purpose: (1) to introduce *transmediality* as a relevant dimension in relation to contemporary reading practices, and (2) to showcase a method that can be useful for investigating reading experiences by going beyond the empirical reticence of the classical reader reception field.

Case and method

In order to showcase a process of transmedial reading, I have chosen a relatively new addition to the *Star Wars* transmedial universe: the first volume (containing six issues) of the comic book series *Star Wars: Darth Vader* drawn by Salvador Larroca and written by Kieron Gillen. The series has 25 issues (compiled in four volumes), published during 2015 and 2016, and follows the character of Darth Vader in the time between the *Star Wars* films *Episode IV: A New Hope* and *Episode V: The Empire Strikes Back*. The series is so new that it is not hard to find *Star Wars* audiences that have not yet read it, also because comics have much less mainstream appeal than films. At the same time, it depicts one of the best-known characters in the transmedial world, so that readers have both previous knowledge and most likely affective attachments of various kinds. The events covered in the first volume fall in between two of the "old" films, rather well known by audiences, which makes the comic book series an excellent object of study to trace specific transmedia connections.

For this experimental approach, I am inspired by the work of two researchers that have contributed to our understanding of reading as connected to our lifeworld: Louise M. Rosenblatt and Nina Mikkelsen.

Rosenblatt's work on transactional reading is key because she insists on the affective dimension of reading, going beyond cognitive understandings: "[T]he reader infuses intellectual and emotional meanings into the pattern of verbal symbols, and those symbols channel his thoughts and feelings. Out of this complex process emerges a more or less organized imaginative experience" (1995, 25). Likewise, Mikkelsen's typology of the many dimensions of reading, which she calls literacies, also takes readers' emotions, biographies, and social life into account (Mikkelsen 2005). Her interviewing method, as presented in the book *Powerful Magic* (2005), has also directly informed my setup, although my readers are older than hers, and I did not engage in group sessions. This chapter is based on six individual interviews with young Danish transmedial fans of *Star Wars* aged between 13 and 19 years, two girls and four boys, showing varying degrees of investment in the fictional universe. I will identify them by their gender (B/G for boy or girl) and age in the quotes.

The interview proceeded as follows. I first invited each participant to read the comic book (48 pages; it is a compilation of the first six issues) on their own, before the interview. The interview started with us talking about the expectations they had had before reading the book, and then we embarked on a surface "joint reading," where we together turned pages and talked about the content and progression of the story. As we went on, they described and explained the comic art and talked about what they thought and felt at every turn. My focus was on getting them to verbalize their interpretive and creative engagement with the *worldness* of the story: how did it add to the mythos, topos, and ethos they already knew, and at the same time, how did the new story change their idea of that world? As introduced above, transmedial reading is not just about tracing new information, but also about interweaving it with the personal story of reception of each reader.

I did not use a rigid interview guide with a set order of questions. Instead, I had a picture of the transmedial experience model with me as a visual reminder to address the different experiential lines and sense-making operations. For instance, I asked questions like: what were your expectations before you started to read? Can you make a summary of what you just read? How does it fit with what you already knew? How is it different? As for the "experiential threads," I would for example ask the reader to explain a specific scene to me in order to comment on compositional and sensory issues, or prompt them to elaborate when they connected what we were seeing to their own personal stories. Usually, the conversation would start very close to the actual comic book and then moved back and forth between the part (the panel, the page, the book) and the whole (the transmedial world), allowing each reader to expand on their own topics of interest, and encouraging a safe space that allowed them to concentrate on the impact the transmedial universe had had on their lives. The transcriptions revealed a messy process, where topics were rarely well defined, as aesthetic impressions, interpretation, affect, and anecdotes were mixed together. I have here used the transmedial experience model to organize this mild chaos in four focus areas ("What were you expecting?," "What do you see?," "How does this make sense?," and "What does it mean to you?"), even though many utterances span several categories.

What were you expecting?

Cognitive operations: anticipating and reflecting. Experiential threads: emotional, social

The interview always began by me asking the reader to reflect on the expectations they had had before reading the comic book, which mostly had to do with the emotional thread (their previous personal relation to Darth Vader) or with placing this new work in the network of products. Often, readers reflected on extra-diegetic elements, like Disney's *Star Wars* development strategy, or the buzz from social media around different kinds of products. Sometimes this question did not elicit a lot of response, if the interviewees were too eager to get started with the comic book, so I asked it again at the end of the interview, which yielded more success.

The most shared expectation was that of recognition, of getting to revisit the known sites and themes. This was often formulated in spatial terms: "I was just looking forward to coming back to the *Star Wars* universe" (G15), like returning home. The characters are old friends, and the stylish drawings summon rich audio-visual memories. Most interviewees had strong expectations as to the "look and feel" of the universe. One even expressed fear of opening the comic book in case they had "botched it" (B19); if it felt wrong, it would be a disaster. When I prodded for more concreteness as to what the look and feel was made of, the answers were very varied: cool colors, the impression of a limitless galaxy, white clothes and red lasers, metal, the possibility of flying off, accurate weapons and uniforms, darkness. Turning the first pages, some let out a satisfied sigh as these expectations were met, and all readers agreed that the authors of the comic book had "totally nailed it" (B19). Even the first images strongly recall the past by remediating the films, as the yellow inclined letters that seem to glide across a starlit background are followed by an opening shot at the ocre desert of Tatooine, where the whole saga started. The emotions attached to readers' expectations are hard to verbalize (maybe it is too embarrassing), but I observed an intense look of concentration and smiles of satisfaction as the images did rise to the challenge. Perhaps the expression of affect becomes clearer when readers consider the protagonist's character as nobody had neutral feelings about Darth Vader. They were aware that their perception of him was about to change because the comic book series is expressly dedicated to going in depth with his character. And he already meant something to them: "I was really little when I saw the old movies.

Darth Vader stayed with me as this mythical terrifying being. He was pure evil. This thing, that he could choke people with his thoughts ... man. I had nightmares for years. I think I hoped to be scared again. I think they do it; he is scary" (B17). Readers reminisced about dark movie theatres or video evenings with their families, about toys and computer games. Two of them mentioned that they could almost hear the iconic music in their head as they turned the first pages, in a remarkable synesthetic moment.

What do you see?

Cognitive operations: recounting and reflecting. Experiential threads: compositional, sensual

All the readers I interviewed, even those who did not consider themselves hardcore fans, could read more things in the story than I could. As they embarked on literal recounting of what they had read (while we leafed through the book), they pointed to details and explained twists of the story that had escaped me, like how Darth Vader avoids standing on the floor trap when visiting Jabba the Hutt. In the transmedial model, this is referred to as the compositional thread (the components of the story), often taking the images as its starting point (sensory), but becoming interpretive in sophisticated ways. Some of this refers to encyclopedic aspects of the fictional world, which not all readers master equally well: details about droids, battleships, weapons, and uniforms. For instance, half of my readers mentioned that the Imperial Palace we see in a picture is the old Jedi Temple, while the other half either did not realize or did not think it was worth mentioning. These details are not merely registered, but connected to overarching meanings, like when an informant mentioned that Darth Vader "still uses a Nubian ship like Padme's" (G13). "So what?" I asked. And she explained that this could be a sign of his attachment to the memory of his dead wife, from the time where he was still called Anakin, an emotional residue that complicates the figure of Darth Vader as an emotionless monster.

Transmedial universes are big networks of meanings where there is always one more story to be told: a secondary character with a crucial secret, a peripheral planet that hides a whole civilization, a legend from the past that can be revived ... Even well-known facts and events can be seen in a new light when a fresh perspective is adopted, and it would seem that fans never tire of learning more. Fan fiction has long operated in this terrain, filling the gaps of meaning in fictional universes, telling untold stories or showing other points of view. Now, however, it is transmedial producers that fulfill this mission. My readers were critical about excessive "fan service," referring critically to the way in which producers take the easy way out to please non-exigent fans. The balance is hard to hit, for readers want their favorite elements to return, but it cannot just be in any way: "[I]f you make a beloved character appear out of nowhere, say Luke Skywalker, for a short cameo that has no weight whatsoever in the story, that brings nothing new; those are lazy nostalgia points. That sucks" (B15). So it turns out that more is not always better. These transmedial readers are not only interested in getting more of the same, they want "necessity," as another put it, more depth, a crucial (other) point of view. When they see, they are not interested in just recognizing; they also want their opinion to change, their image of the world to shift. All six readers pointed to the sequence at the end of the volume, where Darth Vader discovers he has a son, as the most memorable part of this particular reading session. In the films, we never see this moment, and here it is told with flashbacks to Anakin and Padme's life. However, Vader does not miss his old life; he seems to feel disgust. He is silent and unmoved as he for the first time realizes the extent of the emperor's betrayal, and in a panel gazing into space he declares: "He will be mine. It will all be mine." The readers appreciate the lack of sentimentality, the way that this broken man once more sets himself up for tragedy. Only the possibility of a new reading justifies a new retelling: "This is really what the character deserved. In the original trilogy, he was a bit of a ridiculous villain [...] Then in the prequels he is this creepy horny teenager and I lost all respect for him. The *Clone Wars* saves him, really, that he gets his reason to be, but it is like he has been a bit out of focus. Here you *see* him. And it is so well done!" (B17).

How does this make sense?

Cognitive operations: interpreting and connecting. Experiential threads: compositional, spatio-temporal

This focus area is of course very much related to the previous one, as all explaining becomes an act of connecting the dots across a galaxy of stories. The compositional thread is always meta when reading *transmedially*, as any act of interpretation requires knowledge from several sources. An interpretation is a palimpsest of insights, gathered across years of reading, watching, and playing, and put into play here. A quote can illustrate this, as one interviewee made an effort to explain to me the causes and consequences of Darth Vader's falling from the emperor's grace:

B15: A part of me thinks that it is very unfair that Palpatine is so pissed with Darth Vader, I mean he was this close to saving the Death Star. Have you seen *Rogue One*? [...] On the other hand, he is a Sith, that is the way of the Sith, you know. They are not a bunch of boy scouts. He thought Anakin was the perfect apprentice, but now he doesn't trust Vader. Vader hasn't reached the potential that Palpatine hoped he would, and now his body is destroyed ... [...]
Interviewer: Where do you know all this from?

180 *Susana Tosca*

B15: I don't know. All over, the *Clone Wars*, *Legends*, the novels, the Wookieepedia, reddit, YouTube, we really have talked a lot about this.

Some of this information comes from the film *Rogue One*, but a lot of it has become ingrained in such a way that this reader cannot really explain how he knows. Interpreting and connecting is not a straightforward affair, and my interviewees distinguish between facts that are "canon," even different categories of canon, and the many speculations that fill the Internet, as the fan community (the interpretive community) collectively struggles to make sense of new story developments or of content that seems to contradict something they already knew.

What does it mean to you?

Cognitive operations: reflecting and appropriating. Experiential threads: emotional, social

Transmedial reading is not just about neutrally parsing information. Readers appropriate the stories in different ways, deciding what the overarching meaning is. In some cases, the reflection moves from exegesis into eisegesis:

> We never see what he thinks, but we get it, you know. You cannot show Darth Vader's thoughts, he is like a god, you cannot look into such a character, but here you can see how he moves, how he talks, how the others react to him. I liked the flashbacks, where we see images of what he is thinking without words, you need to connect the dots yourself. [...] Like when he murders all those Sand People and there is no explanation. We know why (G15).

I made a point of asking the rest of my readers about this scene, and it turned out that there was a lot of disagreement about what the motivation behind Anakin/Vader's action could be: from plain anger to a wish to damn himself by doing something terrible to calculated rage to a prefiguration of the way he would later kill the Jedi younglings. But is it a problem if nobody is connecting the dots in exactly the same way? To paraphrase Umberto Eco (1990), what are the limits of the text? A text like this is partially open, precisely to allow each reader to interpret it according to their previous knowledge of the transmedial world and also their personal idiosyncrasy. The interesting point is that all these interpretations are backed by actual connections to points in the galaxy of texts. Are they all equally valid? Perhaps what strikes me is that the decision of which dots to connect to is not neutral, but filtered through the situated experience of each reader.

This becomes even clearer when I asked the readers to reflect on what the text means in relation to their own lives. Some feel a big distance to Darth

Vader, a mythical figure that cannot have anything to do with their regular teenage lives in Denmark. But for others, Darth Vader is a character that makes them reflect on their relation to their own father, dwelling on the topic of a son who opposes his father in some way, or generally about disappointment, about broken expectations that can go both ways. As one put it:

> You know how you come home with a bad grade or your friends have thrashed the house in a party you were not allowed to hold or something. That look on your father's face. I mean. My father is a nice guy, nothing to do with Palpatine. It is not like that, but you get this: You are found lacking, when you really wanted to be accepted. At that moment, there is no place in the world for him. Nothing makes sense (B17).

One has to wonder about this reader's change of pronouns in his answer. He is talking about "him"/Vader, but he is also talking about "you"/himself, as the experience of disappointing your father can well be said to be universal.

Transmedial reading findings

I began this chapter by introducing transmedial reception as a cognitive meta-position that makes readers hyperaware of networks of connections, a sort of reading surplus, since no transmedial text can be considered in isolation. The example case presented here has hopefully shown that it is also just as much an embodied, affective, and social experience. Filling the gaps of the transmedial universe was an obvious source of pleasure for the interviewed readers, who enjoyed the sense of mastery in recognizing references as well as the challenges of the cognitive process. The reward is knowledge and depth. As one of the readers said, processing all the new information about Darth Vader made the character suddenly come into focus. Even though the constant effort to connect across a network of references required a somewhat detached meta-attitude, this was not experienced as alienating or disruptive, but as engrossing, coincidental with my previous work about *palimpsestuous* reception (Tosca 2020). The readers were also proud of being able to see more layers in this text than me. They reveled in a sense of owning the fictional world, as a secret world not everybody can enter. The social dimension of reading also became very clear, as readers referred to online fora or conversations with friends where they had discussed interpretations and crowdsourced knowledge, speculating about the fictional universe's development. In this way, reception also prompts productive activity, in the forms of readings that are offered to the community and validated in collective processes of interpretation. As for the biographical aspect, it was harder to get the readers to talk about their own personal connection to the topic, which is no doubt a weakness of the method, since vulnerable issues are difficult to open up to with an unknown person. Despite this, there was a vividness to their memories that was very touching, as they shared deeply impressive experiences.

The difficulty of verbalizing the personal affective dimension and the near epiphanic quality of the reception makes my small study resonate with Gitte Balling's empirical work about the articulated reading experience (2016). For her, the good story has a double dimension as related to the actual text (if it is well written in various ways that provide aesthetic pleasure) and the experience of reading it (what it does for its reader). The linguistic (in the case of a comic book, there is also the visual language) goes hand in hand with the phenomenological and psychological, and the aesthetic experience becomes visible. There is for me no doubt that transmedial reading is a source of aesthetic experiences, with its own intense pleasures. Other research has suggested that the interpretive energy and multiplatform social competence of transmedial readers can be transferred to other domains, constituting its own kind of emerging literacy (Scolari et al. 2018). The current explosion of meta-cultural genres (memes, parodies, retellings) across platforms like TikTok, Snapchat, and YouTube would seem to confirm this. Transmedial content is appropriated and repurposed in many different ways, as readers/viewers become makers, using shared fictional universes as ways to connect with their peers in new visceral ways. Transmedial reading serves as a necessary preamble for all this productive activity, which shares the same qualities of being intensely affective, situated, and very, very social.

Note

1 The term "sensual" is used in the original model by McCarthy and Wright and will therefore also be used throughout this chapter; though a more precise term for this category of experience would be "sensory."

References

Balling, Gitte. 2016. "What is a reading experience?" In *Plotting the Reading Experience: Theory/Practice/Politics*, edited by Paulette M. Rothbauer et al., 37–53. Waterloo, Ontario: Wilfrid Laurier University Press.
Eco, Umberto. 1990. *The Limits of Interpretation*. Bloomington, Indiana: Indiana University Press.
Freeman, Martin, and Gambarato, Renira. 2018. *The Routledge Companion to Transmedia Studies*. New York: Routledge.
Hall, Jonathan. 2020. *Reaction Formations: Dialogism, Ideology, and Capitalist Culture*. Leiden: Brill.
Heap, James L. 1977. "Toward a phenomenology of reading." *Journal of Phenomenological Psychology* 8, no. 1: 103–113. 10.1163/156916277X00141.
Kinder, Marsha. 1991. *Playing with Power in Movies, Television, and Video Games, from Muppet Babies to Teenage Mutant Ninja Turtles*. Berkeley, California: University of California Press.

Klastrup, Lisbeth, and Tosca, Susana. 2004. "Transmedial worlds – rethinking cyberworld design." In *2004 International Conference on Cyberworlds*, edited by Masayuki Nakajima, Yoshinori Hatori, and Alexei Sourin, 409–441. Tokyo: IEEE Computer Society. 10.1109/CW.2004.67.

Mikkelsen, Nina. 2005. *Powerful Magic: Learning From Children's Responses to Fantasy Literature*. New York: Teachers College Press.

Rosenblatt, Louise. 1995/1938. *Literature as Exploration*. New York: Modern Language Association of America.

Rosenblatt, Louise. 1978. *The Reader, The Text, The Poem, The Transactional Theory of The Literary Work*. Carbondale, Illinois: Southern Illinois University Press.

Scolari, C. A. et al. 2018. "Transmedia literacy in the new media ecology: Teens' transmedia skills and informal learning strategies." *El profesional de la informacion* 27, no. 4: 801–812. 10.3145/epi.2018.jul.09.

Tosca, Susana. 2017. "Time, memory and longing in transmedial storytelling." In *Clash of Realities 2015/16, On the Art, Technology and Theory of Digital Games. Proceedings of the 6th and 7th Conference*, edited by Gundolf S. Freyermuth, 159–174. Bielefeld: Transcript-Verlag.

Tosca, Susana. 2020. "Beyond immersion. Gin Tama and palimpsestuous reception." In *Comics and Videogames. From Hybrid Medialities to Transmedia Expansions*, edited by Andreas Rauscher, Daniel Stein, and Jan-Noël Thon, 240–254. London and New York: Routledge.

16 Readers between media: sixth-grade students tuning in to literature in different formats

Ayoe Quist Henkel

Introduction

The chapter will empirically analyze the reading experiences of sixth-grade students in their meeting with a fantasy story that they read either as an illustrated print novel, an audiobook, or a digital narrative. On a phenomenological and postcritical basis, it will analyze aspects of reading experiences which can be divided into two categories: partly formal aspects associated with sensory experiences of the three different formats and partly substantive aspects related to attunement, identification, and the existential resonance of the story. Theoretically, the analyses are based on literary materialism (Hayles 2002, 2004, 2008, McGann 1991) and theories that contribute with knowledge of the reader's attachment to literature (Gumbrecht 2004, 2011, Felski 2008, 2015, 2019, 2020a, Løgstrup 2018). The analysis sets out to identify various aspects of what can be characteristic of the reading experiences of 11–12-year-olds when they read through different formats (audio, paper, and digital), how they express their thoughts about literary reading, and how they make use of literature.

Reading experience in a school context – theoretical framework

There is no strong tradition of research into reading experiences and especially not when it comes to empirical studies of students' reading experiences. This seems rather paradoxical as there are long-standing and well-established research traditions in the case of "reading" as a phenomenon and competence in school and in the case of "experience," which is often studied from a psychological or phenomenological approach (for a detailed review of research into reading experiences, see Henkel et al. 2021, 3–4). As Skjerdingstad and Rothbauer write in the opening chapter of one of the few books with "reading experience" in the title: "To experience and to read are both highly complex phenomena that involve body, sense, and affect; at the same time, they entail cognitive processes taking place in certain historical and geographical settings" (Skjerdingstad and Rothbauer

2016, 1). In other words, the reading experience is a complex as well as a very open concept involving many different aspects of a cognitive, affective, material, physical, reflexive, social, or institutional character. In the specific case of reading literature in different formats (audiobook, illustrated print book, digital narrative) in a school context, additional aspects such as identification, engagement, and reasons for reading become relevant. In recent years, Rita Felski has criticized literary research for having removed literature from its readers through formalism, the "hermeneutics of suspicion" (from Ricoeur) and critical distance (Felski 2008, 2009). In the most recent example, *Hooked. Art and Attachment* (2020a), Felski attempts to rethink the foundations of aesthetic experience, offering an explanation as to why and how we get hooked on literature and art in the first place. Even though Felski's criticism is directed at literary research, the same criticism could be directed at the development of literature teaching in primary education. Recent studies show that what often characterizes literature teaching is objectification and dissection of the literary text with the aim of finding literary tools, applying analytical patterns and literary terms, and setting clear and assessable goals (Rørbech and Skyggebjerg 2020, Hansen et al. 2019, Oksbjerg 2021). This chapter will focus on the students' reading experiences and, inspired by Felski, study the attachment established by the students – described as attunement, identification, and interpretation (Felski 2020a) – and extend her terms with what I call "existential resonance" inspired by the philosopher K. E. Løgstrup, who points to the deep existential significance literature can have in the form of realizations and "long-sightedness" (Løgstrup 2018). By taking Felski as my point of departure, the analytical approach to the interviews is inspired by postcritique (Felski 2020a, 2020b) and its emphasis on the affective aspects of reading literature and the way aesthetic experiences become possible in the meeting between the student and the literary text.

Another important aspect of this study is the significance of the materiality of the three different formats for the reading experience. Here, the focus is on the multisensory experience and interaction. The materiality perspective views literary texts and their expression forms as more than just representations, since, being haptically embedded, they have an impact on the experience and the "Stimmung" (Gumbrecht 2011). They generate and challenge the body's interaction with the world, and the multisensory exchange with an illustrated print book, a computer, or the interface of a tablet is of considerable significance for the attribution of meaning during the reading (Hayles 2002, 2004, 2008). Like McGann (1991, 8), Hayles emphasizes the "embodiment" of literature (Hayles 2002, 31, 32, and 107). The notion of textual embodiment corresponds with the understanding of the sensory and special haptic appeal of texts. Where McGann and Hayles analyze the materiality of texts, including their embodiment, this analysis will focus on the students' interaction with the different textual "bodies" of the three versions, centered on how materiality creates attachment. The background for the following analyses is the premise that literature is a sensory, embodied, linguistic, and abstract phenomenon embedded in a material context, and the analysis will – as described earlier – focus on formal aspects associated with sensory experiences of the three different formats and substantive aspects related to attunement, identification, and existential resonance.

Data

The chapter is based on empirical material from the research project Reading Between Media.[1] The data consist of four focus group interviews with 12 students mixed according to who read the story *Tavs* as a paper book, an audiobook, and a digital narrative, respectively. *Tavs* (Hübbe and Meisler 2012, 2013) is a Manga-inspired story about the 13-year-old boy Tavs (meaning "silent" in Danish), who, grieving the loss of his twin brother and having to move to Tokyo with his family, has chosen to stop speaking. He travels into a fantasy universe where he fights various creatures and meets love in the shape of a cat and his brother who tries to lure him into the underworld. The paper book comes with illustrations, the audiobook with sound effects, and the literary app with sounds and interactive "hot-spots" where the reader must contribute to make the story continue (Figure 16.1).

Figure 16.1 Screenshot from Hübbe and Meisler (2013) iPad-version.

The first two focus group interviews took place a couple of hours after the students had started reading the story, and the last two interviews were conducted when they had nearly finished or had finished reading the story. Each focus group had three participants: one student from the group reading the paper version, one student from the audio group, and one student from the digital story group. The students had been chosen by their teachers according to their desire to speak about their reading experiences as well as the extent to which they were representative of readers in the sixth grade.

Attunement as *Stimmung* and presence

According to Felski, one of the three major ways in which readers can be attached to literature is attunement: "To become attuned is to be drawn into a responsive relation – to experience an affinity that is impossible to ignore yet often hard to categorize. Being attuned is not primarily an issue of representation, of the 'aboutness' of the work of art, but its presence" (Felski 2020a, 41). So, attunement means tuning in to an experience, to have a sense of empathy or immersion that in turn creates a sense of attachment and the relation in mood and emotional engagement established between text and reader, and, not least, the experience of presence which will be further explained below. In *Stimmungen lesen. Über eine verdeckte Wirklichkeit der Literatur*, Hans Ulrich Gumbrecht suggests that a new openness to *Stimmungen* may enrich our understanding of experience with literature. He shows how *Stimmungen*, which can be translated into English as "atmosphere" or "mood," is a concept with a long history in aesthetics; it is about much more than mere subjective empathy and can be linked to text-immanent relations as well as text-external ones (Gumbrecht 2011, 25 ff).

In the focus group interviews, the students are asked: how would you describe the mood and atmosphere in *Tavs*? – a difficult verbalization to make. Still, the students try to put their impressions into words. First, they talk about the moods of the literary characters: "He was, like, a bit sad, actually" (girl, paper). "He was sort of happy and sad at the same time" (girl, digital). "Well, I think it was sort of sad, because the mother ... and, like, the brother had just died, and it was a lot about him, and about Tavs missing him" (boy, digital). Second, they describe the overall mood of the narrative, e.g., "somewhat bad and also somewhat good" (boy, audio), and "dull mood, neither good nor bad ... it becomes a little bit lighter" (boy, digital). These statements express a dimension of the mood perspective which is linked to the literary artifact itself. The other dimension of the mood perspective is linked to the way the literary artifact creates mood and attunement in the reader. In the analyses, it becomes apparent that the students to a great extent experience mood through the material aspects of the narrative, as they often point to the interplay between text, picture, and sound, or to the specific characteristics of each expression form as being crucial to the experience.

Gumbrecht writes:"[T]extuelle Töne, Atmosphären und Stimmungen [sind] nie ganz unabhängig von den materiellen Komponenten der Texte" (2011, 12). Several of the students who read the paper book or the digital story are positive toward the visual materiality of the pictures, for example, "because there is some depth, there are, like, several layers" (girl, paper), or they emphasize the "cartoon-like" element and "drawings which sort of move a bit sometimes like a movie, and I thought that was rather neat" (girl, digital).

Readers of the illustrated novel as well as readers of the digital narrative refer to meta-fictive aspects where the text is integrated in the pictures, thus generating visual creation of meaning. One of them says, "in some pictures, the text had sort of crept into the picture. This made the story much more exciting to read because you felt as if ... there was a picture, for example, where the cat is looking at a wall where the text is up on the wall. This made the story more exciting because you could feel as if you were the cat who was looking at the wall where the text was" (boy, paper). Here the student experiences a concrete form of presence through the materiality of the narrative, a presence that is conducive to his empathy and imagination. Gumbrecht emphasizes presence as an aesthetic experience that is crucial to *Stimmung* where it is not about analyzing, interpreting, and understanding, but about the feeling of presence that literature, music, and art can promote and which is of value in itself.

During the interviews, the students often used the word "imagine" (Danish: "forestille") and imagined scenarios in the story, for example, "I imagined being in the park where he sat" (boy, digital). They also made visualizations, for example, "I imagined the giant hall where he is on the stage and cannot see the people but only hear all the sounds" (girl, digital), and they literally imagined being the main character: "Well, sometimes I imagine, for instance, if it says that he walks into the swinging cage, then I imagine being inside the cage which swings back and forth" (boy, paper). Here the student creates inner scenarios based on the narrative and experiences an intense, almost physical presence in the narrative. Gumbrecht in particular describes presence as spatial rather than temporal, as appealing to the senses and causing moments of intensity (Gumbrecht 2004).

The students become attuned through formal aspects related to their sensory experience with the three different formats. When asked which senses they use when reading the story in the different formats, they mention sight and hearing in particular in connection with the audiobook: "[I]t was really nice to be sitting there, just listening to the story" (audio, girl). Referring both to the audiobook and digital version, they highlight the sound effects, for example, "the effects are good; they added a good effect to the story" (audio, boy), and the "creepy sounds" which make the story "exciting" (digital, boy). As mentioned earlier, the students often point out the relation between text and picture, for example, "it was a bit funny sometimes where the text was sort of like *in* the pictures, and it was like a comic book" (paper, boy), and "the pictures and the sound effects made it exciting. I mean, there was also music" (girl, digital). In addition, the readers of the digital version stress the interactivity, describing how you could also use "a bit of feeling, because you have to touch the screen sometimes" (digital, boy), and "that it is positive that you have to press some white stars and touch the text" (girl, digital), here referring to an interactive spot where the text "collapses" and the reader can move text fragments, accentuating the disturbed mind of the main character.

Altogether, it is evident that the materiality of the pictures and sounds stimulates interest and is valued positively by the students, and, especially when the expression forms are incorporated in several relations, the students are attentive. For example "there were pages where the text was sort of jumbled and that made it even more exciting. Because it was different than when it just appeared on lines and looked the same all the time, to be read from the top and down. It was more slanting, like" (boy, paper). Generally, the students are often attuned through elements that are linked to the media specificity of the three different formats. The media-specific understanding of literature focuses on the triangulation between form, content, and media (Hayles 2002, 31, Hayles 2004). The students experience intensity and immersion because of the relations between text, picture, and sound, and they become engaged by the multisensory aspects of the narratives, prompting them to read with their senses up front. At the same time, the multisensory aspect of the reading situation provokes feelings and moods which greatly influence their empathy and absorption of the narrative.

Attunement as identification

Next to attunement, Felski describes the second way in which the reader can become attached to literature as identification. Overall, she seeks to refine and defend artwork that is often seen as naïve and sentimental and instead present it as the very soundboard of the reader's attachment. Rather than distancing us from the literary characters by analyzing them objectively, she finds that it is important that we involve ourselves and identify with the characters and use them in relation to our own lives. Parallel to reception theories, Felski draws on the concept "Umwelt" (Felski 2019, 2020, 85 ff) to capture the experience of being related to fictional characters – not only during reading, but as a quality in the form of an acquaintance or a relation the reader carries with him into his everyday life. Felski emphasizes that the reader can relate to many different aspects of a character: "[O]ne can identify with *aspects* of a character, emotions, motivations, beliefs, self-understanding, physical characteristics, experiences, or situation" (Felski 2020a, 82, emphasis in original).

When the students read *Tavs*, they especially identified with the relationship between parents and children and Tavs' vulnerable and lonely situation. One student says:

> I think what is important is that his parents seem not to care that he does not have any friends and that, yes, well, they think only of their careers and do not consider whether he wants to go to for example Japan or not. They do not consider that he does not know the language and so forth. I do not really feel that his relationship to his parents is close. I rather feel that they force him to go and do not really understand how much he really misses his brother when he is all alone all the time (girl, digital).

Another student joins in: "I think the parents – it is like Maria says – it is neglect ... they do not consider the boy's feelings, and that is very interesting" (girl, paper). For the students, it is very much about emotional empathy and identification with the main character and the conditions of his life; they feel an allegiance with him (Felski 2020, 96). Another central element in identification is, according to Felski, recognition (Felski 2008, 2020), which is generally very pronounced in the students' reading. They especially recognize feelings in the narrative: "It is sort of the same feeling Tavs has ... At least it is easy to take something from a book and then maybe not the exact same things happen, because in a book it is often wilder than what you experience yourself" (girl, paper).

Felski enhances the diversity of identification, but one prominent aspect in the students' comments and reflections on their reading of the narrative, which she does not include, is the significance of imagination, defining their experience and empathy/attunement. The following quotes are expressions hereof: "Often, when I read, then I imagine what is happening. For example, when the father says, 'How about you go and hug her.' Then I try to see it in my head. And also where he was sitting in the train and a boy came and tried to take his book – where he then moves – well, then I try to visualize it like that" (girl, digital). "You can imagine having a little fantasy image in your head. When you describe so much about a person, you have a picture of the person you describe" (girl, audio). These two quotes point to the importance and power of imagination and the creation of mental images for the students' experience. Also, imagination is important for the students' empathy and how they relate to the story. One student says, "Yes, I found it sad and a bit ... . You could almost imagine what it was like to lose a brother" (boy, paper).

Attunement as interpretation and existential resonance

The third major way in which the reader can be attached to literature is described by Felski as interpretation, that is, "[i]nterpreting as relating" (Felski 2020, 123). This does not mean establishing poetic, discursive, or historical relations; it means *relating* by involving the reader in the reading through his interests, experiences, sympathies, and identifications and including this involvement in literary studies and humanities. In one of the focus group interviews, three students talk about how they can all relate to the feeling of being alone, different, or missing or having lost someone. One student says that she knows what it is like "to feel alone, because yesterday we were working on planning tomorrow and I found myself in a group where I do not really talk to anyone – there I felt rather: 'Oh, where should I sit,' and so on. I think this is very much the way he [the main character] feels" (girl, digital). Another student continues by saying,"[H]is brother was in Norway, and he is in Tokyo. I recognize this because me and my family we live in Denmark and the rest of my family live in Lithuania, so it is the same" (girl, audio). And a third student agrees: "My parents are divorced, so I often feel as if things are decided without me – it is quite frustrating. And when we have family gatherings in my father's girlfriend's family, I don't know anyone, so who do I talk to? ... Where do I go? I mean, everyone is talking to someone, and I feel ... I just feel left out" (girl, paper). The students recognize the main character's feelings of loneliness and loss from various events in their own lives and interpret the literary text in relation to their own circumstances. The sources and strengths of their identifications are very different, ranging from a specific situation in school the previous day to more general living conditions such as being a bilingual child or a child of divorce. This short conversation and exchange of experiences between the three students also show that even though the identification is emotional, it is also reflecting, as pointed out by Felski (ibid., 98). Attunement as interpretation can be the key to engagement in a text and a chance to gain insight into and perspective on one's own life.

Throughout the interviews, the students recognize feelings and relations between people in the narrative. Many of them draw parallels to their own lives; they especially recognize the relationship between child and parents, for example, the experience that "sometimes your parents just will not listen to you" (girl, paper). Another student relates to the feeling of moving from one country to another and losing friends: "I come from Poland, but if I lived in Norway like Tavs and had to move to Tokyo, then I think that perhaps they should have asked him. Because in a way, he loses his friends, because he had this friend ... that good friend" (girl, digital). For one student, the recognition of feelings and empathy is significant, as the student has experienced death close to home: "That Teo [the dead twin brother], he was sort of ... a creation of death." The student repeats this view of the brother as symbolizing death: "The only ones I might feel a bit sorry for, that was Teo and Tavs. Tavs, he has lost Teo. He wanted him back, but knew that was not possible. But then he got this idea that he could. I felt sad about this, because I ... I have lost my mother. Teo is evil, and somehow he is a creation of death" (boy, digital). According to his teacher, this boy identified with and reflected on the narrative to a surprising degree, which could partly be because he got caught up by the media specificity of the digital narrative – the interplay between text, picture, sound, and interaction – and partly because he recognized the experience of having lost a close relation. For this student, the narrative took on existential resonance.

From what literature states to what it does in a school context

By studying the 12 students' reflections on their reading, partly focusing on their sensory interaction with the three different media versions and partly focusing on their attachment to this particular literary text, a diverse picture emerges where the school context can either promote or impede attunement. An example: "That is why I like to read books. It is because I feel I lose track of time. When you read, you get totally absorbed in it. That is why I got mad when we had to write down notes about every chapter [laughs], because then you had to tear yourself away from it again" (boy, audio). Reading can make you forget yourself, and generally, the students express a high degree of attunement, immersion, and identification in their reading of *Tavs*. This identification is neither naïve nor simple; it may just lead to an experience,"not just of finding oneself but of leaving oneself" (Felski 2020, 83), potentially giving the readers perspectives on something in their own lives. However, by teaching the students formalism and reflection on texts, the school context may distance them from the text and maybe even rob them of their deep reading experience and engagement. With Felski, Gumbrecht, and postcritique, there is potential in a school context to move away from what literature *states* to what it *does* to us as readers and as humans. With reference to Toni Morrison, Gumbrecht describes the affective appeal of literature as being "touched like from inside" (Gumbrecht 2011, 12). It is important to read for meaning and life interpretation AND for mood, feeling, and presence, just as the students in the interviews do. Perhaps literary texts that make use of various expression forms such as text, picture, and sound have a special kind of appeal to the students' empathy and attachment. Felski says, "to become attuned: forms of alignment, a coordinating of senses, affects, bodies, and objects that can happen with or without linguistic support" (2020, 72). Especially sensory and emotional empathy with the text is prominent in the students' reading experiences, as seen in the interviews. One of them says, "it sounds really strange, but sometimes you can sort of feel … or if a person is in a wet place, then you feel it – or if something scary happens, then you get goose bumps or something. Also when something happens, if there is a climax in a book, then I feel really, 'Ah!' I just want to read on, because I want something else to happen. It is like you really have to get to the bottom of this" (girl, paper).

Note

1 The research project Reading Between Media is a collaboration between Aarhus University and VIA University College, Denmark, funded by the Novo Nordisk Foundation.

References

Felski, Rita. 2008. *Uses of Literature.* Malden, Massachusetts, and Oxford: Blackwell Publishing.
Felski, Rita. 2009. *After Suspicion.* In *Profession* 8:_28-35.
Felski, Rita. 2015. *The Limits of Critique.* Chicago: University of Chicago Press.
Felski, Rita. 2019. "Identifying with characters." In *Character. Three Inquiries in Literary Studies*, edited by Amanda Anderson, Rita Felski, and Toril Moi. Chicago and London: University of Chicago Press.
Felski, Rita. 2020a. *Hooked. Art and Attachment.* Chicago and London: University of Chicago Press.
Felski, Rita. 2020b. "Postcritical." In *Further Reading*, edited by Matthew Rubery and Leah Price. Oxford and New York: Oxford University Press.
Gumbrecht, Hans Ulrich. 2004. *Production of Presence: What Meaning Cannot Convey.* Stanford University Press.
Gumbrecht, Hans Ulrich. 2011. *Stimmungen Lesen. Über eine Verdeckte Wirklichkeit Der Literatur.* Munich: Carl Hanser Verlag.
Hansen, Thomas Illum, Elf, Nikolaj Frydensbjerg, Gissel, Stig Toke, and Steffensen, Tom. 2019. "Designing and testing a new concept for inquiry-based literature teaching. Design principles, development and adaptation of a large-scale intervention study in Denmark." *L1-Educational Studies in Language and Literature* 19: 1–32.
Hayles, N. Katherine. 2002. *Writing Machines.* Cambridge, Massachusetts: MIT Press.
Hayles, N. Katherine. 2004. "Print is flat, code is deep: The importance of media-specific analysis." *Poetics Today* 25, no. 1: 67–90.
Hayles, N. Katherine. 2008. *Electronic Literature: New Horizons for The Literary.* University of Notre Dame Press.
Henkel, Ayoe Quist, Mygind, Sarah, and Svendsen, Helle Bundgaard. 2021. "Exploring reading experiences in three media versions: Danish 8th grade students reading the story *Nord*." *L1-Educational Studies in Language and Literature* 21: 1–19.
Hübbe, Camilla, and Meisler, Rasmus. 2012. *Tavs.* Copenhagen: Høst & Søn.
Hübbe, Camilla, and Meisler, Rasmus. 2013. *Tavs.* iPad version. Copenhagen: Høst & Søn.
Løgstrup, Knud Ejler. 2018 (1983). *Kunst og Erkendelse. Metafysik II. Kunstfilosofiske Betragtninger.* Aarhus: Klim.
McGann, Jerome J. 1991. *The Textual Condition.* Princeton University Press.
Oksbjerg, Marianne. 2021. "Undervisning med litteraturlæremidler på mellemtrinnet." PhD diss., Aarhus University.
Rothbauer, Paulette M., Skjerdingstad, Kjell Ivar, McKechnie, Lynne E. F., and Oterholm, Knut, eds. 2016. *Plotting the Reading Experience: Theory / Practice / Politics.* Wilfrid Laurier University Press.
Rørbech, Helle, and Skyggebjerg, Anna Karlskov. 2020. "Concepts of literature in Danish L1-textbooks and their framing of students' reading." *L1-Educational Studies in Language and Literature* 20, no. 2: 1–23.
Skjerdingstad, Kjell Ivar, and Rothbauer, Paulette M. 2016. "Introduction: Plotting the reading experience." In *Plotting the Reading Experience: Theory / Practice / Politics*, edited by Paulette M. Rothbauer, Kjell Ivar Skjerdingstad, Lynne E. F. McKechnie, and Knut Oterholm. Wilfrid Laurier University Press.

Section V
Aesthetics and Digital Reading

Introduction to Section V

When conceptualizing the reading condition, we need to approach the reading act as an experiential process that unfolds in (a particular) time and space. Understanding the reading act as a sensory situation that emerges in part from the affordances of the medium suggests a phenomenological stance for analysis. In this section, we investigate the aesthetics of digital reading through for instance the concept of "aesthetic atmosphere" by the German philosopher Gernot Böhme (2001) and Lutz Koepnick's concept of "resonance" (2021). In particular, the section takes as its point of departure the *situatedness* of digital reading atmospheres as especially decisive in the present digital reading condition. A concrete, physical space that people move through and are affected by becomes part of the situation on new terms when reading takes place via apps, audiobooks, and augmented reality (AR) technologies. When a reader reads a print book, engages with a literary app, or listens to an audiobook, the experience produces an aesthetic situation and a sense of place which we will address in the chapters of this section. Technology in this sense distributes readers on new terms. New reading experiences as well as new reading environments make it necessary to broaden the phenomenological perspective to a more situated and technologically grounded concept of situated experience. A concept that investigates and takes into account which conditions *digitality* creates.

As evident from the previous sections, one of the main focuses of this volume is the role of technology in relation to reading experiences. The digital reading condition must be investigated as an interplay between situational, technological, and relational/aesthetic matter. In this section, this will be reflected on more than one level:

Digital technology is increasing the simultaneity of reading and writing. We read, and at the same time, we are being read by technologies. The relationship between humans and technologies changes alongside our reading habits; humans are increasingly being produced or at least distributed by the technologies that surround us. This is also part of the changing landscape of ways in which we approach texts and, in continuation hereof, our reading habits.

DOI: 10.4324/9781003211662-27

This notion of how technology changes our world as well as our perception can be related to the more affective, distributed sense of subjectivity that we also subscribe to in this section (Kassabian 2013). This is a way of outlining the reading situation as an interplay between text interfaces in several possible media versions, surroundings that affect these texts as well as a reader position that is exposed to the surroundings in a resonant manner. We read and are read in continuous dynamic processes. We could name this interplay between technology, perception, and environments a post-phenomenological position (Ihde 2007), adding the affordances of all three as important actors when discussing reading as meaning production. This section thus focuses on the framing of reading situations produced by the digital condition. We will address the contexts in which reading takes place and the ways in which they affect reading experiences.

The chapter "Situated reading" by Maria Engberg and Birgitte Stougaard Pedersen discusses multisensory aspects of experience and reading and emphasizes the situated, everyday experience of digital reading. It addresses multi- or cross-sensory interactions, which are part of the reading of various digital interfaces as a situated practice. Via sensory autoethnography, the chapter bridges the gap between the aesthetics of experience and a sociological perspective of everyday reading practices. It identifies the characteristics of the everyday digital reading condition in terms of the interplay between technology, everyday behavior, and practices and sensory aspects of how we interact with digital interfaces.

In the chapter "Reading: atmosphere, ambience, and attunement" by Birgitte Stougaard Pedersen, the aspect of *situatedness* or reading context is related to atmosphere via a philosophical approach. The chapter investigates the interplay between environment and reading through the concepts of ambience, attunement, and atmosphere, addressing how these aspects can relate to digital reading or multisensory reading practices in a broader perspective, including and beyond sound studies perspectives. What is the reading context, and how does it relate to, intermingle with, and challenge the reading? In continuation hereof, one of the aspects that we pursue has to do with the way we interpret the production of meaning when accessing texts in contexts. This is done by investigating the interplay between Citton's concepts of figure and ground.

In the chapter "Resonance and the digital conditions of reading," Lutz Koepnick further develops the concept of resonance for the analysis of different modalities of reading, insisting that digital reading takes place in a multisensory complexity of perception and attention. Koepnick discusses the role of digital reading in the landscape of attentional economies of new media, inspired by thoughts on ambient listening and hyper reading. The chapter explores practices of digital reading, reflecting and challenging traditional binaries between active engagement and passive consumption, hereby inviting a general questioning or reframing of prior normative models of reading.

References

Böhme, Gernot. 2001. *Aisthetik: Vorlesungen über Ästhetik als allgemeine Wahrnehmungslehre*. Paderborn, Germany: Wilhelm Fink.

Ihde, Don. 2007. *Listening and Voice – Phenomenologies of Sound*. New York: State University of New York Press.

Kassabian, Annahid. 2013. *Ubiquitous Listening: Affect, Attention, and Distributed Subjectivity*. Berkeley, California: University of California Press.

Koepnick, Lutz. 2021. *Resonant Matter: Sound, Art, and the Promise of Hospitality*. New York: Bloomsbury.

17 Situated reading

Maria Engberg and
Birgitte Stougaard Pedersen

Throughout this book, our focus has been to describe and analyze the changing ways in which reading happens today via digitally mediated devices and interfaces. Likewise, we are interested in understanding the ways in which mediation affects how reading engages the human sensorium and shapes meaning-making, aesthetic experience, and literary engagement. In this section, we shift our gaze to understand how any given situation and place inflect the digital reading condition of these mediated experiences. The aim of the chapter is to delve deeper into what characterizes such concrete everyday situated digital reading experiences, and how digital mediation makes the situation and place of the reading an integral part of the experience. We are inspired by Johanna Drucker, who in her chapter "Sight" asks if "where we read [is] as important in constituting a text as what we read?" (2020, 170). What we call situated reading in this chapter involves analyzing how reading digital texts or audiobooks on the phone happens, and how the domesticated use of smaller digital devices, primarily the smartphone and the tablet, has moved reading into new situations of everyday life. This change is neither new nor drastic, but has occurred incrementally over the past couple of decades. Reflecting on this change, Drucker notes that "what texts *do* and how they *work* is not determined simply by what they say and how they look, but *where* and under what *conditions* they perform their work" (ibid., 167–8, emphasis in the original).

We and our fellow authors in this book have outlined commonalities across digital media devices and apps, along with the multisensory engagements that have become commonplace today. However, it is also in situated moments, described in detail, that we can engage further with individualized media consumption and reading. Situated reading is made up of the combination of media affordances, the ways in which apps and services function, the audiovisual or tactile dimensions of the mediated experiences, and whatever happens around the reader.

In this chapter, we will provide two autoethnographic examples that describe the intricate media choices and modes of consumption that go into digital reading. They show how particular situations and places of reading

DOI: 10.4324/9781003211662-28

impact and influence the reader's understanding of the reading as a whole. Digital technologies allow for an emphasis on the ability to link to the reader's surroundings. Although any narrative can draw upon the time and place of its reading, and of course the readers themselves can have experiences of reading that include memories of where they were when they read the text, these digital narratives seek to draw on place, through location-aware technologies such as global positioning systems (GPS), or situation by pointing toward different sensory modes. In each activity, the situation and place play important active roles.

To actively place a reading activity in a place that matters to the reading has forebears in literature and art. Digital site-specific or situated narratives have continued in this tradition, using the affordances of location awareness in mobile devices. In the audio walks of Janet Cardiff and George Bures Miller (Cardiff and Bures Miller 2022), the experience is intertwined with the reader's movements in space: what you hear and what you see and feel around you is intimately connected, by design. Blast Theory's mixed-media narratives (such as *Rider Spoke* and *Too Much Information*) create an experience in which reading, listening, and exploring the work along with the space in which it is set are part of the overall experience (Blast Theory 2022).

We find it interesting that these mixed-media formats emerge within distinct institutional frames, the artworld on one side and a literary community on the other, though they actually share a number of properties and qualities.

Literary works that query the function of narrative through experimentation with form can of course be seen as esoteric or highbrow. However, smartphones and tablets have radically changed what kinds of mediated experiences are possible, and experimental art and mainstream literary services and apps are starting to resemble one another. Also, the institutional and format borders increasingly start to mingle, for instance, the release of a podcast service by the music streaming platform Spotify and streaming services providing audiobooks via infrastructure formerly belonging to channels of music (Have and Stougaard Pedersen 2019, Sullivan 2019).

Before moving on to autoethnographic descriptions of everyday reading situations, Michael Bull's perspectives on listening practices in urban spaces from 2007 can provide an interesting point of departure and a testament to how social media platforms have transformed media practices in a relatively short time period. In his studies of audio culture and mobile listening practices, Bull underlines the risk of creating physical and cognitive listening bubbles that potentially isolate the music listener. He saw the iPod culture of the first century of the new millennium as "changing the way we perceive our social environment" (Bull 2007, 40–1). From a position within sound studies, Bull pointed to the interplay between private and public created by iPods as mobile devices. These oscillating movements between social and individual, public and private have only continued as both media technologies and social platforms have evolved, and our media consumption patterns along with them.

Bull's studies positioned the act of listening to music in a public space, leading to what he in 2007 called aural solipsism. Since then, a number of scholars have revised or nuanced Bull's position, including Gram (2012) who claims that listening to music in a public space may indeed intensify the listener's experience of the given milieu (ibid., 113). Have and Stougaard Pedersen (2016) point to the potential *relationality* toward the surroundings that audiobook reading in public spaces can bring about. Reversely, Mack Hagood highlights the possibilities of sonic self-control in *Hush: Media and Sonic Self-Control* (2019), in which he suggests that these sonic "microspaces of freedom" away from disturbing sounds are part of what drives a lot of our use of digital media technologies, what he calls "orphic media" (ibid., 2–3). In all these scholarly accounts, the listening moves beyond the mediated experience itself and seeps into the experience of the world.

One thing that has changed since Bull wrote about iPod culture is, of course, that we no longer use iPods. Today, almost every person carries a smartphone, and on that smartphone a huge number of activities are available. People use their phones for all sorts of communication and media consumption, not least through social media platforms. And as Jason Farman has noted (2015), storytelling with mobile media has transformed how we "produce and practice space" (ibid., 1).

All in all, we communicate more, on a number of platforms, in almost every space that we move through daily. Moreover, we communicate and document our reading experiences digitally. For instance, we post pictures of our latest reading experiences on Instagram, we rate them on Goodreads, and we discuss whether one performing narrator is better than another in audiobook communities on Facebook.

In describing commonplace, yet particular and situated reading experiences, we employ auto-ethnography and a sensory ethnographic approach that attends to the "sensory embodied and affective routines of everyday life" (Pink and Leder Mackley 2013, 678). Putting into words what happens during a reading experience can be particularly difficult, anecdotally or in an empirical research context. In order to bridge the gap between an individually perceived intellectual, emotional, and sensory experience and the apparatus – the text, images, sounds, etc. – of that experience and attend to the situation in which it takes place, we draw on Sarah Pink's understanding of sensory ethnography as "a way of approaching the world that accounts for the ways in which we are emplaced – that is, how we are part of the everyday environments in which we live, how we perceive these environments and how we contribute to their constitution (2015, 118). Here, we focus on the particular situation and environment of digital reading, and the auto-ethnographic stance allows us to "consider ways others may experience similar epiphanies; [auto-ethnographers] must use personal experience to illustrate facets of cultural experience, and in so doing, make characteristics of a culture familiar for insiders and outsiders" (Ellis, Adams, and Bochner 2011, 276).

Reading situations

Reading on the phone I: ubiquitous reading

Birgitte: When I read *Beautiful World, Where Are You* (2021) by Sally Rooney, my entire reading, as usual these days, took place on my phone via the streaming service Mofibo, which is a part of Storytel. For some time, Amazon and others allowed you to choose an extra feature when ordering an e-book that made it possible to switch between e- and audiobook. Today, the possibility of continuously switching between text and audio is embedded in most new titles as a default on streaming services such as Mofibo and Storytel.

You can press either "listen" or "read" every time you open the app. You are able to switch throughout the reading, and the app keeps track of your bookmarks. What type of reading does this produce and afford? For me, the act of reading becomes even more ubiquitous, flexible, and varied, accommodating the rhythms and routines of a typical day. When I go to work in the morning, I either go by train, by bike, or by car. For all these types of transport, the audiobook works perfectly. When I go for a longer walk in the afternoon, find time to do some knitting, or cook dinner at night, the audiobook is the natural and preferred choice, as it allows me to do other things while listening. At night and in the morning, I enjoy reading e-books in bed with the lights dimmed.

Almost all my audio reading is conducted while I am engaged in other activities. Some are calm – driving a car or knitting – while others are more bodily varied – bicycling, walking, cooking. These reading experiences take place in different situations, and they draw on diverse sensory engagements – engagements that affect the way I experience the literary narrative. The audiobook and the e-book mutually influence each other. For instance, the voice of the performing narrator is central to the audiobook experience. The performing narrator of Rooney's novel on Audible is Aoife McMahon; in the Danish version it is Sicilia Gadborg Høegh. The English version is read in a fast tempo, and it is relatively dramatized. The voice performance is very professional and dramaturgically varied (Ihde 2007). Her diction has a rather varied pitch level, and she changes her voice slightly when shifting between the novel's narrators, Eileen, Simon, Alice, and Felix. Felix is performed with a rather deep and rough voice. The performing narrator applies a clear Irish dialect in direct speech and a more general, speaking voice in other parts.

Intriguingly, as I continuously switch between e- and audiobook, the voice of the performing narrator stays with me in some sense when I open the e-book app at night. The small pages on my phone illuminating the dark room take on a sense of the rhythm and tone of the performing narrator's voice. The letters on the digital interface are delivered to me with an auditive resonance. I hear an echo of the sound of the speaking voice while I read, and new dialogues between the imagined physical voice and the voice of the text itself emerge.

Mobile places and digital reading practices

As the reading situation described above exemplifies, digital audio is becoming more and more important as a reading medium. When presenting audiobook research to research communities in different parts in the world, we have noticed that the discussion always becomes lively and passionate. This is because many audience members want to share details from their personal audiobook experiences. Often, in these lively and engaging accounts, the voice of a specific performing narrator is described in detail, or the reading situation is discussed. Moments like, "whenever I drive along this specific turn in the road on my way home, I know exactly where I was in the audiobook that I listened to while turning just there." The audiobook, the voice, and the narrative details amalgamate with the place and the landscape, and the memory hereof remains part of the embodied sensory memory of the lived experience. This can of course also be the case with printed book experiences. However, the way the moving body participates in audiobook reading in some ways intensifies the synesthetic meaning-making processes, and the multisensory aspects of reading in such mediated situations create new modes of reading and remembering.

The meeting between audio reading experiences and localities and landscapes sometimes results in a specific atmosphere that sticks to a place. A kind of resonance emerges, Koepnick (2021) argues, in which places, words, and voice are entangled. The Danish poet Morten Søndergaard finds that after having listened to poetry while cutting fruit trees, the poems were left hanging in the trees. To support this observation, cultural geographers often talk about rhythm and places of mobility on different levels. In *Geographies of Rhythm* (2010), Tim Edensor suggests that "regular rhythms of mobility […] produce a sense of mobile place" (2010, 6), a sense which is embodied, material, and sociable, or, in Scheller and Urry's words, a "dwelling-in-motion" (quoted in Edensor 2010, 6). In this sense, mobile activities can create rhythms that are both experienced as floating and spatial at the same time. The experience of a mobile place can also create a sense of place via the transport itself, that is the rhythm of the body walking, the circular movements of your legs forcing the bike to move, or the rhythm of the train moving through the landscape (ibid.).

Reading on the phone II: networked reading

Maria: Networked media allow reading to be shared and brought into conversation with other readers' experiences. While I read a novel by Colson Whitehead on my Kindle app, I can look at popular highlights to see what passages of the text have resonated with other readers, and I can add my own notes and highlights. Before I started reading the novel, I had read some reviews in magazines and newspapers (in digital and print forms) as well as on the social networking site devoted to reading, Goodreads, now a subsidiary of Amazon. There I could choose between more than 3,500 reviews on this particular novel (in January 2022) and over 60,000 reviews and comments on the author's works. These networked reading practices are digitally remediated and amped-up versions of non-digital social practices – the digital equivalent of a book club, only much larger and with drastically wider reach. This awareness of being able not only to access works online, but to get relevant information or connect with other readers with relative ease is part of the digital reading condition today, even if not every reader chooses to take part. There are other, more distinctly situated, networked forms of digital reading. With GPS, Wi-Fi, and other location-awareness components, my smartphone and tablet can pinpoint where I am when I read on them.

As part of a research project exploring the potentials and pitfalls of digital archives, I cooperated with colleagues from art history, philosophy, and design on creating a semi-fictional, semi-historical narrative based on the life of a young girl in early 20th-century Copenhagen called *Finding Alberta* (Engberg 2017). The work is reminiscent of the by now many historical narratives, published on webpages or via apps, that use smartphone location awareness, primarily GPS, together with digitized cultural heritage material. While active, *Finding Alberta* used the reader's GPS coordinates to bring sections of the narrative forward, and when I started the application and looked at the first screens, the digitally mediated narrative of young Alberta's arduous life in the very streets of Copenhagen where I found myself standing provided an evocative layering. Of course, the urban environment in which I found myself was very different from that of the book, but there was something intriguing and almost ghost-like about seeing the house in which she first stayed right in front of me. As the app urged me to move toward the next point in the narrative, to the next place in the city, I was forced to take into account the interplay between history and the current cityscape, and Alberta's narrative took on a dual interpretative dimension of familiarity, on the one hand, because of my own physical sensation of being in the same street, and distance, on the other, because of the difference in time between her reality and mine.

Everyday reading, time, and *relationality*

At the start of this chapter, we outlined the aim of exploring how digital mediation reinforces the relation between the situation and place of the reading and the reading material as such. This *relationality* is described in the "Reading on the phone" examples above, and although they are individual and anecdotal, they resonate with the broader digital reading condition.

Reading experiences such as these are highly dependent on the particular milieu as well as technological affordances and of course the texts that are read. Our examples focus on the relation between technology, literary content, and everyday situations and to a lesser degree reflect upon the *relationality* between the reading subject and the environment. From the point of view of "aural solipsism" in Michael Bull's sense, the ways in which we make the world around us our own through the sounds we bring to it, there is a continued need to understand how this affects digital reading. Does the act of reading, digitally mediated, reach out toward the surroundings? Or, as print novels have been viewed historically, are such reading acts a way for us to withdraw from our surroundings and other people? What we argue here is that digital technologies often create fluid and changing reading situations. For instance, readers of mobile digital interfaces, such as audiobooks or augmented reality-based literary works, reach out toward and become enriched by the smells, sights, sounds, and tactile qualities of the surroundings. However, audiobook reading can also be a way to block off the sounds of the surroundings and immerse ourselves in a different sonic space.

Mobile media continue to confound and question the notions of private and public spaces and the activities associated with them, and digital reading practices become part of such discussions. You can read in every small interval of your everyday life, you can transform the otherwise "lost time" of a commute into "quality time," and the mundane experience of doing the dishes after dinner can become an immersed reading experience. The criticism that one can level against this view of digital audio reading is that it poses that reading experiences need to be convenient and sleek moments of multitasking, which ensure that we exploit every possible moment of our day in the most efficient way (see also Chapter 12).

No matter whether we view these heterogeneous reading activities as part of a larger condition of digital culture or as a fundamental transformation of the cultural practice of reading in general, they are becoming ubiquitous (see also Chapter 19) and require that researchers reflect on them. Such reflections include understanding how they affect the other activities of our everyday lives as well as our reading routines. The situational aspect of reading acts prompts reflection and shifting scholarly attention because of the medialization and digitization of literary systems as a whole. Once the marriage of reading and the printed book no longer seems as naturalized as it still does today, perhaps we can begin in earnest to reflect on how and in which situations we read.

References

Blast Theory. 2022. "Blast theory." Blast Theory. https://www.blasttheory.co.uk/.
Bull, Michael. 2007. *Sound Moves: iPod Culture and Urban Experience.* New York: Routledge.

Cardiff, Janet, and Bures Miller, George. 2022. "Janet Cardiff & George Bures Miller." https://cardiffmiller.com/.
Drucker, Johanna. 2020. "Sight." In *Further Reading*, edited by Matthew Rubery and Leah Price, 167–178. Oxford: Oxford University Press.
Edensor, Tim (Ed.). 2010. *Geographies of Rhythm: Nature, Place, Mobilities and Bodies*. London: Routledge.
Ellis, Carolyn, Adams, Tony E., and Bochner, Arthur P. 2011. "Autoethnography: An overview." *Historical Social Research / Historische Sozialforschung* 36, no. 4 (138): 273–290.
Engberg, Maria. 2017. "Augmented and mixed reality design for contested and challenging histories." Museums and the web, Cleveland, Ohio, January 30, 2017. https://mw17.mwconf.org/paper/augmented-and-mixed-reality-design-for-contested-and-challenging-histories-postcolonial-approaches-to-site-specific-storytelling.
Farman, J. 2014. "Storytelling with mobile media: Exploring the intersection of site-specificity, content, and materiality." In *The Routledge Companion to Mobile Media*, edited by Gerard Goggin & Larissa Hjorth, 528–537. New York: Routledge.
Gram, Nina. 2012. "Når musikken virker," PhD diss., Aarhus University.
Hagood, Mack. 2019. *Hush: Media and Sonic Self-Control*. Durham, North Carolina: Duke University Press.
Have, Iben, and Stougaard Pedersen, Birgitte. 2016. *Digital Audiobooks. New Media, Users and Experiences*. New York: Routledge.
Have, Iben, and Stougaard Pedersen, Birgitte. 2019. "The audiobook circuit in digital publishing: Voicing the silent revolution." *New Media & Society* 22, no. 3: 409–428.
Ihde, Don. 2007. *Listening and Voice – Phenomenologies of Sound*. New York: State University of New York Press.
Koepnick, Lutz. 2021. Resonant Matter: Sound Art and the Aesthetics of Vibration (New Approaches to Sound, Music, and Media): Sound, Art, and the Promise of Hospitality. Bloomsbury Academic.
Kukkonen, Karin. 2021. "Reading, fast and slow." *Poetics Today – Modes of Reading* 42, no 2.
Pink, Sarah. 2015. *Doing Sensory Ethnography*. 2nd ed. London: Sage.
Pink, Sarah, and Kerstin Leder Mackley. 2013. "Saturated and situated: Expanding the meaning of media in the routines of everyday life." *Media, Culture & Society* 35, no 6:677–691. 10.1177/0163443713491298.
Sullivan, John L. 2019. "The platforms of podcasting: Past and present." *Social Media & Society* 5, no. 4. 10.1177/2056305119880002.

18 Reading: atmosphere, ambience, and attunement

Birgitte Stougaard Pedersen

This chapter will discuss the interplay between environment and reading through the concepts of attunement, atmosphere, and the ambient, addressing how such situational and affective aspects of interaction with the surroundings relate to and shape digital or multisensory reading practices. The chapter, through philosophical reflections, proposes modes of communication that reconfigure the interplay between reader and context in the reading experience, enhancing the dynamic interplay between figure and ground.

The concept of attunement, originally stemming from developmental psychology (Stern 1985), has recently gained popularity within sound studies (Koldkær Højlund 2017, Thibaud 2017), and it describes the ways in which we engage with, produce knowledge from, or otherwise tune in to sounding environments. Within literary studies, Rita Felski develops the concept from a different angle in her recent book, *Hooked* (2020), also presented in Chapter 16. Gernot Böhme's concept of atmospheres designates a phenomenological approach to studies of the surroundings' qualitative character, dealing with how we connect to moods around us (Böhme 2001). In this chapter, I wish to test three concepts – attunement, atmosphere, and the ambient – against a reading situation, expanding the use of the concepts beyond sound studies and concrete architectural spaces. Ambient concerns a certain kind of character of the surroundings, a type of perception that is inattentive, a background character, or a subliminal affect (Schmidt 2013). This concept is important for understanding multisensory reading, for instance, audiobook reading or reading literary apps. The chapter will also reflect on the genre of ambient literature, literary works that are site-specific and interactive regarding sensory aspects.

As we can learn from Johanna Drucker, a lot of texts are read *"in the landscape,* an environment whose specific qualities are also, arguably, integrated into the productive reading of the work" (Drucker 2020, 169–70, emphasis in the original). Sound studies often emphasize the auditory environment as decisive for our being and attention toward inhabiting concrete sounding spaces. How are these auditory aspects essential parts of a reading situation? Reading always happens in a context, and the three concepts discussed in this chapter all address and enhance, in different

DOI: 10.4324/9781003211662-29

ways, the importance of milieu-related aspects of meaning-making processes. These can relate to both places, media, and bodily interactions and all take part in renegotiating the importance and dynamic shifts between what we scientifically could call figure and ground.

Figure and ground in context

Experiencing environments always involves processes of perceptually organizing the elements of this environment. There will be things that remain in the background, the sound of rain or the distant sound of traffic from the ring road. There will also be things that you cannot avoid paying attention to, the sound of an ambulance, the huge advertisement with its salience-producing effect. Late capitalism is always looking for new ways of producing attention in what has been called the economy of attention. When we pay attention to something, we extract figures from the ground. The French philosopher Yves Citton calls for a counter response to this striving for attention, pleading for an aesthetics that pays attention to the ground as ground. His idea is that if we shift sense regimes from the hegemony of *visuality*, which is discussed in Chapter 5, to the auditory, the olfactory, or the senses of taste, this figure/ground relationship will appear less hierarchic, will form a closer, multi-sensory interplay between figure and ground, giving attention to "the ground as ground" (Citton 2023 forthcoming).

Imagine a situation including this relationship of figure and ground: you are sitting on the train reading a printed book, experiencing the (very physical) noise of the person opposite you snoring, or the noise coming from another passenger's headphones close by. It may disturb your concentration, making the bubble of immersed reading somewhat porous. However, you could also regard the friction of the surroundings as something not solely disturbing your bubble, but as a part of the reading experience that is possibly enriching it. How do we perceive the qualitative aspects of the ground as ground? The notion of presenting context as noise can be found in the canonized model of communication by Shannon and Weaver from 1949, a mathematical model that has been used to develop a theory of communication by arguing that human communication can be reduced to six key aspects: sender, encoder, channel, noise, decoder, and receiver. The reason why I introduce this early model of communication to the general discussion on relationships between figure and ground is that it regards context as *noise*.

Calling the context noise, which is the argument that I wish to draw attention to in this chapter – both to clarify and to challenge – builds on a linear idea of communication processes. Noise in these ideas of communication can disturb the otherwise "perfectly" transmitted decoding process of information. Of course, in later communication models, context is included, for instance in Stuart Hall's model. And from the 1980s and 1990s, sociological aspects as well as updated concepts of subjectivity as performed or distributed in poststructuralist thinking and gender studies have been taken into account when discussing communication. This seems further intensified when the digital era makes it necessary to include the aspect of interactivity or to produce an increasingly dynamic relation between text, interface, and user.

The way in which we conceptualize the reading experience in this volume explicitly aims to enhance the reading process or reading rhythms as a dynamic interplay between (1) the technological interface, (2) the meaning of the text itself (if one such exists), (3) the reader, and (4) the specific context. Attunement, ambience, and atmosphere might foreground the importance of "ground aspects" of a communication situation, pointing explicitly to qualitative aspects of the situational space of experience.

The purpose of this chapter is thus, by foregrounding the "ground as ground" (Citton forthcoming 2023), to enhance the singular, dynamic, and qualitative aspects of a reading situation. I hereby consider the relations between technology, reader, and situation, between figure and ground, as increasingly renegotiated and intensified. And I enhance the importance of the multisensory aspect of perception. Including the situation as such when discussing reading experiences, the multisensory aspects of for instance the auditory or olfactory aspects of perception might to a lesser degree create static and hierarchical figure/ground relationships.

Experiencing the surroundings while reading can appear disruptive. However, taking in the experience of the surroundings as part of the reading can also, if we expand the idea of reading beyond that of a solely hermeneutic process, create a productive friction that actually adds to and changes the aesthetic and bodily aspects as well as the cultural hierarchies of the reading experience.

In this chapter, I wish to propose an alternative way of outlining the multisensory reading experience, placing the distributed subject in a central position and thereby enhancing the reading situation, turning it into a potentially productive, atmospheric, or resonant space (Koepnick 2019, 2021). Here, I bring Koepnick's idea of resonance into dialogue with Yves Citton, who in *The Ecology of Attention* (2017) points to the complexity of reading rhythms:

> The assertion that I never pay attention alone can [...] be understood in two very different ways. It may indicate [...] that even when I seem to be alone looking at the page of a book, newspaper or website, which is absorbing my attention, this is the result of a very complex interplay of media enthrallment, selective alignments [...] profit-hunger and the will to resist. [...] But it may also designate a collection of more specific, localized situations, where I know I am not alone in the place in which I find myself, and where my consciousness of the attention of others affects the orientation of my own attention.
>
> (Citton 2017, 83)

Reading rhythms emerge in increasingly complex situations and are made up of a number of interests and levels of attention; thus, the reading context becomes more and more interesting to study, as also stated by both Pryce and Rubery (2020) and Drucker (2020). The surroundings interact with the reading process in feedback loops, to use a term from the German theater scholar Erika Fischer-Lichte. However, the reading "subject" of our mode of situated reading does not appear to be essentialist in Fischer-Lichte's sense. On the contrary. The reading subject is an affective body distributed by technology, human interaction, and place.

Reading can take place via the ears, sight, the body moving, and touch. In most cases, we read with several senses, as we have touched upon in previous chapters (5, 7, and 8). I will now proceed to exploring multisensory reading by sketching three different imagined contextualized reading situations that can help develop a reconfigured mode of the digital reading condition.

First reading situation

You hear the screams of seagulls, as you stand close to the river and read the story on your smartphone screen accompanied by the seagull-sound effects in your in-ear headphones. When you walk away from the spot, the story on the screen disappears, and you enter into new areas where new stories emerge on your screen, as does music which appears and disappears while you move. This is a glimpse of James Attlee's work, *The Cartographer's Confession*, a piece of ambient literature from 2017, which combines fiction and non-fiction and locative digital technology on the physical locations of the riverbank near Tate Modern in central London.

Ambient literature performs the reading situation per se as ongoing digital and embodied feedback loops. As Amy Spencer puts it in her article "Reading Ambient Literature: Immersion, Distraction, and the Situated Reading Experience" (2021), "[a] work of ambient literature is a situated literary experience delivered by a pervasive computing platform, such as a smartphone, that responds to the presence of a physically present reader to deliver a story" (Spencer 2021, 299). Ambient literature as a genre involves and engages its reader in a singular, specific context and uses this context as well as digital technology as a driver in the story. In some examples, ambient works also engage with all kinds of data surrounding the reader, and "in some works of ambient literature walking can become a narrative feature of the work, and a reader becomes physically engaged in a work (Spencer 2021, 299)" This is the case in *The Cartographer's Confession* by James Attlee (2017), introduced above (Figure 18.1).

The work consists of an app that includes music, sound effects, visuals, and texts. It presents itself in a geographically distributed number of stories about different 20th-century events – historically linked to specific places near the south bank of the Thames River in London. The reader becomes an embodied co-creator of the work, carrying her smartphone around the area

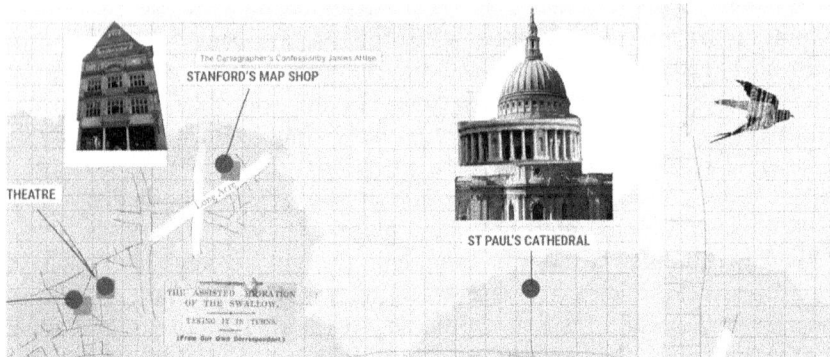

Figure 18.1 A screenshot from *The Cartographer's Confession* by James Attlee, Illustration by Grace Attlee, App producer: Emma Whittaker.

of Tate Modern and Borough Market in Central London, via GPS technology tapping into specific stories related to the locations she passes by.

The reading situation is multisensory in every sense, as an inherent part of a book's or app's affordances. You need to move around, you need to be in place to get the full output of the story, just as you have to read texts visually, listen to the sounds of the river, the birds, and the jazzy background music of the artifact.

Second reading situation

Imagine this reading situation: you are reading the audiobook *Outline* by Rachel Cusk (2018). You read via your earbuds while walking in the same area – the busy bank of the River Thames. The novel has an interesting narrative strategy not really presenting the antagonist to the reader. We do not really get to know the person telling the story; we experience her descriptions of meetings and dialogues with a number of people, and by her way of unfolding these characters we implicitly get to know her. However, in a way, she remains an outline to the reader. The plot or storyline of this book is not easy to hold on to while listening in the city. In that sense, the sounds of tourists passing by and the street musicians playing in front of Tate Modern create a kind of friction that makes it difficult to follow the plot. But do we really need to understand this as noise? Can the ambient character of the soundscape contribute to the atmosphere of the reading experience? There is no doubt that it affects the way you tune into the novel. The text is unfolding close sensory descriptions, just as the author paraphrases detailed conversations. The text is affected by the way I as a listener in a concrete situation tune into the voice of the performing narrator, creating a mood or an immersed sense of the situation as a whole.

Third reading situation

You are sitting on a bench in front of Tate Modern reading the same book – in a printed, paperback version. The place, the smells, and the background noise of people talking and laughing plus the jazzy tune of the saxophone player also become part of this reading situation. The boundaries between foreground and background are more apparent. I concentrate on the act of reading, my body is not moving, the sounds and smells around me remain liminal background phenomena, though they are still vibrant parts of my reading experience. And, similar to the tableau regarding the audiobook experience, the sense of this specific, singular place and this particular novel will forever be linked in my memory.

How can we describe this attunement, atmosphere, and ambient character from a theoretical point of view? The concepts arise from related, yet distinct disciplinary perspectives.

Attunement

The concept of attunement in sound studies deals with how we perceptually adjust to the auditory qualities of specific surroundings. In this sense, attunement is relational. Daniel Sterne talks about affective attunement as a non-verbal tuning into the surroundings. According to Sterne, attunement has to do with emotional resonance and is primarily an intersubjective matter. This outline of affect attunement enhances the subjective approach to communication situations while also conceptualizing affect as something that is related to subjective emotional states, which differs from the affective register outlined in for instance Brian Massumi's notion of affect (2002). Rita Felski's discussion of attunement takes place in a different arena, not as a psychological concept, but relating to the affective turn in theory. According to Felski, attunement related to reading deals with a responsive relation between reader and text, a relation that underlines aspects of presence instead of reading for meaning. The "howness" of reading is substituted by an appeal to the senses or "moments of intensity" (Felski 2020, 67–8; see Chapter 16).

Within sound studies, the concept of attunement designates an evaluation of listening experience – how do listening subjects tune into specific sounding surroundings.

How can we translate this to something that can be as observed and described related to the process of digital and multisensory reading? Attunement can possibly be productive as a metaphor for experiencing multisensory digital literary interfaces. The idea is that attunement create affects that take part in the knowledge production and reading experience regarding time, awareness, and attention.

Attunement deals with how inner rhythms act in correspondence with rhythms of the setting. In the reading experience, the rhythms of the body, the rhythms of the text, as well as the rhythms of the surroundings are put into vibration. They can create friction, and they can intensify one another. The attuning activity performs relational aspects of the situation. How does the reader tune into the story in the setting? The three examples embody attunement on different conditions: the ambient piece of literature in itself creates a rhythm of the body walking – just as it deliberately uses sound effects and music to create a certain and designed sonic mood that the reader can attune into. Both regarding the audiobook and the printed book, reading in this situation can be performed in a number of different settings. You can lie down on the lawn outside Tate Modern and listen to the audiobook with your eyes closed, or you can walk along the river and these modes will affect the way you attune into the story world. The printed version does not allow you to walk or to close your eyes. However, the sounding as well as the olfactory aspects can still make your attunement in one reading situation differ from your attunement in another reading situation. The attunement concentrates on a subject's or receiver's correspondence with surroundings; it enhances the *relationality* of the multisensory reading experience.

Atmosphere

In Gernot Böhme's phenomenological approach to the study of atmosphere, the concept designates the way we connect to and interact with moods around us as non-linguistic dimensions of expressions or surroundings (2001). In that sense, atmosphere also has to do with the relations between subject and surroundings in a given situation. However, comparing the concept to attunement, atmosphere can be present in a space when you enter it. The atmosphere of a poetry slam event differs from the atmosphere of a poetry reading; it performs differentiated cultural values and habits that affect the specific atmosphere. According to Böhme, an atmosphere is not a product of a subject's projections of inner sentiments to the surroundings; it belongs to the experience of a concrete space. Can the experienced space of reading an audiobook during a walk create an atmosphere? The atmosphere will be subjectively experienced, and in this sense the audiobook reading situation creates a singular meeting between a changing sense of place, a body that may be moving around, and a specific literary interface.

Listening to Rachel Cusk while walking around London attunes us to a specific mood that we can be pulled into – because we become immersed in this specific story and its literary style in a specific sensory situation. This space can in itself have a touch of a certain feeling; however, the feeling derives from the meeting between the story, the interface, the listener's movements and mood, and the surroundings. Atmospheres are attuned spaces, and they are, according to Böhme, a "quasi-subjective" phenomenon as well as a spatial quality of the surroundings. The genre of ambient literature has to a wide extent created and designed a multisensory atmosphere, deliberately producing a combination of movement of the body, visuals, sound, and specific geographical places. In that sense, it creates a specific, designed atmosphere where the sensorial interplay is choreographed. What acts as figure and ground in the experience of ambient literature is to a certain degree part of the design. For instance, the sound of a seagull calling creates a certain sense-of-sea feeling, which adds to the ambient atmosphere.

Ambience

Ambience also designates a spatial concept. However, the ambient part of the atmosphere enhances parts of our sensory attention that usually slumber unconsciously in the background of our perceptive apparatus.

The noun form of the concept, ambience, is often related to concrete, physical architectural settings (Thibaud 2017), while its adjective form, ambient, is related to aspects of a musical style or genre. An ambient experience can be described as a qualitative perception that is inattentive, a background character that has subliminal affect (Schmidt 2013).

Ambient reading can be related to multisensory reading, for instance when dealing with the character of the reader's interaction with the surroundings while reading, how figure and ground change places in ongoing dynamic processes. Ambient literature is a named genre-producing artifacts that combine digital interfaces with possible mobile reading experiences and specific places, as presented earlier.

In the audiobook experience, the sound of the voice reading to you via your earbuds is the main sensorial input. However, the reading situation can attune to the voice, just as the voice can attune to the surroundings. The audiobook reading atmosphere appears dynamic when it comes to the experience of figure and ground.

The sound of people talking in the background while you are reading the printed version of *Outline* can correlate with or increase affective aspects of the aesthetic experience without you being aware of this. It can be annoying, but it can also amplify your investment in the people the novel introduces you to. Compared to the audiobook reading experience, the figure/ground constellations of reading a printed book can in most cases be said to seem more stable, since your senses appear more fixed qua the body's reading position.

In both reading experiences, the ambient character of the surroundings can influence an affective register without the reader noticing, a sensory engagement that can correlate with the use of underscore music in TV series and documentaries (Have 2008). It creates an affective force and direction in your reading. In that sense, the "ambient" corresponds to the experience of *an affective quality* of the surroundings.

Figure/ground reconfigured

I have now outlined how these concepts can help us characterize multisensory reading experiences. I will in the following sketch possible operational distinctions between them: Which of the concepts deal with the surroundings primarily, and which deal with the subject attuning her attention to something?

In taking the qualitative aspects of multisensory reading experiences into account we need to highlight the interplay with the surroundings on different levels of intensity as well as the differentiated and dynamic interplays between subject, object, and milieu as well as between what is experienced as foreground and background, respectively. In this outline or mode of reading – in continuation of Shannon Weaver – "noise" is considered an important and meaning-producing component of the reading experience.

Building on the knowledge we have gained from the concepts of attunement, atmosphere, and the ambient, I do not propose an alternative model of communication, rather I enhance and address how attunement deals with classical phenomenological aspects of an experience that takes place in a context. The reading situation takes attunement into account as performing continuous emotional feedback loops between the reader, the text, and the surroundings, hereby concentrating on the reader's distributed and dynamic correspondence with these surroundings. The atmosphere of the reading situation is a more democratic concept, dealing with the interplay of context, receiver, and text, and it is experienced as a more stable spatial quality of the surroundings. The ambient is an affective quality that colors an engagement in the reading situation, but often remains subliminal.

The multisensory reading situation consists of a number of entities that are less stable and more fluent than the entities in the traditional, historical models of communication. The reader acts as a distributed subject, and this places the reader in a more porous position, also formed and produced by technologies. On the one hand, this chapter points to the reader as the central position for studying multisensory reading experiences, but at the same time, we phase out the privileged subject position and, as a result hereof, the certainty of the relations between reader and surroundings and between figure and ground. Yves Citton proposes that we focus our attention on the ground as ground, and that we need to rethink attention in relation to aesthetics. Knowing and acknowledging this, I have outlined the central positions of an oscillating mode of communication, where ground as ground is "foregrounded" as having severe meaning for reading experiences. However, the elusiveness of the interplay between reader, interface, and surroundings suggests that multisensory reading is performed through attunement, atmosphere, and the ambient, in itself questioning the idea of models as such.

This chapter has sought to operationalize the three theoretical concepts which to different extents take the dynamic interplay between the surroundings, channel, reception, and technology into account, investigating how we can conceptualize and process multisensory reading experiences. When enhancing the distributed meaning-creating aspects of the surroundings, qualifying the aspect of "noise," the chapter outlines how feedback loops tap into the decoding process and reverb to the transmitting agent. The language of the ground as ground has been foregrounded, hereby underlining the importance of rhythmic, affective interplays between the reader and the surroundings in every single multisensory reading experience.

References

Attlee, James. 2017. *The Cartographer's Confession*. https://apps.apple.com/gb/app/the-cartographers-confession/id1263461799.
Böhme, Gernot. 2001. *Aisthetik: Vorlesungen über Ästhetik als allgemeine Wahrnehmungslehre*. Paderborn, Germany: Wilhelm Fink.
Citton, Yves. 2017. *The Ecology of Attention*. Cambridge: Polity Press.
Citton, Yves. Forthcoming 23. "Automatizing attention vs. a public right to hear." *The Aesthetics of Attention*. Special Issue of *Nordic Journal of Aesthetics*. No 65.
Cusk, Rachel. 2018. *Outline*. Faber & Faber Fiction.
Drucker, Johanna. 2020. "Sight." In *Further Reading*, edited by Matthew Rubery and Leah Price, 167–178. Oxford, UK: Oxford University Press.
Felski, Rita. 2020. *Hooked. Art and Attachment*. Chicago & London: The University of Chicago Press.
Frandsen, Finn. 2013. "Kommunikationsmodeller." Medie- og Kommunikationsleksikon. Samfundslitteratur. https://medieogkommunikationsleksikon.dk/kommunikationsmodeller/.
Gumbrecht, Hans Ulrich. 2003. *The Production of Presence*. Redwood City, California: Stanford University Press.
Gumbrecht, Hans Ulrich. 2012. *Atmosphere, Mood, Stimmung: On a Hidden Potential of Literature*. Redwood City, California: Stanford University Press.
Hall, Stuart. 1973/1980. "Encoding/decoding in the television discourse." In *Stencilled Occasional Papers* 1973–75, no. 7. Centre for Contemporary Cultural Studies, University of Birmingham.
Have, Iben. 2008. *Lyt til TV*. Aarhus, Denmark: Aarhus University Press.
Howes, David. 2005. *Empire of The Senses: The Sensual Culture Reader*. New York and Oxford: Berg.
Howes, David. 2011. "Hearing scents, tasting sights: Toward a cross-cultural multimodal theory of aesthetics." In *Art and the Senses*, edited by Francesca Bacci and David Melcher, 161–181. Oxford: Oxford University Press.
Howes, David. 2019. "Multisensory anthropology." *Annual Review of Anthropology* 48, no. 1: 17–28. 10.1146/annurev-anthro-102218-011324.
Howes, David, and Classen, Constance. 2014. *Ways of Sensing: Understanding the Senses in Society*. New York: Routledge.
Ihde, Don. 2007. *Listening and Voice: Phenomenologies of Sound*. 2nd ed. Albany, New York: State University of New York Press.
Ingold, Tim. 2000. *The Perception of The Envionment*. London: Routledge.
Koldkær Højlund, Marie. 2017. "OVERHEARING – an attuning approach to noise in Danish hospitals." PhD diss., Aarhus University.

Koepnick, Lutz. 2013. "Reading on the move." *PMLA* 128, no. 1: 232–237.
Koepnick, Lutz. 2019. "Figures of resonance." *SoundEffects – An Interdisciplinary Journal of Sound and Sound Experience* 8, no. 1.
Koepnick, Lutz. 2021. Resonant matter: sound art and the aesthetics of vibration (new approaches to sound, music, and media): sound, art, and the promise of hospitality. Bloomsbury Academic.
Massumi, Brian. 2002. *Parables for the Virtual. Movement, Affect, Sensation.* Durham, North Carolina: Duke University Press.
Rubery, Matthew, and Leah Price. 2020. "Further reading." Oxford: Oxford University Press.
Schmidt, Ulrik. 2013. *Det Ambiente: Sansning, Medialisering, Omgivelse*. Aarhus, Denmark: Aarhus University Press.
Stern, Daniel N. 1985. *The Interpersonal World of the Infant*. Routledge.
Shusterman, Richard. 1998. "Somaesthetics: A disciplinary proposal." *Journal of Aesthetics and Art Criticism* 57, no. 3: 299–313.
Spencer, Amy. 2021. "Reading ambient literature: Immersion, distraction, and the situated reading experience. Modes of reading." *Poetics Today* 42, no. 2: 301–315.
Thibaud, Jean-Paul. 2011. "The sensory fabric of urban ambiances." *Senses and Society* 6, no. 2: 203–215.
Thibaud, Jean-Paul. 2017. "Installer une atmosphère." *Phantasia* 5: 127–135.

19 Resonance and the digital conditions of reading

Lutz Koepnick

Text today proliferates as never before. Digital screens surround every niche of our lives with printed words, creating vast environments of ceaseless reading, scanning, and scrolling. Electronic writing commands our bodies like the sea rules the hearts and minds of a sailor. We touch letters on our monitors to activate them, and we carry our monitors to allow figures of writing to touch us, to energize, pause, and direct our pathways. We read on the move and in mid-stride, and we move text around to move us. Meanwhile, letters fly by across electronic surfaces everywhere without our doing. Some of this writing screams for attention. Some of it seems to know that it will never be noticed at all, that it will only be perceived at the very edges of attention, like the pattern of a wallpaper, the background noise at the airport.

Meanwhile, as much as digital culture propels us to read at all times, it also reads us as never before: our movements in and across space, our shopping habits, our usage of data sets, our listening to music, our eye movements, our attention spans. We may with good reason resist social media's efforts to read the reading of its users 24/7, but the ubiquity of algorithms reading the activities of human bodies and minds at the very least indicates a dire need to rethink what may count as reading under digital conditions in the first place. Reading today comes in many shapes and sizes, and in many cases, it no longer involves the cherished image of the reader as a cognitively focused and intentionally motivated, isolated and monadic, goal-oriented, and hermeneutically proficient subject. Nostalgia for reading's analog past may be one response. The true challenge, however, is to recognize today's digital entanglement of machines and minds, of reading and being read, as an invitation to question, reframe, and enrich normative models of reading – and to insist on the future design of sustainable rather than exploitative environments of text usage.

Responding to this expanded field of reading in our digital present, Holger Schulze has recently called for a radical revaluation of what may count as good and pleasurable reading (Schulze 2020). As he transposes Annahid Kassabian's (2013) reappraisal of semi-attentive listening into the language of literary criticism, Schulze challenges traditional norms of deep,

DOI: 10.4324/9781003211662-30

focused, and sustained reading. The 21st-century ecosystems of textuality and reading, Schulze argues, require us to rethink a reader's subjectivity as distributed and to release our understanding of the practice of reading from dominant frameworks of hermeneutic understanding, cognitive decoding, or critical analysis. No approach to contemporary reading, according to Schulze, can do without taking the presumed lightness of hyper-reading – of skimming, scanning, surfing, discontinuously consuming, or half-attentively ignoring figures of text – seriously. Hyper-reading may be one among other practices of engaging with text, but as Schulze rightly insists, it deserves much more attention than traditional literary scholarship has been willing to grant. Hyper-reading blissfully disregards the demands of a text's integrated totality and unity, and precisely therefore it is "generative" (Schulze 2020, 40). It defies traditional binaries between active engagement and passive consumption: today's hyper-readers, as they embrace particles of texts as engines of the imagination, redefine the very act of reading as an act of writing.

Similar to how Kassabian's notion of ubiquitous listening asks us to explore the acoustical unconscious as a ground for rethinking existing norms of attention, Schulze's concept of hyper-reading encourages us to think of reading, not as something that unfolds in a sealed vacuum between textual objects and a reader's eyes, but within much larger environments of signs, sensory perceptions, materialities, and movements. In this chapter, I want to add another dimension to this ecological approach to reading and argue that the expanded field of reading in our digital present requires us to think of all reading as ecological, as deeply entangled with the media, materialities, spaces, and atmospheres that surround it. The central concept of this effort is what I call resonant reading. Though, as I argue, resonant reading undergirds all acts of reading, it required the ubiquity of text in the digital age to become fully graspable as such.

Like Schulze's techniques of hyper-reading, resonant reading stresses the generative aspects of semi-attentive and incoherent, post-hermeneutic and post-critical, embodied and affective practices of absorbing textual particles. Unlike Schulze's deliberate techniques of fraying the borders of the text, however, resonant reading may not qualify as a technique at all. It highlights the way in which texts touch readers, readers touch texts, possibly long before they intend to or know it. And in doing so, it not only asks us to radically expand cognitive or semiotic frameworks of reading to account for the ubiquity of text under digital conditions but to challenge the widely held view that the prevalence of digital media today increasingly erases the vibrancy of resonant interactions.

The touch of reading

The term resonance resists unequivocal definition. Natural scientists consider resonance the causal and predictable occurrence of transduction: the process by which one vibrating object or entity incites another to vibrate because the latter's own so-called natural frequency is identical to the first's frequency of vibration. Playing the middle A on your piano will cause a nearby tuning fork to vibrate, should it be tuned to the standard pitch of 440Hz. When it comes to human affairs, however, we primarily use the term of resonance to describe the opposite of clear and causal relationships: relations strikingly fuzzy and often unpredictable in nature, causes and effects whose exact logic exceeds our understanding. For the humanist, resonance identifies certain atmospheric values, a vibrant and affective ecology of connectivity, effects funneled through affects that register in bodily and sensorial ways. In contrast to scientific terminology, then, everyday language resorts to the concept of resonance whenever we cannot name exact causes and linear influences.[1]

Natural scientists will readily admit that resonant transduction will often play itself out above or below the thresholds of human perception. They may be less inclined, though, to think of it as a phenomenon that draws our attention to the multiplicity of flows, vibrations, materialities, and movements that inhere to anything we typically regard as object. Hence, they may also be less inclined to question how we tend to coagulate, to reify, such multiplicities into what we consider as object. Instead, humanists may applaud the affective, atmospheric values of resonant relationality. They may speak about texts, poems, images, films, and photographs as if they possessed the reverberant force of music. But rarely will they be prepared to question the humanistic subject as the very pivot of such resonant encounters, that is, to understand resonance as a force that may question the very way in which we think about the borders of the subject and how this subject experiences meaning or utilizes certain media to construct the world as meaningful.

As a term associated with the work of audible and inaudible sound waves, resonance at first seems ill suited to describe acts of (silent) reading, digital or not. *MS Slavic 7* (2019), a small art house film directed by Sofia Bohdanowicz and Deragh Campbell, offers intriguing images to think otherwise. Though the film primarily deals with written marks on seemingly old-fashioned paper, it provides rich insights to conceptualize resonant reading as a practice that spans the historical divide between analog and digital ecosystems of reading. Just as importantly, the film locates the true nemesis of resonant reading, not in today's expanded field of digital screens and their pressure on normative models of focused attention, but in the Cartesian underpinnings of classical print culture, the disembodied academicism of textual appropriation and concentrated, semiotic reading. In doing so, the film is of great value to think through the place of resonance under the digital conditions of reading today.

MS Slavic 7 tells the story of Audrey (Deragh Campbell), who after being appointed the literary executor of her great-grandmother's poetry travels to Houghton Library at Harvard University to go over the correspondence between her great-grandmother, Zofia Bohdanowizowa, and Polish writer Józef Wittlin. The film's title refers to the library's call number for the archival box containing the correspondence. Set over three days, *MS Slavic 7* is a slow film, but the pensive delicacy of its images, the slight rustling of its sounds, is arguably the film's very point. Reading takes time; it here evades the protocols of goal-oriented, task-driven action. What is perhaps most remarkable about its visual choreography, however, is the persistence with which Bohdanowicz frames Audrey's encounter with the library's holdings as a profoundly embodied, sensorial, and haptic enterprise. Again and again, Audrey literally lays her hands on the letters and their written words to read, transcribe, and translate them. Audrey's attention to the literary estate is guided by her fingertips rather than her eyes, and the camera is quite relentless in focusing our own gaze on the tactile probing of Audrey's fingers. Bohdanowicz tries whatever cinema can do to communicate the sensation of touch through moving or barely moving images.[2] Like Audrey, we are asked to sense what we see, to read with our hands rather than our eyes, to understand reading and writing as deeply embodied practices far removed from how certain historical traditions have envisioned them as a spiritual communion, as transcendental or ecstatic events, as out-of-body experiences (Figure 19.1).

Materialities matter in *MS Slavic 7*. Each particle has a bearing on Audrey in its own right: the curve of a letter, the texture of a piece of paper, the folds and crevasses of a single page. Reading, for Audrey, is not an intentional technique of a sovereign subject trying to secure (or deconstruct) meaning from a static textual object, nor a quasi-spiritual communion with a distant other. Instead, it is a practice of wayfaring, in Tim Ingold's sense,

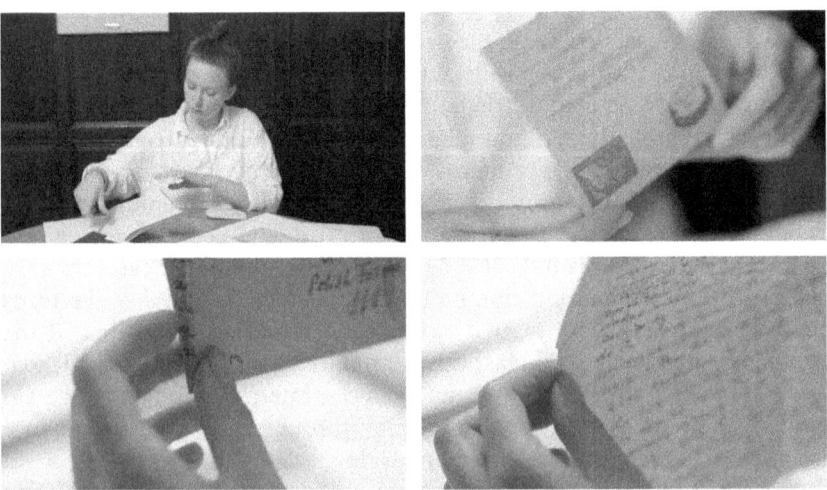

Figure 19.1 A scene from *MS Slavic 7* (2019) by Sofia Bohdanowicz and Deragh Campbell.

an effort to inhabit writing and textuality as an environment and echo chamber. It is a practice in which to read is to breathe and think, dream, and move *in* the movements of writing and *along* the sensory vibrations and reverberations of a text, rather than to penetrate a text's surfaces or use it as a mere vehicle of intellectual transport (Ingold 2011, 145–55). Resonant reading, in Audrey's sense, means to allow the reader's body and mind to be swept and carried away; it means to experience meaning as *that* movement, as the confluence, the co-presence of multiple movements, histories, temporalities, and stories within the space of the present. Resonant readers such as Bohdanowicz's Audrey read words and letters to sense and immerse themselves in the unpredictable fluxes of their medium, to experience the marks others have left on paper as sensuous gestures and traces, as knots in a tangled mesh rather than points connected by lines across seemingly stable surfaces.

Resonant reading and writing, as featured in *MS Slavic 7*, taps into the mimetic, even the animistic, as theorized by Walter Benjamin (1999, 721–22) or Michael Taussig (1993). It treats writing as a form of drawing, and reading as a way of following marks on paper. Resonant reading thus seeks to recover the original meaning of "text," understood as a fabric, a mesh of interwoven threads and lines produced by gestural movements, not a stable, linear, and fully integrated object transporting the reader's eye conveniently from point A to point B. To read, in this way, is first and foremost to experience the binding of mind and world, perception and cognition, sense and meaning in ongoing movements and gestures. It is initially not about the effort to impose form on matter, extract meaning from verbal objects, isolate information from noise. It instead – like Audrey – values the "that" as much as the "what." It in fact thinks of engaging text in analogy to how spiders spin and navigate their webs: as a weaving of threads, not extrinsic to eye and body, but integral to a spider's very movements, as an interplay of multiple forces, the ground and infrastructure upon which spiders base their very interaction with the world.

Such reading at first seems profoundly out of touch with and even antithetical to what digital readers do when they prepare for exams, browse newspapers, study scientific papers, or follow the directions of their GPS. Doesn't such reading, one might ask, belong entirely to the world of analog media and sensorial imminence? As I will argue in the next section, however, *MS Slavic 7* itself offers compelling reasons to think of resonant reading as a practice that not only echoes and illuminates Schulze's participle poetics and Kassabian's account of ubiquitous listening under digital conditions, but requires our world of digital interfaces and screen environments to become visible as such in the first place: It is what we all do, knowingly or not, when navigating our world of digitally expanded textuality.[3] Audrey's reading, like the irreverent or distracted hyper-readers of our digital present, valorizes becoming and ongoing transformation over any sense of finality or conclusiveness. It never has any definite end, output, or deliverable in sight,[4] and it flourishes not in spite but because of the way in which the digital has reshuffled the case of reading. As such, Audrey's resonant reading not only offers alternatives to the normative image of the writer and reader as a cognitively centered subject and willful agent but urges us to think of pre- and post-print cultures as soul mates.

Reading beyond the gatekeepers

In his influential writing on resonance, sociologist Hartmut Rosa has argued that the landscapes of digital screens in our present largely undercut the possibility of resonant experience such as Audrey's, understood as the affective suspension of strict divisions between self and world. Resonance, he suggests, withers in a world dominated by digital interfaces, not only because our world's technological regimes lead to what he considers a mechanized and disembodied "uniformity or mono-modularization of our relationship to the world" (Rosa 2019, 92),[5] but also and just as importantly, because our primary media – smartphones, tablets, touchscreen computers – heavily rely on various forms of symbolization, on written code and algorithms at their operational level, on an abundance of words and letters, links and textual information at their surface, all of which thwart the sensorial and non-cognitive intensities of resonance. While networked communication tools might afford us to spend time with each other, exchange thoughts and ideas, perhaps even trigger or trade emotional values, they are largely ineffective, Rosa's implies, when it comes to providing viable infrastructures of affective attunement.

The nervous excitations and bodily contortions of texters on public transport systems provide anecdotal evidence that Rosa's argument requires correction: their reading clearly vibrates with the writing of others, touches on and is touched by the writing of tele-present interlocutors, regardless of the fact that letters and emojis require digital code to become visible on screen. The artistic interventions of a Jenny Holzer, Jason Rhoades, or Ben Rubin, as they feature digitally generated text in gallery settings or public architectural spaces, offer other good reasons to reconsider whether algorithms and digital code indeed obstruct the work of resonance. The installations of these artists embrace digital text and technology as a medium of creating space, of sensory world-building, of affective reorientation. They invite users and viewers to navigate a fleeting world of digital text as affective spaces in which writing creates physical environments, regardless of whether readers fully grasp what is on display or not. Holzer and Rubin know as much as eager texters, that much of what we consider the digital inhabits the world of sensory relationships in analog form. Words and images on screen may require invisible code to come into being, but any screen itself is of course as much part of and shapes our physical environment, our architectures of being, as the leaves of a tree, the frame of a panorama window, or the solidity of a brick wall. What is essential about the digital condition of reading in our contemporary age, they tell us, is not textual ontologies relying on code and algorithms, but how digital technologies have dramatically expanded the phenomenology of writing and reading in private and public spaces, have largely expanded the environments for reading, and as a result now cause us to think of reading as an inherently ecological question and of resonance as something that today, pace Rosa, rarely takes place in the absence of digital technologies.

MS Slavic 7 is well aware of this. The film shows Audrey's resonant reading – her desire to touch and be touched by words from the past – as fundamentally different from the practice of a librarian who at various junctures of the film gets a real kick out of his power to regulate access to the letters and materials. As we learn in the opening images, he is a smart reader of filmmaker Jean-Pierre Melville's essays, even in their original language. Unlike Audrey, who knows everything about the hand that produces and defines manuscripts as media of readerly interest, the librarian knows nothing about this. He only reads with his eyes, and he only reads to better understand a world in which most things, including the act of reading, primarily pivot around a purified sense of sight. Just as importantly, however, the film introduces this gatekeeper as a reader who uses his printed book as a medium to block the digital screen that sits right in front of him, between him and his clients. Paper trumps pixels, his posture proclaims, the lure of the physical book outperforms the distracting displays of digital screen culture. As much as he wants to police Audrey's multisensory approach to reading, he thus also poses as a navel-gazing humanist for whom the pixels and fragmentary nature of digital reading present a severe threat to the academy, its maintenance of professional status and interpretative authority, the moral authority presumably embedded in the ability to focus on, assess, and be absorbed by the pages of a bound book (Benesch 2021, 12) (Figure 19.2).

Audrey gets in trouble with this gatekeeper, not only because her understanding of seeing and reading texts vastly exceeds the merely ocular, but also because her practice of reading – like the undulation of pixels on screen – defies the rhetoric of boundedness and control, the finality, the normative value of introspection, attention, and disembodiment historically invested in the printed book. Reading, for her, is far too complex and important an activity, too multilayered and spatial a matter, to be entrusted to the eye or a willful and willfully integrated subject alone. Resonant reading, for her, instead presents a practice of mimetic entanglement, of ambient attachments. To read is to walk with individual texts, walk through them, inhabit and be inhabited by them similar to how we immerse ourselves in a work of installation art or an architectural structure, unable to ever grasp their totality, their wholeness, their formal unity from ever-shifting points of view. And this is precisely where Audrey's mode of reading meets the reading amid digital conditions that Schulze calls hyper-reading: a reading often joyfully ignorant of normative frameworks of decoding and meaning-making, a reading that simply reads for the sake of

Figure 19.2 A scene from *MS Slavic 7* (2019) by Sofia Bohdanowicz and Deragh Campbell.

reading itself and often hovers at the edges of cognition, a reading whose primary point is not to grasp things from a distance like the Harvard gatekeeper, but to inhabit, to probe, and to attune our movements to impermanent ecologies of text in all its particularity, its *particleness*.

One of the film's most iconic shots shows Audrey soundly asleep on her bed surrounded by manuscripts, as if she was a vessel crossing the high seas. Sleep, for Audrey, is one among other ways to live with and inhabit the movements of letters, to engage with and be engaged by writing – and not an insignificant one at all, for that matter. Though no digital technologies are in sight, the shot emblematizes the conditions of reading in an age of digital text production, dissemination, and reception as much as it highlights the extent to which texts and their readers can form vibrant environments beyond the librarian's norms of focused and disembodied attention. Like Audrey's sea of manuscripts, digital media today ask us to think of reading – like Audrey – as an impermanent habitat whose role far exceeds the function of semiotic input and output devices meant to shape what happens in people's brains. Far from obliterating resonant interactions, the digital conditions of reading today in fact make us understand as never before that resonance – its affective power, its logics of touch and movement – has always provided the material base, the infrastructure, the anchor, and the engine of our being as readers, including print culture's ideal of a cognitively centered, goal-oriented, semiotic, and hermeneutic reading. All reading starts with floating in and along the currents of texts, before it may progress to the task of understanding, decoding, analyzing, and critiquing it. We need to know Audrey's as well as our contemporary hyper-readers' art of reading with our eyes wide shut, of reading at the threshold of attention, of reading while asleep or navigating ambient textual spaces, in order to recognize, meet, and challenge the normative regime that print culture has historically imposed on us (Figure 19.3).

Digital resonance

Humanists bypassing the physics of resonance often celebrate resonant interactions – the transduction of vibrational energies – as an automatic good. But let us not make any mistake: the aerostatic flutter that brought down the Tacoma Narrows Bridge on November 7, 1940, counts as much as an instant of resonant transduction as the damage your car's suspension may suffer from the rotation of a misaligned tire. Therefore, we would be mistaken to welcome what I understand here as resonant reading in the age of digital media as an automatic good. It would be as foolish as to claim that gravity, poetry, or painting as such are good and desirable. What I do

Figure 19.3 A scene from *MS Slavic 7* (2019) by Sofia Bohdanowicz and Deragh Campbell.

want to claim in closing, however, is that the expanded field of reading in our digital present offers much more than a mere training ground for modes of resonant reading.

Bruno Latour has argued that "resonance compels us to call into question the notion that the nature of things resides in their essence and that this essence can be exhausted by a sign, a discourse, or logos" (quoted in Erlmann 2015, 177). Here, he draws our attention to certain Enlightenment traditions that have sought to pit reason against resonance, the first representing critical detachment, agency, culture, and freedom, the second embodying presence, proximity, touch, submission, nature, and necessity. Veit Erlmann has shown in masterful detail how the prevalence of these binaries has obscured the extent to which, even in the context of Enlightenment thought itself, resonance and reason, affect and abstraction, often end up needing each other, both energizing, grounding, and vindicating the operations of its presumed other (Erlmann 2010).

To reclaim resonance against all odds of the digital, in fact, to argue that the digital may foster expanded ecosystems for the resonant co-existence of mind and matter, does not mean to endorse a return to some dark age of premodern, pre-Enlightened, vitalistic, or animistic unreason, let alone advocate a gay science of desirable illiteracy. On the contrary. Resonant ecologies and interactions may not produce automatic goods. They can be generative, but they may also be harbingers of destruction, of violence. They foster forms of distributed subjectivity, but they can also destroy subjects and objects altogether. But in its very stress on the material aspects of audition and the physical immediacy of vibratory transactions, the idea of resonance has never simply served as an echo chamber, a mere other, let alone an opponent of practices, institutions, ideas, values, and hierarchies associated with the world of cognition. As much as the flows of resonant reading undergird semiotic reading like a basso continuo, the melodic arrangements of a Bach sonata, so do the movements of vibrant matter energize even the seemingly coldest, mechanical, and dull gadgets of digital culture. Far from ushering us into a mindless and soulless era of mechanized dematerialization, then, the expanded field of text in the digital age reveals a profound, yet often forgotten truth about the nature and art of all reading: whenever we try to detach reading from the echo chambers of resonance, we render its logos mute and lifeless.

Notes

1 For a longer discussion of the difference between scientific and humanistic approaches to resonance, see Koepnick (2021, chapter 1).
2 For more on cinema and touch, see e.g., Marks (2000).
3 This argument can be seen as a variation of Lisa Gitelman's (2006) important claim that the history of media is inseparable from the stories they tell and the stories different users tell about them. See also Bolter and Grusin (2000) and, of course, McLuhan (1964).

4 In this, the term of resonant reading registers transformational changes in contemporary criticism and scholarship as well, as analyzed more recently by N. Katherine Hayles: away from normative modes of scholarly writing praised for its "crystalline prose," its rhetoric of precision, control, and endurance; and toward collaborative digital research ecologies that engage metaphors such as "contagion, extension, mutation; remixing, recombining, upgrading disseminating; extensible, exportable, importable" (Hayles 2021, 119).
5 The figure of resonance has received considerable scholarly attention across numerous disciplines over the last decade. For other accounts, see Farland (2013), Price (2011), Erlmann (2010), and Koepnick (2021).

References

Benesch, Klaus. 2021. *Mythos Lesen: Buchkultur und Geisteswissenschaften im Informationszeitalter.* Bielefeld, Germany: Transcript Verlag.

Benjamin, Walter. 1999. "On the mimetic faculty." In *Selected Writings, 1926-1934,* translated by Rodney Livingstone et al., edited by Michael W. Jennings, Howard Eiland, and Gary Smith. Cambridge, Massachusetts: Belknap Press.

Bolter, David, and Grusin, Richard. 2000. *Remediation: Understanding New Media.* Cambridge, Massachusetts: MIT Press.

Erlmann, Veit. 2010. *Reason and Resonance: A History of Modern Aurality.* Cambridge, Massachusetts: MIT Press.

Erlmann, Veit. 2015. "Resonance." In *Keywords in Sound,* edited by David Novak and Matt Sakakeeny. Durham, North Carolina: Duke University Press.

Farland, David. 2013. *Drawing on the Power of Resonance in Writing.* Scotts Valley: CreateSpace.

Gitelman, Lisa. 2006. *Always Already New: Media, History, and the Data of Culture.* Cambridge, Massachusetts: MIT Press.

Hayles, N. Katherine. 2021. *Postprint: Books and Becoming Computational.* New York: Columbia University Press.

Ingold, Tim. 2011. *Being Alive: Essays on Movement, Knowledge and Description.* London: Routledge.

Kassabian, Annahid. 2013. *Ubiquitous Listening: Affect, Attention, and Distributed Subjectivity.* Berkeley, California: University of California Press.

Koepnick, Lutz. 2021. *Resonant Matter: Sound, Art, and the Promise of Hospitality.* New York: Bloomsbury.

Marks, Laura U. 2000. *The Skin of the Film: Intercultural Cinema, Embodiment, and the Senses.* Durham, North Carolina: Duke University Press.

McLuhan, Marshall. 1964. *Understanding Media: The Extensions of Man.* New York: McGraw-Hill.

Price, Peter. 2011. *Resonance: Philosophy for Sonic Art.* New York: Atropos Press.

Rosa, Hartmut. 2019. *Resonance: A Sociology of Our Relationship to the World,* translated by James C. Wagner. Cambridge: Polity Press.

Schulze, Holger. 2020. *Ubiquitäre Literatur: Eine Partikelpoetik.* Berlin: Matthes & Seitz.

Taussig, Michael. 1993. *Mimesis and Alterity: A Particular History of the Senses.* New York: Routledge.

Conclusion: the digital reading condition

Maria Engberg, Iben Have, and
Birgitte Stougaard Pedersen

Multisensory and situated reading

This volume has offered a palette of perspectives to give a better understanding of the digital reading condition (or conditions) and how to approach it conceptually and analytically from different academic fields, including sensory and aesthetic studies, learning and educational studies, as well as media and literary studies. We have explored the digital reading condition from a macro level of philosophical and theoretical discussions and down to individual readers in schools and everyday life, whose reading practices we have studied empirically. We have brought the voices of readers into dialog with the voices of academic scholars to understand contemporary reading practices and explore theoretical approaches to analyzing them.

An important insight is that many of the characteristics of the digital reading condition are not new simply because they are digital, their affordances and conditions shaped by digital media. Rather, the digital reading condition includes an understanding of how reading has always been multisensory and included aural and tactile perceptive modes. Many of the reading conditions mentioned in this volume have long traditions, although they have changed over time, and we have sought to resist the tendency to think of "old" reading cultures and practices compared to "new." However, many practices have become more widespread, as different material, cultural, and technological possibilities have become more accessible and affordable in the digital reading condition. In this book, our aim was to focus on the kinds of reading that are conditioned by the digital and new kinds of reading possibilities that are offered through digital affordances. From that follows that we operate with a more inclusive understanding of reading than is usual in academic literature: an expanded understanding of digital reading toward the multisensory.

With the term multisensory reading, we want to include forms of reading not traditionally associated with reading, such as audio reading, interactive reading, and reading across different media and technologies. We also want to establish the multi-sensing body as a premise for reading, whether you

DOI: 10.4324/9781003211662-31

read printed books, e-books, audiobooks, app books, or alternate between them. That requires an interdisciplinary approach that includes a polyphony of voices and research perspectives.

A key point of our argument is that reading never happens in a vacuum. The reading body will always be present in time and space somewhere. Therefore, we speak of situated reading. Partly appealing to a phenomenological epistemology, the book situates reading experiences in specific and changeable contexts, each with shared commonalities and qualities associated with each unique situation. This qualitative approach provides an important addition to existing quantitative studies in the various fields that study digital reading, primarily education and pedagogical studies. In this book, we contribute with historical, cultural, and aesthetic knowledge to the expanding field of scholarly studies of digital reading. It is important for our scholarly approach to challenge ruling conceptions of what constitutes reading and what constitutes so-called "good" reading, often associated with learning outcomes and recall of facts rather than literary experience. The different examples, scenarios, vignettes, and case studies provided in this book – some derive from empirical studies, some represent common phenomena – demonstrate the nuances and various kinds of experiences individual readers get from various reading situations today.

This book cannot alone provide a full picture of the digital reading condition. We have prioritized some perspectives over others. Therefore, the chapters in this book should be viewed as contributions to a larger landscape of scholarly work. Our hope is that we have succeeded in establishing a meaningful and fruitful exchange of approaches to reading in digital manners that can contribute to and promote future dialogue.

Personal and social reading

Many studies have pointed out that it is not always the reading practice itself that is important to readers, but rather the whole context of reading, that is, the reading situation. We find this as early as in Janice Radway's pioneering study of popular reading experiences, *Reading the Romance* from 1984. What she thought would be a study of the content of the novels in question and the impressionable community of housewives in the Midwestern American town of Smithton considered subjects to a patriarchal, gender-stereotypical worldview turned out to reveal a much more nuanced picture. She found that the context, the very reading situation was the most important part of the women's reading experiences. Following in the scholarly path paved by Radway's seminal study, we want with this book to democratize the readers' experience, focusing on why people read without judgments of literary quality or literacy. It is not only the literary value, but also the values of reading that are important. There is a scholarly need to expand and democratize notions of literacy to include the wider range of reading styles that emerge in our contemporary digital media culture. As Jay Bolter has pointed out, today we live in a media plenitude that is not purely digital, but increasingly so, and digital technologies challenge and change the role of printed books and along with them the reading practices they support (Bolter 2019).

Reading communities have experienced a blossoming, as online platforms support digital reading cultures. In this book, we have chosen to focus on how the digital reading condition impacts the reader in terms of sensory and technological dimensions. Further, we have opened for analyses of the reading situation in terms of place and time. However, although some chapters describe social aspects of reading, we do not analyze in depth how social reading, social media communities, and networking facilitate reading in a digital age. Social reading in a digital context is often associated with newer social media platforms such as Goodreads, BookTok, Bookstagram, or BookTube and fan fiction in general, but as Dorothee Birke has recently argued, "sociality and self-fashioning have been integral aspects of book culture for centuries" (2021, 149).

Compared to Radway's and Birke's sociological perspectives on reading communities, this book has taken a slightly different approach by focusing on different practices of reading, primarily from the perspective of individual's meeting with texts. The ambition of this book has been to expand the context of reading beyond sociological studies and include the sensory and aesthetic aspects of contemporary reading experiences as well. Theoretically, the sensory and aesthetic dimensions of any (reading) experience resonate with recent post-critical thinking that seeks to enhance the curious and delightful aspects of reading experiences as a corrective to former habits and cultural norms related to critical reading or the hermeneutics of suspicion (Felski 2015). For our purposes, the idea of multisensory reading can encompass both critical and post-critical approaches. Affective registers of experience that are activated during reading can lead to a renegotiation of what is viewed as culturally valuable in terms of reading. A multisensory understanding of digital reading broadens the notion of what is considered to be a focused or deep reading experience. This in turn goes against the culturally dominating universal idea that printed text is the most important medium for engaged modes of reading.

Out of many: polyaesthetics, multisensory, polymedia, transmedia, and plenitude

The digital reading condition is characterized by multitude. Many media forms coexist in the current media landscape; older media forms live alongside newer ones. Printed books and e-books, multimedia narratives and audiobooks. The ways in which narratives can be created, published, and distributed multiply, supported by the affordances of digital media. We have not focused on how business models for publication are changing, nor how social media communities support social and shared reading activities (briefly described above), but they do form part of the diverse media landscape in which the practices of reading that we have focused on here reside. Media studies scholars, sociologists, and communication scholars have in recent years shown how different media channels support and foreground varied media use by producers and consumers alike. Concepts such as polymedia (Madianou and Miller 2012), polyaesthetics (Engberg 2014), transmedia (Jenkins 2006, Phillips 2012), and Bolter's analysis of the digital plenitude (2019), along with older terms such as multimedia and multimodality, all point to the varied and complex media culture in which the digital reading condition should be understood.

It is not primarily a question of how the digital overtakes print; rather, narratives can employ many different channels of publication, many modes of creation and aesthetic form: audiovisual, visual, audio, textual, tactile, locative, and so on. In the wake of this continued exploration and cultural development of narrative media, new or altered reading practices emerge. If there is one lesson to take from this book's varied contributions, it is that current digital media cultures demand a conceptual broadening of how reading practices are to be analyzed and understood. Mirca Madianou and Daniel Miller described this multitude as an "environment of affordances" in which "each individual medium is defined in relational terms in the context of all other media" (2012, 170). Similarly, we see that the digital reading condition must attend to the various choices made by creators, writers, and producers and their impact on the affordances of reading environments.

Institutional perspectives

The digital reading condition is not only relevant to discuss in relation to books and the literary field. The Internet has made possible a multitude of digital texts and digital writing – private and public texts, long-lasting and temporary texts, factual, and so on. In journalism and news reporting, multimodal and multisensory texts have been gaining ground in the last decade. So-called immersive journalism (De la Peña et al. 2010) uses the multisensory affordances of technologies such as Virtual Reality, Augmented Reality, and 360° video to create a first-person, embodied, and intimate experience of news. In journalism, then, we can see some of the multisensory registers highlighted by this book begin to establish themselves alongside other forms of writing.

The focus of this book has been the meeting between the reader and the digital literary text. Thus, we only cover parts of the circuit of mutually dependent parts of text production, distribution, and reception. Obviously, the conditions of digital production as well as distribution are important for the digital reading condition and must be taken into account to address the whole picture of the digital reading condition. In this book, we have sought to present a nuanced picture of the reception side, and much like Jerome McGann (1991) who developed a theory of textuality based on a richer understanding of the complexities of writing and text production, this book has presented an assemblage of approaches to digitally mediated literary texts based on understanding reading and experience. Never far away from the conceptualization of the digital reading condition, technological infrastructure and cultural contexts shape how digital texts are perceived, read, and understood. Similar to recent decades' development in film, TV, radio, and music industries, the book market and publishing industry are slowly experiencing a takeover by streaming services companies like Audible in the U.S. or Mofibo/Storytel in Europe. This development is most distinctive and widespread in relation to literary streaming services offering unlimited digital audiobook and/or e-books by subscription. Also, Spotify, as a music distribution platform, is increasingly moving toward the field of audio texts, for instance by introducing podcast services.

This concluding chapter has pointed to contextualized perspectives on the digital reading condition which the book has focused on, but not exhausted. We have pursued the aesthetic and sensory experiences of audible and digital interfaces and studied how they can contribute productively to creating immersed reading experiences. We hope that the book has projected and outlined how the digital reading condition is characterized by a complexity that not only leads to distracted reading experiences. From a sensory perspective, the digital reading condition in new ways orchestrates reading situations and can potentially enrich our everyday lives with new, immersive and engaging, reading practices.

References

Birke, Dorothee. 2021. "Social reading? On the rise of a 'Bookish' reading culture online." *Poetics Today* 42, no. 2. 10.1215/03335372-8883178.

Bolter, Jay David. 2019. *The Digital Plenitude: The Decline of Elite Culture and the Rise of New Media*. Cambridge, Massachusetts: MIT Press.

De la Peña, Nonny, Weil, Peggy, Llobera, Joan, Ausia's Pome's, Elias Giannopoulos, Spanlang, Bernhard, Friedman, Doron, Sanchez-Vives, Maria V., and Slater, Mel. 2010. "Immersive journalism: Immersive virtual reality for the first-person experience of news." *Presence: Teleoperators and Virtual Environments* 19, no. 4: 291–301. 10.1162/ PRES_a_00005.

Engberg, Maria. 2014. "Polyaesthetic sights and sounds: Media aesthetics in the fantastic flying books of Mr. Morris Lessmore, upgrade soul and the vampyre of time and memory." *SoundEffects - An Interdisciplinary Journal of Sound and Sound Experience*, no. 4: 1. 10.7146/se.v4i1.20370.

Felski, Rita. 2015. *The Limits of Critique*. Chicago: University of Chicago Press.

Felski, Rita. 2020. *Hooked. Art and Attachment*. Chicago and London: University of Chicago Press.

Jenkins, Henry. 2006. *Convergence Culture: Where Old and New Media Collide*. New York: New York Press.

Madianou, Mirca, and Miller, Daniel. 2012. "Polymedia: Towards a new theory of digital media in interpersonal communication." *International Journal of Cultural Studies* 16, no. 2: 169–187. 10.1177/1367877912452486.

McGann, Jerome. 1991. *The Textual Condition*. Princeton, New Jersey: Princeton University Press.

Phillips, Andrea. 2012. *A Creator's Guide to Transmedia Storytelling: How to Captivate and Engage Audiences Across Multiple Platforms*. New York: McGraw-Hill Education.

Price, Leah. 2019. *What We Talk About When We Talk About Books: The History and Future of Reading*. Basic Books.

Radway, Janice. 1984. *Reading the Romance*. North Carolina: University of North Carolina Press.

Index

360-degree circle 31
360° photography 81
360° video 79, 81, 233
3D 42, 64–65, 79–82
3D graphics 80

accelerating society 136, 141
acoustemological 89
acoustic space 30–31
act of reading i, 1, 15, 16, 21, 27, 73, 75, 124–125, 203, 206, 213, 220, 225
actor 93, 159, 198
actress 93
aesthetic 2, 15, 23, 47, 48–49, 51, 53, 59–60, 65, 71, 77, 95, 121, 137, 148, 162–167, 169, 170–171, 173–175, 177, 182, 185, 188, 197, 201, 210, 215, 230–234
aesthetic code 173
affective 18, 20, 94, 173, 175–176, 181–182, 185, 192, 198, 202, 208, 211, 213, 215–217, 220–221, 224, 227, 232
affective body 211
affordances 1, 20, 22, 82, 90, 114–115, 118, 121, 129, 137, 152, 173, 197, 198, 200–201, 206, 212, 231–233
AI (artificial intelligence) 85
algorithmic data 30
algorithmic journalism 85
alphabet 30–31
Amazon 18, 20, 36, 39, 83, 113, 203, 205
ambience 198, 208, 210, 215
ambient 91, 198, 208, 211–216, 225, 227
ambient literature 208, 211, 214–215
ambient sound 91
amphitheaters 89

Anakin (Star Wars) 178–180
Ancient Greeks 89
anthropology 59
atmosphere/moods/presence 126
attachment 127, 129, 164–166, 175, 178, 184–185, 187, 189, 192, 225
attention economy 209
Attlee, James 211–212, 217
attuned spaces 214
attunement 148, 164, 184–187, 189–192, 198, 208–211, 213–214, 216, 224
Apollo 11, 82
app (application) 3, 18–19, 21, 41–42, 44, 58, 68–71, 73–77, 80, 82–83, 89, 91, 103, 105, 111, 113, 186, 197, 200–201, 203–205, 208, 211–212, 231
Apple Macintosh 39, 43
AR (augmented reality) 42, 80–81, 197, 206, 233
Army 89
arousal 139
ASMR 93
attention 16–17, 20, 33, 47, 50, 52, 58, 64, 66, 69, 79–80, 85, 88, 90, 116, 119, 126–127, 136, 138, 140, 150, 165–171, 173, 198, 206, 208–211, 213, 215–216, 219–222, 225, 227–228
audio 5–6, 19, 22, 27, 29–31, 35–36, 39–40, 42, 44, 47, 51–52, 57–58, 62, 65, 79–80, 82–85, 88–92, 95, 111–112, 124–125, 128–129, 132, 135–141, 147–148, 177, 184, 187–188, 190–192, 201, 203–204, 206, 230, 233–234
audio articles 83
audio cassettes 137

Index

audio characteristics 31
audio formats 58, 65, 80, 83–85, 125
audio grooming 92
audio immersion 84
audio journalism 80, 83–84
Audio Long Leads 84
audio media 39, 85, 89, 91, 137–139, 141
audio news 83–84
audio newspaper 83
audio output 83
audio production 79
Audio Publishers Association 136, 138
audio reading 6, 27, 62, 88–90, 95, 112, 124, 132, 135–141, 147, 203–204, 206, 230
audio messages 83
audiovisual 14, 17, 29, 30, 48, 57, 61, 66, 80, 91–92, 126–127, 130–133, 233
audiovisual environments 126
audiovisual litany 61, 66
audiobook i, 1, 3, 5, 12, 14, 17–18, 23, 27, 31–32, 36, 39, 46–48, 57–58, 65–66, 85, 88–95, 111–112, 124, 126–132, 135–141, 147–148, 184–186, 188, 197, 200–204, 206, 208, 212–215, 231–232, 234
auditory experience 60
augmented reality (*See* AR)
authenticity 85
autobiographical 94–95
auto-ethnography 202
autonomy 112, 135, 140

background noise 139, 213, 219
Baldwin, Nathaniel 89
Barlow, John Perry 98–99, 106
Baron, Naomi 23, 51, 54, 90, 96, 111–112, 116, 119–121, 125, 131, 133, 135, 142
being absorbed or immersed 82, 126–127, 130
being attentive 124, 131
Bell, Alexander Graham 29, 89, 102
Bell, Alice 47
Benjamin, Walter - "The Work of Art in the Age of Mechanical Reproduction" 40, 44, 223, 229
between reading *see* reading
binary alphabet 30
biographies 116, 174, 176
bird song 28

blog posts 32
board games 64
bodily movement 66
bodily sociality 92–93
body language 28, 171
body movements (dance) 28
book covers 91
bookishness 76, 89
bookshops 91
book page 132
born-digital i, 1, 12, 14, 36, 47, 63–65, 80, 83, 112, 126
born-digital literature i, 1, 14, 47, 64
Braille 27, 90
Breeze, Mez 64–66, 118
Bråten 48, 54
Bull, Michael 133, 201–202, 206

cannibalize 136
canon or canonize 28, 35, 39, 99, 114, 153, 156–157, 180, 209
Carr, Nicholas 3, 7, 85–86, 113–114, 116–117, 122, 133
Cavarero, Adriana 92, 94, 96
cave paintings 27–28
Cayley, John 12–13, 22, 24, 47
Ciccoricco, David 47
China 29
children 6, 13–14, 41, 46–50, 52–53, 58, 68–71, 73–77, 132, 148, 152, 157, 163, 173, 189
Citton, Yves 198, 209–210, 216–217
churches 29
cinema or cinematic 29, 81, 84, 127, 222, 228
cinematic reality 81
clay 27
Clone Wars (Star Wars) 179–180
close reading (*See* reading)
closure 31–32
coaching 140
coded signs 27, 29
codex book 29
coding sessions 126
cognitive 4, 20, 31, 46, 48, 51, 60, 65, 91, 112, 117, 119–121, 124, 131, 135, 138, 140–141, 147–149, 156, 175–181, 184–185, 201, 219–220, 224, 227; cognitive apparatus 48; cognitive approach 4, 60, 91, 148; cognitive science 48; cognitive operation 175, 177–180
colors 121, 131, 177, 216

collective reading (*See* reading)
comic books 148, 173, 175–177, 182, 188
communication models 139, 209
commuting 136, 138–139, 141
compact cassette tape 89
comparative textual media 19
competent citizen 51
comprehension 12, 22, 46, 48, 53, 64, 90, 111, 119, 130
computer 3, 12, 14–16, 30, 35–40, 43, 46, 68–69, 71, 73–77, 82, 90–91, 99, 101–105, 115–117, 124, 126, 140, 147, 151, 153, 162–165, 167, 169–171, 178, 185, 224
computer screen 36, 46, 124
concentration 90, 114, 170, 177, 209
consumer 39, 43, 64, 84, 136, 233
consumption 2, 12, 18, 23, 36, 52, 83–84, 136, 139, 198, 200, 202, 220
Connor, Steven 59–60, 62, 66
context as noise 209
Cope and Kalantzis 50–51, 54, 154, 160
cooking 18–19, 95, 136, 138, 141, 203
COVID-19 82, 138–139
critical reading 6, 20, 112–114, 121, 232
critics 37, 137, 141
cross-modal learning 50
cross-sensory 91, 198
Csikszentmihalyi, Mihaly 140, 142
cultural artifacts 65, 91
cultural hierarchies 20, 28, 44, 60, 210
cultural transformation 30
cultural values 13, 51, 65, 112, 137, 159, 214
curious reading (*See* reading)
Cusk, Rachel 212, 214, 217
cyberspace 23, 98–99

daily duties 136
Danish 29, 47–48, 51–52, 80, 83–84, 94, 124, 135–136, 138, 150–157, 162, 176, 186, 188, 203–204
Danish National Library 136, 138, 155
Danish secondary school 52
Dann and Spinelli 129, 133
DARPA (Defense Advanced Research Projects Agency) 102
Darth Vader (Star Wars) 175, 177–181
Darwin 28, 33
decoding 27, 29, 46, 48, 57, 209, 217, 220, 225, 227

deconstructive 93
deep body 92
deep reading (*See* reading)
deep-dives 84
democracy 44, 85
Derrida 93, 96
The Descent of Man 28, 33
descriptions, thick *see* thick descriptions
device 1, 3, 5, 18, 22, 36, 41–43, 58–59, 63, 65, 68, 70, 73, 76, 89, 91, 117, 153, 200–201, 227
diction 93–94, 129, 203
digital audio files 89
digital audio journalism 80, 84
digital footprints 30
digital games 64
digital journalism 79–81, 85
digital literature i, 1, 14, 46–47, 57, 148
digital media culture 12, 30, 35, 83, 233
digital narrative structures 65
digital orality 32
digital reading practices i, 1, 3–4, 6, 26–27, 30, 33, 51–52, 62, 66, 125, 150, 152–153, 204, 206
digital screens 82, 116, 219, 221, 224–225
digital-only 83
digital technologies 5, 14–16, 18, 21–22, 36, 46, 59, 62–63, 75, 80, 85, 114–116, 119–121, 150–151, 158, 201, 206, 225–226, 232
digitized speech 32
digitized society 2, 49, 53
disabilities 137
discourses 14, 22, 33, 41, 138, 153, 228
Disney 156, 177
distant reading (Moretti) 20, 114, 117
distracted reading 6, 20, 48, 111, 140, 234
distraction 85, 119, 125, 151, 211
distributed subjectivity 93, 228
disturb 28, 93, 128, 139, 166, 189, 202, 209
documentaries 80–81, 215
driving 103, 105, 136, 138, 203
Drucker, Johanna 21, 24, 118, 133, 200, 207–208, 211, 217
dynamic 16, 38, 62, 69, 72–74, 112, 125, 135, 140, 159, 163, 169, 198, 208–210, 215–216
Dufrenne, Mikel 60, 66
Dyson, Frances 81, 84, 86

e-reading 16
e-singles 83
earbuds 89, 91, 127–129, 212, 215
ear reading 31
cecology of attention 210
Edison, Thomas 29, 89, 137, 141
EDVAC, computer 35
efficiency 135–136, 139
Egypt 29
eisegesis 180
Eisenstein, Elisabeth 26, 88, 96
Elbro, Carsten 48, 54
electric typewriter 29
electricity 29
electronic cultures 29
electronic literature 12, 23, 71, 118, 171
electronic media culture 31
electronic texts 16, 32
electronica 139
emails 18–19, 32, 104, 116
embodied 4, 11, 15, 18, 21, 44, 51–53, 57, 64, 84, 89, 91–94, 102, 112, 115, 120–121, 124–125, 131, 135, 140, 181, 186, 202, 204, 211, 220–222, 224, 227, 233
embodied co-creator 211
embodied reading 57, 112, 135, 140
emerging literacy 182
emotional 11, 31, 80, 85, 127, 129, 164, 166, 173–178, 180, 187, 190–192, 202, 213, 216, 224
emotional immersion 127, 129
emotional news 80
emotional thread 177
empirical studies 4, 6, 22, 52, 58, 141, 184, 231
engagement 6, 15, 17, 20–21, 52, 57–58, 60, 63, 65, 79–81, 88, 90, 95, 109, 111–112, 121, 132, 139, 147–148, 156, 163–164, 170–171, 174, 176, 185, 187, 191–192, 198, 200, 203, 215–216, 220
enjoy-dos 136
enjoyment 118, 139
Ensslin, Astrid 47
Entertaining news 80
environment 4, 12, 14–15, 22, 26, 33, 39, 42, 46, 50, 81, 84–85, 101, 121, 126, 131, 148, 197–198, 201–202, 205–206, 208–209, 219–220, 223–225, 227, 233
eReolen 132, 136, 138, 141
erudites 88

ethos 31, 176
eurocentric 29
European bourgeoisie 29
everyday aesthetics 59
everyday life 18, 21, 120, 135, 141, 189, 200, 202, 206, 230
exegesis 180
expectations 76–77, 114, 171, 174–177, 181
experience 1–5, 11–12, 16, 27, 31, 37–38, 42, 46–47, 51–53, 57–66, 73, 79–82, 84–85, 89–95, 111–113, 118–121, 124–132, 135–136, 139–141, 147–148, 157, 162–170, 173–177, 180–182, 184–192, 197–198, 200–204, 206, 208–217, 221–224, 231–234
experience-centric approach 174
experiential threads 174, 176–180
experiments 77, 85, 153–155
externalize memory 61
extended reality (XR) 81

facial expressions 27–28
fake news 85
fallacy 138
fans 176, 178
Feld, Steven 30, 33, 89, 96
Felski, Rita 20–21, 24, 122, 124–125, 127, 131, 133, 148, 162, 164, 166, 172, 184–185, 187, 189–193, 208, 213, 217, 232, 234
fictional universe 148, 173–174, 176, 178, 181–182
figure ground 209–210, 215–216
film studies 127
films 40, 173, 175, 177, 179, 221
Finnemann, Niels Ole 29–30, 32–33
first-person experience 84, 148, 165, 233
Fischer-Lichte, Erika 211
fitness 136, 138
flesh breefings
flexibility 65, 93, 119–120, 137, 141
flow 1, 80, 83, 104, 111, 125, 127, 135, 140–141, 167, 169, 221, 228
flow radio 80, 83
focus groups 139, 141, 186–187, 191
focused reading i, 1, 3, 22, 116, 139
food commercials 95
form, content, and media (Hayles) 125, 189
France 83
Funkhouser, Chris 47

games 17, 36, 64, 68, 74, 77, 147, 163–165, 167, 169–171, 173, 178
gender 102, 129, 176, 210, 231
Germany 83
global positioning systems (GPS) 42, 201, 205, 212, 223
Google 37–38, 42, 43, 83, 100–101
Grimshaw, Mark 127, 133
grunts 27–28
The Guardian 82, 84
Guldager, Katrine Marie 94, 96
Gumbrecht, Hans Ulrich 125, 127, 130, 133, 184–185, 187–188, 192–193, 217
Gutenberg, Johannes 29, 35, 63

habit 2, 15, 19, 46, 51–52, 124, 135, 139, 147, 197, 214, 219, 232
haptic 2, 4, 57, 62, 64, 66, 90–95, 129, 132, 185, 222
Harry Potter 52, 173
Hartley, John 32–33
Havelock, Eric Alfred 26
Hayles, N. Katherine 12–14, 17, 19, 20–23, 37–38, 44, 47–48, 54, 63–64, 69, 71, 73, 76, 78, 88, 96, 111–112, 116–117, 122, 125–127, 133, 162, 164, 171–172, 184–185, 189, 193, 229
headphones 52, 83, 85, 89, 91, 93, 136, 140, 209, 211
hegemony of visuality 209
heritage 31, 42, 157, 205
hertz 92
hexagon 175
hierarchy of the senses 61–62
hip-hop 139
hoarse 94
Homer 88
Horton and Wohl 93, 96
host 80, 85, 93, 103
Howes, David 59, 61–62, 65–67, 217
human perception 27, 29, 59, 221
human senses 57, 63
human sensory perception 47
Husserl, Edmund 59, 67
hyperlink, -ed 22, 38, 80, 116
hyper reading 20, 22, 38, 114, 116–117, 198, 220
hypertext 12, 16, 22, 35–39, 43–44, 47, 117–118
hypertext literature 47

idiosyncrasy 180
Ihde, Don 61–62, 67, 198–199, 203, 207, 217
The Iliad 88–89
imagination 128, 165, 169, 174, 188, 190, 220–221
immaterial 68, 71, 73, 91–93
immersed reading 125, 132, 140, 206, 209, 234
immersive experience 80, 84, 127
immersive journalism 58, 79–82, 84–85, 233
immersive journalistic 65, 80, 82, 85
immersive technologies 57, 65, 80–82, 84–85
immersion 6, 81, 84, 111–112, 124–129, 131–132, 136, 140, 162, 165, 167, 171, 187, 189, 192, 211
Innis, Harold Adam 26, 33
intensify immersion 127
intensity 92, 111, 114, 129–130, 165, 188–189, 213, 216
intentionality 33
interactive 1–2, 12, 17–18, 30, 36, 38, 64, 71, 73, 76, 80–81, 84, 90, 111, 121, 124, 128, 132, 148, 162, 167–168, 174, 186, 189, 208, 230
interactive journalism 81
interfaces 3–5, 19, 21–22, 52, 57, 59–60, 62–66, 79, 91, 101, 103–105, 112, 124, 130, 132, 147, 198, 200, 206, 213, 215, 223–224, 234
Internet 17, 29–30, 32, 38–41, 43, 57–58, 80, 85, 88, 91, 98–106, 114, 135, 137, 151–153, 155–156, 180, 233
Internet cloud 91
internet-based audiobooks 88
interpretation 15, 20–21, 32, 93, 167, 177, 179–181, 185, 190–192
intertextual 37, 75, 156, 173
interviews 4, 80, 83–84, 126, 141, 148, 163, 168–170, 175–181, 185–188, 191–192
intimacy 85, 92–93, 95, 129, 132
intimacy contract 129

Jabba the Hutt 178
jazz 139, 212–213
Jedi Temple 178
Jewitt, Carey 48, 54
Jones, Caroline A. 59, 67

journalism 58, 79–86, 127, 233
journalistic news 79
journalistic storytelling 81, 84

Kassabian, Anahid 198–199, 219–220, 223, 229
kinesthetic 89
knowledge 20, 32–33, 48–51, 53, 59–62, 80, 85, 117, 124, 132, 151–152, 154, 156–157, 164–167, 169, 175, 179–181, 184, 208, 213, 216, 231
knowledge production 50, 59, 62, 213
Koepnick, Lutz ix, 20, 24, 116, 119–120, 122, 197–199, 204, 207, 210, 218–229
Koldkær Højlund, Marie 208, 217
Kress, Gunther 48, 50, 54, 154, 160

L1 teaching 48, 147, 150–154, 157–159
lab-test 90
landscapes i, 1, 5–6, 16–17, 22, 27, 47, 63–64, 80, 95, 102, 124–125, 131, 197–198, 204, 208, 224, 231–233
language 2, 27–29, 32–33, 46–49, 60–61, 94–95, 100, 118, 120, 125, 147, 149–150, 152, 159, 162, 165, 171, 182, 190, 217, 219, 221, 225
language comprehension 48
late capitalism 209
lazy reading 62
learning environments 50
Lessig, Lawrence 40, 44, 99, 106
librarians 137, 225, 227
libraries 37, 39, 91, 113, 136, 138, 155, 221–222
lifeworld 175
linguistic communication 28
linguistic symbols 27
list services 32
Listening and Voice 61
listener 60, 84–85, 92–95, 129, 131, 139, 201–202, 212, 214
listening situation 128
literacies 3, 12–13, 44, 46–53, 147, 149–150, 154, 157–159, 176
literacy i, 3, 11, 13, 15–16, 31–32, 39–41, 46–47, 49–51, 53, 80, 114, 119, 147, 149–150, 153–154, 156–159, 182, 228, 231
literacy, UNESCO definition 49
literary studies i, 1–3, 16, 20, 47, 52, 71, 80, 117, 190, 208, 230

literate culture 29, 61
literary value 139, 231
literate 26–30, 37, 61, 119
locative reading 43
locative media 42
Logan, Robert K. 32–33
logocentrism 93
Lombard and Ditton 127, 133
long reads 80, 83–84
loudspeakers 90–91
Luke Skywalker 178
lungs 92

macro perspective 28
mainstream journalism 79
management 138–140, 151
Manchester Mark I, computer 35
Mangen, Anne 4, 7, 20, 25, 51, 54, 116, 120–121, 125, 131, 133
manuscript cultures 29
manuscripts 29, 35, 225–227
Marks, Laura U. 64, 67, 91, 95–96, 228–229
Massachusetts Institute of Technology 28
Massumi, Brian 213, 218
material apparatuses 64
materialities 12, 14, 21–22, 27, 36, 43–44, 57, 64, 126, 220–222
materiality 2, 5–6, 11–12, 14–15, 17, 20–21, 23, 31, 42, 48–49, 58, 68–71, 73, 75–77, 88–91, 111, 114, 116, 121, 125–127, 129, 147, 164–165, 185, 188–189
materiality of texts 49, 164–165, 185
McLuhan, Herbert Marshall 11, 13, 26, 29–31, 33, 61–64, 67, 228–229
meaning 4–5, 21, 27, 29–30, 48, 50, 52–53, 60–63, 65–66, 68, 70–71, 73, 75, 103, 118, 125, 136, 139–141, 149, 151, 154, 165, 167, 169, 176, 178, 180, 185, 188, 192, 198, 200, 204, 209–210, 213, 216–217, 221–223, 225, 231
meaning effects 125
meaning production 21, 125, 198
media cultures 1, 12, 14, 17, 26, 30–31, 35–36, 42–44, 52, 83, 233
media ecology 26
media matrices 26–27, 32–33
media matrix 11, 26, 30, 32–33
media semiotics 29
media technologies 11–12, 14, 26, 28, 32, 63–64, 89–90, 98, 202

242 Index

media use 46, 52–53, 120, 233
media-historical perspective 27, 30
media-specific analyses 21, 125
Medium Theory 26
Memmott, Talan 47
memorability 90
memory 29, 32, 61, 90, 111, 113, 119, 178, 204, 213
Mencia, Maria 47
mental representation 127
mental space 139
merchandise 173
Merleau-Ponty, Maurice 60, 67, 165, 172
Mesoamerica 29
Mesopotamia 29
meta-level 173
metal 91, 177
metaphorical 41, 64, 74, 92
Meyrowitz, Joshua 26, 30, 33
Michailidis, Balaguer-Ballester, and He 127, 134
microphones 89, 93
mixed reality 81
mixture of modalities 124
mobile audio reading 88
mobility 89–90, 129, 137, 141, 204
mobile setting 66
modal 46, 50–52, 92
modern societies 135–137
Mofibo 51, 94, 138, 203, 234
mono-modal 49, 128
mono-sensory 28, 88
monopoly 88, 101
mood 126, 130–131, 138–140, 169, 175, 187, 189, 192, 208, 212, 214
mood management 138–139
mood-balancing 139–140
mouth 28, 92, 94
movement 1, 27–28, 36, 49, 63–64, 66, 68, 72, 77, 92, 125, 149, 165–170, 201, 204, 214–215, 219–221, 223, 226–228
moving images 27, 222
mp3 files 91, 137
multichannel sound 84
multiliteracies 12–13, 46–47, 49–51, 53
multiliteracy skills 50
multimedia 39–41, 43–44, 46, 81, 121, 232–233

multimodality 40, 46–50, 233
multisemiotic 30
multisensorial 136, 140
multisensory i, 1–2, 6, 12, 14, 26–28, 30–31, 33, 46–47, 52–53, 55, 57–60, 62–66, 76, 79, 80, 84–85, 88–91, 95, 112, 118, 120–121, 124–126, 128, 130–131, 147–148, 164, 185, 189, 198, 200, 204, 208–217, 225, 230, 232–233
multisensory perception 31, 63
multisensory practice 91, 124
multisensory reading, and – culture 12, 26–28, 30–31, 33, 47, 53, 55, 57–58, 85, 88–89, 95, 124–125, 130–131, 147–148, 164, 198, 208, 210–211, 213–217, 230, 232
multisensory situations 65
multitasking 52, 112, 136–141, 206
music 3, 12, 52, 72, 74, 76–77, 89, 91–92, 131, 137–139, 166, 169, 178, 188–189, 201, 202, 211–212, 214–215, 219, 221, 234
music streaming 139, 201
must-dos 136

narration 28, 32, 127
narrative 2, 26, 32, 46–47, 51–53, 57, 65, 73–74, 76–77, 82, 84, 100, 114, 118, 127–129, 140–141, 148, 162, 164–168, 170, 171, 184–191, 201, 203–205, 211–212, 232–233
narrative suspense 127–128
navigation 64, 91, 148, 152, 156, 162, 165–171
network 1, 12, 16, 22, 30, 37–38, 58, 92, 98–105, 117, 173, 177–178, 181
Neumark, Norie 93, 96, 129, 134
The New London Group 50–51, 114, 154, 157–158
The New York Times 38–39, 81–82, 113
news communication 79–80, 85
news shows 80
noise-canceling 91, 136
non-critical 137
non-normative 137
normative conceptions 27–28
North American 42, 135, 138
Northern European 135
Novo Nordisk Foundation 124, 192

objects 6, 15, 19, 23, 63, 73, 81, 88, 92, 99, 167–169, 192, 220, 223, 228
obligations 135, 156
ocularcentrism 11, 61
The Odyssey 88
Ong, Walther Jackson 11, 13, 26, 29–33, 88, 97
operators 89
oral cultures 28–29, 31–32
oral language 61
oral narration 32
oral world of storytelling 31
oral-literate-electronic schema 26–30
oral-literate-electronic-digital reading condition 28, 30
orality 11, 31–32, 94
Orality and Literacy: The Technologizing of the Word 31–32
organs 92
outdoor exercising 138

Padme (*Star Wars*) 178–179
palimpsestuous reception 181
Palpatine (*Star Wars*) 179, 181
pandemic 36, 39, 82, 138
paper 4, 19, 27–28, 36–37, 51, 69, 71, 73, 79, 82, 116, 126, 132, 184, 186–192, 221–223, 225
paradox 51, 68, 73, 120, 141, 153, 184
parallax scrolling 80
parasite 136
parasocial relationship 93
Paterson, Mark 59, 64, 67
Peabody Award 81
pedagogical research 3, 46, 48, 231
pendulum 27, 30
perceive 3, 11, 23, 27, 31, 59, 71, 84, 92, 114–115, 135, 139, 165, 201–202, 209, 219, 234
performing narrator 93–95, 129, 202–204, 212
Peters, John Durham 26, 34
phenomenological 4, 20, 91, 127, 130, 132, 148, 162, 164–165, 168–171, 175, 182, 184, 197–198, 208, 214, 216, 231
phonograph 29, 89, 137
phrasing 93
physical body 92
physical presence 64, 73, 188
pictures 27, 69, 72, 74, 76–77, 93, 128–130, 166, 168, 188–189, 202

plastic 91
playback media 91
plenitude, digital 6, 13, 17, 232–233
plots 173–174
podcast listeners 139
podcasts 19, 46, 52, 65, 79–80, 83–85, 129, 136, 139, 147, 201, 234
polyaesthetics 40, 65, 121, 232–233
polymedia 120–121, 232–233
positive psychology 140
presence effects 125
Pressman, Jessica 12, 19, 23–24, 47, 76, 78
primary orality 32
print culture 12, 26, 29, 30, 221, 224, 227
print journalism 80
print reading 23, 116–117, 125
print-centric paradigm 62
printed words 11, 27, 29, 219
printing press 29–30
productivity 118, 136
proper reading 28, 111
proprioception 63–64
proprioceptive engagement 65
Pry 64, 118
Pryce and Rubery 211
psychological 26, 182, 184, 213
public knowledge 85
publishers 2, 17, 83, 136–138, 153
Pulitzer Prize 81
Pullinger, Kate 47, 118

qualitative aspects of a reading situation 209–210, 216
quality time 136, 141, 206

radar 29, 151
radio 17–18, 29, 35, 40, 80, 83, 137–138, 234
raspy 94
re-writing 174
read-aloud recordings 84
reader, context 3–6, 12, 15–16, 18, 20–23, 37–39, 41–43, 48–49, 51–53, 57–58, 63–65, 68–69, 71–77, 80–82, 85, 93–94, 100, 111, 113–121, 127–129, 131, 135–136, 141, 147–148, 162, 164, 166, 168, 171, 173, 175–176–182, 184–192, 197–198, 200–201, 204–206, 208, 210–217, 219–220, 223–225, 227, 230–233

reading: between media 52, 112–113, 124, 147, 186, 192; close 22, 115–117, 120; collective 41, 44; competencies 46–48, 50, 114; curious 51, 53, 232; deep 6, 20, 38, 51, 113–114, 116, 118–119, 132, 192, 232; definition of 5, 27, 29, 35–36, 124; distant 20, 114, 117; habits 2, 46, 52, 124, 147, 197; hierarchies 28, 33; hyper 20, 22, 38, 114, 116–117, 198, 220; locative 43; multisensory 12, 26–28, 31, 47, 53, 55, 57–58, 85, 88–89, 95, 124–125, 130–131, 147–148, 164, 198, 208, 210–211, 213–217, 230, 232; situational 4, 51, 197, 206–208, 210; transmedial 6, 147–148, 173–182; transactional 176
Readingwriting, Emerson 22
reception process 126, 173
reception theories 175, 189
Reddit 180
relationality 94–95, 202, 205–206, 214, 221
relaxing 139
religious ideologies 30
resonant reading 220–221, 223–225, 227–229
resonant space 210
Rettberg, Scott 12–14, 22, 25, 47, 118, 122
rhetoric of language 94
rhythm of reading 93
rock 27
Rogue One (Star Wars) 179–180
romanticist ideas 93
Rosa, Hartmut 120, 123, 136, 141, 143, 224–225, 229
routines 18, 136, 140–141, 202–203, 206
Rustad, Hans Kristian 47
Ryan, Marie-Laure 127–129, 134

Saenger, Paul 88, 97
Sánchez Laws 127, 134
scandinavian 135
scanning 85, 116, 219–220
Schafer, R. Murray 93–93, 97
Schmidt, Ulrik 208, 215, 218
scholars i, 5, 12, 15–17, 20, 22, 26, 47, 57, 61, 64, 116–118, 127, 137, 139, 156, 158, 202, 230, 233
Schulze, Holger 219–220, 223, 225, 229
scientific paradigms 62

screens 5, 27, 36, 46, 52, 82, 91, 124, 205, 219, 221, 224
screen reading 51, 116, 125, 131–132, 147
scribal culture 29
secondary listening 138
secondary orality 32
self-indulgence 135
self-presence 93
sense of atmosphere 130
sensing body 33, 89, 230
sensory: appeals 121, 126; bias 26–27, 30; engagements 6, 57, 60, 63, 80–81, 112, 200, 203, 215; ethnography 202; studies i, 1, 57–60; turn 59, 64
sentimentality 179
separate senses 59
Shakespeare, William 88
shortcut 62
should activity 139
sight 27, 30–31, 40, 64, 66, 188, 200, 206, 211, 224–226
silent 2, 29, 31–32, 41, 57, 88, 90, 93, 179, 186, 221
silent reading 31, 57, 221
singing 28–29
skimming 85, 115–116, 220
smartphone 5, 15, 18–19, 46, 51, 58, 63, 83, 90–91, 124, 135, 137, 151, 200–202, 205, 211, 224
smell 89, 91, 95, 206, 213
smoke signal 27
Snapchat 182
Snow Fall 81
sociability 92
social attention 85
social audio 83
social dimension 174, 181
social interaction 27
social media 17–18, 20–21, 39, 41–44, 52–53, 116, 147, 177, 201–202, 219, 232
solitary 29, 82, 88
solitary activity 88
sonic phenomena 61
sound studies 60–62, 65–66, 84, 198, 201, 208, 213
sound waves 92–93, 221
sound-design 80
sounds 1–2, 27, 31, 57, 60, 64, 89, 91, 125, 128–129, 140, 166–67, 169, 171, 186, 188–189, 202, 206, 212–213, 222

soundscape 79, 212
space 15–16, 18, 28–32, 89, 117–118, 121, 125, 128–129, 131, 139–140, 148, 152, 155, 162–165, 168, 170, 176, 179, 197, 201–202, 206, 208, 210, 214, 219–220, 223–225, 227, 231
space of perception 30
spatial dimension 128
spatial immersion 127–128
spatio-temporal 175, 179
speech recognition systems 32
speaker's voice 129
Spencer, Amy 211, 218
Spotify 83, 139, 201, 234
Star Wars 175–177. *see also* Anakin, Clone Wars, Darth Vader, Padme, Palpatine, Rogue One
Sterne, Jonathan 26, 30–31, 34, 60–61, 65, 67, 89, 97
stimuli 140
storage technologies 91
stories 28–29, 32, 53, 68, 81–82, 173–174, 176, 178–180, 211–212, 223, 228
story world 52, 136, 140, 147–148, 214
storytelling 27–29, 31, 52, 72, 81, 84–85, 88–89, 173, 202
streaming services 51, 83, 91, 132, 136, 138–139, 201, 203, 234
stressful 141
structuralist (post-) 16, 37, 41, 93, 210
subplots 174
subway 138
surfaces 22, 66, 68, 73, 92, 98, 106, 176, 219, 223–224
surroundings 27, 31–32, 53, 57, 59–60, 66, 90, 95, 140, 198, 201–202, 206, 208–211, 213–217
symbiotic reading situation 95
symbols 5, 27, 29, 48, 176, 191, 224
synaesthetically 89
synesthetic 91
synthetic speech 32

tablet 15, 19, 46, 58, 63, 69, 71, 73, 75–77, 91, 124, 185, 200–201, 205, 224
tactile 2, 15, 27, 50, 64, 75, 79, 89–92, 95, 132, 200, 206, 222, 230, 233
tactility 63, 90–91, 165
tactile anaphones 91
tactile interfaces 79
tactile reading 27
Tagg, Philip 91–92
talk radio 80
tape recorder 29
taste 91, 94–95, 209
technology i, 22, 26, 28, 30, 32, 35, 37, 41, 47, 50, 52–53, 61–63, 70, 82–85, 88–91, 111, 115, 118–121, 125, 132, 137, 141, 147, 149, 151–154, 157–159, 197–198, 206, 210, 211–212, 216, 224
technotexts 63–64
The Teenage Mutant Ninja Turtles 173
telegraph 29, 101
telephone 29, 89, 101–102
television 17–18, 29, 35, 40, 80
temperatures 92
temporal immersion 127–128
temptation bundling 139, 141
Tender Claws *see Pry*
tertiary orality 32
text, expanded concept of 51
text messaging 18, 32
text-based Internet communication 32
textual media, comparative 19
textures 60, 92, 222
theatres 29, 83, 178
theGuardianVR app 82
Thibaud, Jean-Paul 208, 215, 218
thick descriptions, Felski 4, 20–21
throat 92
thumbnails (images) 91
TikTok 182
time 15–16, 26, 28–29, 32, 35, 38, 43, 93, 114–115, 119–120, 125, 129, 131, 135–136, 138, 140–141, 147, 152, 155, 163, 165–170, 174, 192, 197, 201, 203, 205–206, 213, 222, 224, 231–232
Toronto School 12, 26–28, 30
touch 2–3, 5, 11, 52, 57, 62–64, 69, 72–73, 76, 90–95, 111, 124, 128–129, 162, 189, 192, 211, 214, 219–220, 222–225, 227–228
touchscreen 90, 224
transactional reading 176
transmedia 6, 52, 147–148, 173–182, 232–233
transmedia connections 175
transmedia content 52
transmedial experiences 174–177
transmedia reception 173–174
transmedia storytelling 52, 173

transmedial reading 6, 148, 173–176, 180–182
transmedial worlds 173–176, 180
transmediality 174–175
transmission 58, 98, 103–104, 139
transmission control protocol/internet protocol (TCP/IP) 58, 98, 103
treble 94
Turing, Alan 30
TV series 52–53, 215
typology 176

Umberto Eco 180, 182
Understanding Media: The Extensions of Man 30
usage 84, 88, 99, 138, 219
user-friendly 137
uses and gratifications 139

Van Leeuwen, Theo 49–50, 54
video 17–18, 22, 29, 35–36, 39–42, 44, 52, 64–65, 79–81, 91, 93, 118, 153, 163–164, 170, 178, 233
visible space 31
visual 2–3, 11, 14, 17, 21, 27, 29–31, 33, 35, 39–40, 42, 47–48, 50–51, 57, 60–62, 64–66, 69, 73, 75–77, 80, 82, 89–92, 95, 117–118, 126–128, 130–132, 136, 165–166, 168–171, 176–177, 182, 188, 190, 200, 209, 211–212, 215, 222, 233
visual culture 48, 61
visual domain 61–62

visual media paradigm 91
vocal representation 129
vocality 94–95
voice 2, 28, 32–33, 72, 79–80, 84–85, 92–95, 116, 126, 129–132, 166, 169–170, 203–204, 212, 215, 230–231
voice of the text 32, 93, 204
voice response systems 32
VR. *See* virtual reality (VR)
VR journalism 80

walkman (Sony Walkman) 137
want-activity 139
wasted time 136
web documentaries 81
websites 3, 39–40, 99, 152, 156, 173
weeding 136
Western culture 59–60, 115
whispering 93
Wiener, Norbert 99
Wolf, Maryanne 3, 7, 20, 25, 118–119, 123
Wookieepedia 180
worldness 148, 174, 176
World Wide Web 1, 14–15, 35, 37, 39, 43, 153
writing machine 37, 63–64

YouTube 41, 53, 93, 147, 156, 180, 182
young readers 6, 20, 52, 145, 147

Zetland 80, 83–84

For Product Safety Concerns and Information please contact our EU
representative GPSR@taylorandfrancis.com
Taylor & Francis Verlag GmbH, Kaufingerstraße 24, 80331 München, Germany

www.ingramcontent.com/pod-product-compliance
Lightning Source LLC
Chambersburg PA
CBHW050301010526
44108CB00040B/2009